C000246804

BEDFORD
1950 – 1986

W. H. Smith was one of many household names seen on Bedford vehicles, in this case being a major user for virtually the entire span of over half a century of production. Here a CF and a TL are posed soon after delivery to the company's Leicester garage in 1981.

© Venture Publications Ltd October 1996.

ISBN 1 898432 09 0

All rights reserved. Except for normal review purposes no part of this book may be reproduced or utilised in any form or by any means, electrical or mechanical, including photocopying, recording or by an information storage and retrieval system, without the prior written consent of Venture Publications Limited, Glossop, Derbyshire.

Companion Volume – Bedford 1923-1950
In course of preparation – Bedford Volume Three – a Retrospect

For details of other transport titles available from Venture Publications Ltd please send a stamped addressed envelope to VPL 128 Pikes Lane, Glossop, SK13 8EH

Front Cover Illustration

The S-type, introduced as 'the Big Bedford' in 1950, began the process of extending the range of models into what hitherto had been the province of the traditional 'heavy' vehicle makers, with its 7-ton load rating and forward-control layout. This SL model, restored in traditional style, is owned by R. Leech of Haslington, Crewe.

Photo John Robinson

Produced for the Publishers
Venture Publications, Glossop, Derbyshire,
by Mopok Graphics, Glossop SK13 8EH
using computerised origination

The British Bus and Truck Heritage

BedforD
1950 – 1986

by

Stuart Fergus Broatch

and

Alan Townsin

Venture *publications*

THIS BOOK, LIKE THE PREVIOUS VOLUME, IS DEDICATED
TO THE MEMORY OF

GEOFFREY KING

A FINE ENGINEER, GREAT WIT
AND A TRUE FRIEND AND GENTLEMAN

Below: The TK, introduced in 1960, was the most popular of Bedford's many successful types, and indeed more were built than of any other British truck model. The half million production mark had been passed shortly before this one was built at the end of the 1970s. The picture conveys the patina of a working truck, in sound order but not fussed over, so typical of the type and still to be found all over Britain, even if no longer the common sight it used to be.

Facing page: Still to be seen from time to time on our TV screens are some of the 'Green Goddess' fire engines, originally purchased by the Home Office in the mid-1950s for use by the Auxiliary Fire Service in the event of major attacks on British cities in a nuclear war. Nowadays some continue to be pressed into service when normal fire service cover is suspended by industrial disputes. This 1953 example on the SHZ chassis with two-wheel drive was restored to original livery with the AFS emblem by the Fire Service Preservation Group.

CONTENTS

INTRODUCTION

In the previous volume, the Bedford story was taken from its origins amid the complexities of the growth of the huge General Motors combine in the United States and its acquisition of Vauxhall Motors Limited, a very 'English' concern, in 1925. The introduction of Bedford as a commercial vehicle marque name came in 1931 and its meteoric growth, to become the leading maker of commercial vehicles in the classes up to 5-ton capacity and in coaches up to the 29-seat class in Britain, was described.

This volume continues from 1950 with the introduction of the S-type models marketed as the Big Bedfords, yet in later years, they would have been regarded as quite modest in size and load-carrying capacity amid the range of Bedford models offered.

The 1950s and 1960s were decades of expansion both in further upward spread of size range and in the numbers of vehicles produced, the latter aided by the opening of the Bedford truck and bus chassis-building plant at Dunstable in 1954. There was also growing variety, despite the use of mass-production techniques to keep costs and hence prices down. This apparent contradiction was achieved by use of a range of standardised units in models carefully tailored to suit the widely varying needs of different markets, the latter being an aspect of the business to which Bedford paid close attention over succeeding decades. These covered a wide range, from the very successful CA and long-lived HA vans to a succession of 4x4 models designed mainly for military use.

Yet the need to aim mainly at large-scale markets and low costs resulted in a degree of conservatism in adopting some kinds of new idea – diesel engines were not offered as a production option by Bedford until the mid-1950s. Yet soon their modest cost meant that more such engines were being made in the Dunstable factory than by most of the traditional makers that had been associated with diesels for road vehicles since the 1930s.

The efficient use of every ounce of material in each vehicle was reflected by Bedford's standard practice of calculating the weight of every single item as it was designed. It indicated an approach to efficient use of materials which sometimes seems to be neglected nowadays, and in related respects Bedford was often a design leader, as with the adoption of 16in wheels instead of the traditional commercial-vehicle 20in size for some medium-weight Bedford models, with benefits in cost and lower loading height, even though in some applications the problems of long-term brake performance were to prove intractable. The VAL twin-steering coach was the most adventurous application of such principles, even though less successful than the subsequent Y-series underfloor-engined two-axle models.

Bedford's most successful truck model of all time and the most popular ever built in Britain was the TK, introduced in 1960 and of which over half a million had been made before it was largely, though not entirely, replaced by the similar but updated TL in 1980. Among the TK's main assets were the 'civilised' standards offered to the driver, from ease of entry to good standards of noise insulation and outstanding forward vision. Yet the TJ bonneted model introduced two years earlier was to prove even longer lived, being favoured in many export markets and surviving beyond the end of Bedford as a GM concern. In a similar way, the SB passenger model first seen in 1950 was to remain in production mainly for export to the end in 1986, hugely outnumbering many more glamorous types.

In the 1970s a further move up the weight scale was made with the introduction of the TM range but here, despite extensive investment and what was in many ways an attractive design, the level of success was much more limited. This was largely because the Detroit Diesel two-stroke engines initially adopted for heavier types and especially articulated models of 32-ton gross combination weight and above proved less successful in fuel-economy-conscious Europe than in its native America.

Competition was becoming more intense at all levels, not only from other British and European makers but increasingly from Japan, whose makers, not least Isuzu, in which GM had taken a shareholding, were becoming increasingly successful. The possibility of a GM take-over of the former State-owned Leyland Truck and Land Rover in 1986, with the prospect of a reinvigorated GM commercial vehicle involvement in Britain, vanished when the British Government withdrew these parts of the former British Leyland empire from sale at that time. The GM decision to close Bedford truck and bus manufacture followed later in the year and though AWD and subsequently Marshall acquired part of the business it was on a scale far smaller than in the days when 'You see them everywhere' was simply a statement of fact.

This book tells the story of that 1950-86 period with the benefit of insight into the atmosphere within what for many years was Britain's biggest commercial vehicle manufacturer.

ACKNOWLEDGEMENTS

As with the previous volume, there are far too many people who have contributed to the authors' interest in and knowledge of Bedford vehicles over the years to attempt to list them all individually. Even so, it is good to be able to put on record our appreciation of many unfailingly courteous and helpful contacts with Vauxhall Motors and its representatives of various kinds over the years.

We would like to thank the following in particular for their assistance in regard to this volume:-

John Alden, former Chief Engineer, Vauxhall Motors Ltd

Mike Bundy and Steve Muspratt, Anna Valley Motors, Salisbury, Wiltshire.

C. Chesterman, for the loan of his extensive brochure and photograph collection.

Commercial Vehicle and Road Transport Club, and in particular Christopher Saleman and Steve Winbush.

Geoffrey King, son of C. E. King, former Chief Engineer, Vauxhall Motors Ltd, and Rita King, his daughter-in-law.

Miriam Carroll and Bob McPhee, Vauxhall Motors Ltd.

Paul Crowther, Director of Operations, and Mr Heath, Brighton Borough Council.

Charlie Hardy, Engineering Inspector (PSV), who sadly died before this book was completed.

C. Rowland, Rambler Coaches, St Leonards on Sea, Sussex.

Leo J. Taylor, latterly in charge of the bus and medium truck groups of engineering staff when Bedford was part of GM and who transferred to AWD. He has provided a valuable insight into engineering methods from the 1960s onwards and many useful items of information, especially in regard to the bus and coach models.

John C. Thompson, for photographs and information on Bedford fire engines, particularly the Green Goddess story – he is co-author of 'The Green Machine' which gives much detail on the former AFS fleets.

David Waterman, Yeates in the South, Salisbury

Dilys and Pauline, for their general help and encouragement.

Margaret, for her patience and skill in producing 'the finished product' from our material.

PHOTOCREDITS

Most of the illustrations in this book were originally issued for publicity purposes by Vauxhall Motors Ltd or, from 1983, Bedford Commercial Vehicles when it had become a directly-owned Division of General Motors. The copies used come from the authors' collections plus those of Colin Chesterman and Leo Taylor, to both of whom we are most grateful. Credit for other illustrations is as follows and, again we must express thanks not only to those concerned but also others who sent photographs in response to a request from the publishers, quite a number of which are set to appear in the third volume.

G.H.F.Atkins	60,70(top)
S.F.Broatch collection	23(top),29,37(centre & foot),112(foot)
D.A.Broom	31(foot)
C.Chesterman collection	1,10,12(all),19(both),20(top & centre) 26(centre),27(foot),31(top),58(top),93(all), 127(lower),128(both)
Commercial Motor	22
M.Fowler	76(top)
M&D and East Kent Bus Club	116(top)
Marshall SPV	156(bottom left)
R.Marshall	147(foot)
R.Pennington	3
J.A.Senior	44
Senior Transport Archive/R.N.Hannay collection	90(top)
W.J.Taylor	2
A.A.Townsin	69(foot)
A.A.Townsin collection	120

The Whittle concern, of Highley, Shropshire, had been a Bedford user since owning one of the first WHB 14-seat buses in 1931. In the post-war years, coach operation was greatly expanded, excursion and tour business being built up so as to serve much of the West Midlands area. By the early 1960s a regular pattern of purchasing a new fleet of Bedford coaches with Duple bodywork annually was established, and frequently these were sold when only a year old, being replaced by a new fleet. The 1976 intake was largely of YLQ models with Duple Dominant 45-seat bodywork, one of which is seen on a local bus service to Bridgnorth. At that date, Bedford was still by far the largest supplier of coach and bus chassis to independent operators in Britain, often outnumbering all other makes put together.

The story so far

Bedford had been chosen as a marque name for the then new commercial vehicle range introduced by Vauxhall Motors Ltd of Luton, Bedfordshire, in April 1931. The first Bedfords, a pair of 2-ton models, the WHG and longer WLG, looked very like the contemporary Chevrolet LQ 30-cwt model already being manufactured for a year or so at the Luton plant, the latter almost indistinguishable from the product as built by Chevrolet in the United States. Chevrolet was the largest division of the huge General Motors combine, and had moved into first place among world sales of cars and trucks, overtaking Ford. Assembly in Britain had begun in 1923, initially at Hendon, on the outskirts of London. Briefly, in 1931, some of the earliest Bedford models were also assembled at Hendon.

Vauxhall had become a General Motors subsidiary in 1925 but the first Vauxhall car dated from 1903, evolving into a much-respected make, its most famous model in production at the time of the GM takeover being the 30/98, a 4.2-litre sports car fully comparable to the vintage Bentley, though less powerful models were sold in larger numbers. Even so, output was modest and the financial position not strong. Over the next few years Vauxhall cars gradually took on a character more akin to their GM cousins, though adapted to British conditions. From 1933-38, the most popular models were the two Light Six models of 12 and 14hp RAC rating which far outsold anything the pre-1925 concern had produced.

High-volume sales were pursued across the range, applying equally to the Bedford models, priced only marginally above the lighter Chevrolet, and sales success was immediate. Yet some elements of the old Vauxhall tradition remained, with several senior engineers, most

The first-generation Bedford models showed their ancestry very clearly, especially the 30-cwt type WS with its close affinity to the Chevrolet LQ. In this scene reproduced on the cover of the April 1933 issue of 'The Bedford Transport Magazine', a 1932 WS van in the fleet of W. H. Smith & Son Ltd turns into Fleet Street, then the home of most national and London evening newspapers, while some AEC NS buses of the London General Omnibus Co wait at the traffic lights at the foot of Ludgate Hill.

The WT was Bedford's first definitive model, setting the standard not only for a whole dynasty of later types from Luton but a series of models from other manufacturers which adopted its snub-nosed semi-forward-control layout. This 1935 WTH tipper of George C. Cross, of Southall, Middlesex, is seen at work supplying materials for house building.

notably C. E. King, Chief Engineer since 1919, continuing to serve the company – King retained this position until 1952. Perhaps the most significant difference between the original Bedford six-cylinder 3,180cc overhead-valve petrol engine and the Chevrolet equivalent – the famous 'stove-bolt six' – from which it was derived was the Bedford unit's pressure-fed lubrication for the crankshaft main and big-end bearings.

Bedford passenger models began with the 14-seat WHB and 20-seat WLB later in 1931, securing 65% of the 9-20-seat market in their first full year, The Chevrolet LQ gave way to the Bedford WS 30-cwt model from 1932, and there was also a similar but lighter 12cwt model, the VYC. The AS 8-cwt delivery van based on the Vauxhall Light Six car appeared in 1933.

It was in that year that Bedford's first definitive model appeared in the form of the WT 3-tonner designed by P. Stepney Acres, with its semi-forward control layout, though production did not begin until the spring of 1934. It created the characteristic look, with radiator set well forward and short bonnet, that was to remain characteristic of much of the firm's output for 20 years. Quite a few of the long-wheelbase WTL chassis were sold with bus or coach bodywork before the WTB was introduced as a purpose-built passenger version for the 1936 season. At the same time the WS 30-cwt and WHG and WLG 2-ton models were given a similar forward-mounted radiator though retaining the normal-control layout, with cab set further back than on the WT range.

This model line-up continued largely unchanged until 1939, though a new engine, generally known in those days as the 28hp, replaced the previous 27hp for all but the small vans from July 1938 (the actual rating under the old RAC system went up from 26.33hp to 27.34hp, but both were rounded up, as usual at the time). It was again a six-cylinder overhead-valve petrol unit of similar general design to its predecessor but incorporated some improvements mainly intended to improve its efficiency, largely the work of Alex Taub, a London-born engineer who had worked on the design of the Chevrolet 'stove-bolt six' but returned to Britain in 1937, joining Vauxhall's staff. Slightly increased dimensions, with $3\frac{3}{8}$in bore and 4in stroke, gave a swept volume of 3,519cc, or 214 cu in, the latter nomenclature was to be adopted as Bedford's usual name for the unit in mildly revised form in the 1950s, as explained later in this volume. Appearance also altered with the adoption of a new style of radiator, with rounded nose and horizontal slats instead of the plainer style with outline much as used since 1931, even though the vehicles' appearance had altered greatly when the radiator was mounted further forward in the mid-1930s.

Also new in 1938 was the Bedford HC 5/6cwt van derived from the Vauxhall Ten car, both being the first four-cylinder models in their respective ranges to have been introduced since the start of the General Motors era at Vauxhall. They were of 1,203cc capacity and much the same general design concept mildly enlarged resulted in the 10/12cwt JC van with 1,442cc engine of June 1939.

This was only one of a whole new range which replaced all previous models except for the small and almost new HC van. The various W-series models gave way to the K, M and O series, covering the 30-cwt, 2-3-ton and 3-4-ton categories respectively, to which a new 5-ton variant of the O-series was also added, differing from the 3-4-ton version largely in terms of suspension and tyres. The general appearance was broadly similar to the equivalent previous models, but there was a new pressed-steel cab with vee-shaped windscreen and the bull-nose radiator had the filler cap mounted externally. Where relevant, short and long versions were indicated by S or L as the second type letter, and a new passenger model was designated OB.

The new range was only briefly in production before the outbreak of war in September 1939. Military versions of the new models, having a broad bonnet with flat front and sloping top, were produced in very large numbers, the OYD 3-ton model being the British Army's standard general duty lorry. In addition, a new four-wheel-drive (4x4) lorry, the QL, was developed and put into production for military use where better cross-country performance was needed, alongside the models derived from the civilian range. Even further removed from peacetime output, Vauxhall Motors was given the job of designing and producing a 21-litre tank engine and then made responsible for the production of the Churchill tank into which it was fitted. Limited civilian output was produced to meet wartime needs for essential transport, perhaps most notably in the form of the OWB 32-seat bus with utility bodywork on what was virtually the OB chassis, apart from minor details. It was the only new single-deck bus available to British operators between 1942 and 1945; the main users tended to be the type of operator previously favouring Bedford coaches, the larger operators tending to favour double-deckers. The wartime civilian OWS and OWL goods models had the military style of front-end.

The long-familiar 'bull-nose' radiator grille first appeared in mid-1938, initially with the cab as used for WT models since 1934. At first the radiator filler was under the bonnet and the headlamps were mounted at the same height as previous models, as seen on this preserved WTL with Kent registration dating from early 1939. The six-cylinder petrol engine, though similar in basic features to that on the earlier models, first appeared in the famous 28hp form on this generation of models – it was to remain in production with only minor changes as standard or an option for succeeding types right up to the TL of the 1980s.

Wartime Bedford models were sometimes still to be found in regular use many years later. This collection of ex-military four-wheel drive QL models and an example of the OWB civilian bus from the same period was in use by Bertram Mills Circus in 1962.

After the end of the war in 1945, what had been the new mid-1939 range of K, M and O civilian models resumed production and as only small numbers had reached operators' fleets before war stopped production, and many of them had been compulsorily acquired for military use, they still seemed modern and 'new'. Demand was immense after six years of war with very few new vehicles built for civilian use, and post-war output tended to be governed by material supplies, also in demand for reconstruction of all types, rather than any problem in selling whatever could be produced.

Even so, the total of Bedford vehicles built since production began reached the half-million mark in October 1947. No other British commercial vehicle maker had reached that point, a remarkable achievement in only 16½ years and underlining Bedford's dominance of the overall commercial vehicle market in Britain as well as a very healthy export trade. Half of that total had been built in wartime, when Bedford supplied the bulk of the British Army's needs for general service lorries, but a high proportion of the rest, still including many examples of even the oldest types, remained in service.

In the post-war period, the distinction between the 3-4-ton and 5-ton models was clarified by the use of a third letter, A or B respectively, in the designation, following the S or L indicating wheelbase. The use of a final, in this case fourth, letter to indicate the type of body fitted, where a factory product, had become standard practice, and thus certain types became familiar, notably the OSBT 5-ton tipper and OLBD 5-ton dropside lorry. The additional cost of these models over their OSAT and OLAD equivalents in 3-4-ton form was only about 5% and the ability to carry the heavier load when needed was of obvious appeal. Also very familiar was the OB, best known with Duple 29-seat Vista coach body – Bedford had entered into a marketing scheme with Duple in the mid-1930s and successive Bedford-Duple coaches dominated the market among independent coach operators.

The HC 5/6cwt van reappeared briefly after the war, but the emphasis swung to the 10/12cwt and in late 1948 the designation of this changed from JC to PC when it was fitted with the steering-column gear change which had been adopted for the new Vauxhall Wyvern LIX car with which it shared its four-cylinder 1,442cc engine and gearbox. However, it retained the styling of the previous model and though modern looking when introduced in 1939, it was beginning to look rather dated by 1950 or so, when new van designs based on post-war car styles were becoming more common.

To some degree, this was beginning to be true of the whole range, and it is perhaps fair to say that in this sense it was becoming the victim of its own success. Bedford's motto 'You see them everywhere' was certainly true, and hence new examples of the types of 1939 design and in large-scale production since 1946 were no longer a novelty by 1950.

Yet sales remained strong, understandably so when a complete Bedford 5-ton lorry was costing about £600. Only Ford – at that date selling its commercial vehicles under the Thames name – was fully competitive on price and its models, using the V8 petrol engine and a cab design more dated than Bedford's, attracted fewer sales, and although Austin (with what was still almost a copy of the Bedford), Commer, and Dodge, both using side-valve engines derived from large car units, offered vehicles only a little more expensive, they had no strong sales point to give a compelling advantage over the Bedford, even though each had their own loyal clientele. In this sense, Bedford's popularity helped to reinforce its own sales figures, as there was a strong dealer network, with service facilities in virtually every town.

The more 'bespoke' makers' products were much more expensive, even a simple four-cylinder petrol 5-ton lorry from a firm such as Dennis cost £850 as a chassis and about £1,100 with cab and body. Similar remarks applied to coaches despite the bodywork contributing more to the total cost, and the same pattern of a complete Bedford 29-seat coach costing less, at £1,736 in 1950, than even the bare chassis of a 'heavyweight' model was still valid. Admittedly the latter would by then be diesel-engined and accommodate 33-seat bodywork, but with body was likely to cost well over double the price of a Bedford OB Vista.

On this basis, a degree of complacency might have been understandable, yet Bedford was about to make a strong challenge in a new sector of the market. Full details of all the models mentioned above are to be found in 'Bedford Volume 1' by the same authors and available from Venture Publications Ltd.

The new range of K, M and O goods models as introduced briefly in the summer of 1939 reappeared in production soon after the war ended in 1945 and continued with only minor changes until 1953. This OSS tractive unit was registered GXX 979 early in 1946 and still carries the Bedford-Scammell lettering on its radiator grille when seen with low-loading semi-trailer as a preserved vehicle. The standard vee-windscreen cab suited the styling of the O-type goods models particularly well.

Spurling built the standard van on the KZ 30-cwt chassis and this ambulance was a derivation of the same basic design, the chassis being offered with softer suspension and low-pressure tyres for this role. This demonstrator, registered in Middlesex as UMY 189, dated from late 1949. Note the chromium-plated bell to give warning of approach when necessary, as used in those days before sirens became standard. The fog-lamp was another desirable accessory when severe urban fog was a common problem in winter.

Furniture van builders tended to build their own cabs as part of the body but the vee-screen effect was sometimes retained in mild form, as in this body built by W. G. Goddard of Oadby, Leicestershire for Whitmores of Wigston on an OL chassis in the latter part of 1949.

9 THE BIG BEDFORDS

Under the publicity name 'the Big Bedfords', a new range was introduced at the 1950 Commercial Motor Show, supplementing existing models. This took Bedford up into the 7-ton class with a new forward-control model known as the S-type, yet it retained the legal speed advantage which had aided sales of the smaller models. There was also a new coach chassis, the SB, of similar design. In many ways, it was a repeat of the coup achieved at the 1933 Show with the WT, although this time production began almost immediately.

The limit on unladen weight up to which operation at 30mph was permissible had been raised from the pre-war figure of 2 tons 10 cwt to 3 tons. This was partly in deference to the scarcity of light materials that had arisen due to the war, leading in turn to wider use of cast iron for major components, some of which had proved beneficial

in terms of rigidity and durability, and the industry had persuaded the Ministry of Transport to allow various higher weight limits to continue. This gave the Bedford design team scope to repeat the process of stepping up the weight-carrying range of its models and yet, by using similar skill in keeping unladen weight down, to venture deeper into the world hitherto thought of as 'heavy vehicle' country. The majority of early S-type trucks with standard bodies met this requirement and could thus run legally at up to 30mph. In practical terms they, like their predecessors were considerably faster than this might suggest – a laden S-type truck bowled along in a very relaxed style at 45mph or so and, though illegal, it became quite common to find vehicles of this class running at well over the legal limit – indeed they tended to be a nuisance to other traffic if they did not.

The first S-type about to leave the production line on 7th November 1950, to an audience of management and senior staff – John Alden, quietly looking on at the extreme right, was to become Chief Engineer in 1963. This was the company's first all-new design for civilian operators since the WT had been introduced in 1933, and it extended Bedford's range in a manner exactly similar to what had been achieved with that model – for the first time Bedford was in the 7-ton class. The unmistakeable styling, dramatically different to that of the existing range, was soon to become familiar in many parts of the world.

This impression by G. Bishop, a well-known automobile artist of the day, appeared on the cover of a brochure for the Big Bedford range and conveys the main markets foreseen for the range, with SLD dropside, SA artic and SST tipper versions all included. The cab could accommodate three as shown, though the middle occupant sitting over the engine cover would have had to sit partly sideways on the optional two-passenger seat.

To power the new range there was a completely new engine, which Bedford generally called the 300 cu in unit. This use of cubic inches was partly a reflection of American practice quite commonly found at Vauxhall, though at least partly related to growing British use of United States engineering standards that had emerged from the war period, when transatlantic co-operation in such matters had grown. Hitherto cubic centimetres or litres had been favoured almost as widely in Britain as continental Europe as a measure of engine size, and indeed this remained so in general conversation between engineers. Even so, this switch to cubic inches was taken up by many British makers for a time in terms of engine designations. There was also a view that they were likely to be more widely understood in terms of world trade, and it was certainly true that American cars and trucks were to be found in many parts of the world.

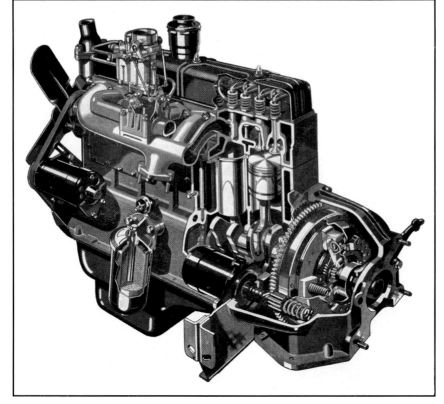

The 300 cu in six-cylinder petrol engine introduced for the Bedford S-type range had obvious resemblances to the existing engine used in the K, M and O range, but introduced important new features such as the seven-bearing crankshaft and renewable slip-fit cylinder liners. After minor teething troubles had been overcome, it became highly regarded as one of the best commercial vehicle petrol engines of its day, giving exceptional life as well as quiet running, save when extended to the top end of its speed range, rarely needed when 40-45mph was regarded as a good cruising speed, and itself illegal as the overall official limit for such vehicles was 30mph.

It so happened that the new Bedford engine, of 3⁷⁄₈in bore and 4¼in bore, had a swept volume of 300.7 cu in, so the round figure designation was quite accurate, even though most British commercial vehicle fleet engineers understood what was implied more readily if the size was quoted as 4.927 litres. As a matter of interest, the RAC rating was 36.32hp, but this had fallen out of use since it was no longer the basis even of car taxation.

It was noteworthy in that the 7-ton class of vehicle, and also the typical forward-control 33-seat coach as built by the traditional 'heavy-duty' manufacturers, had gone over completely to oil (diesel) engines by that date – many such firms had not offered petrol-engined models in this class since before the 1939-45 war. The Big Bedfords, offered only in petrol form at first, had to overcome that situation, but their modest cost made them a proposition – indeed, a considerable share of their appeal, both as goods and passenger models, was to people who were moving up from the Bedford O-series types and still at that date used to petrol engines. The long-wheelbase goods chassis cost £780, though an extra £175 was added to that in purchase tax, then in force. This continued the relationship in which a Bedford was very considerably cheaper than a traditional-style 'heavy-duty' model of similar rating, playing a large part in the sales success achieved.

Its general design, in being an in-line six-cylinder overhead-valve petrol engine with down-draught Zenith carburettor, was in accord with previous Bedford practice, but this new unit had several features moving it into a different class. There were now seven main bearings, for the first time on a Bedford, together with renewable slip-fit cylinder liners and aluminium alloy pistons.

It is not difficult to imagine C. E. King, still Chief Engineer at the time it was designed, taking a certain quiet satisfaction that here was a unit of which the 'old' Vauxhall company could have been proud, with few design compromises in terms of cost-saving, even though efficient

manufacture was given great importance. John Dickson Simpson, a much-respected technical journalist and himself Leyland-trained, described the Bedford 300 cu in unit as the best commercial-vehicle petrol engine of its period, rating it higher than the Rolls-Royce units much favoured by military and fire service vehicle authorities. Teething troubles were experienced with some of the early engines, notably corrosion of cylinder head studs which could lead to failures and some valve trouble, but these were soon overcome and it developed a reputation for long and trouble-free life as well as exceptional refinement.

It was rated at 110bhp at 3,200rpm, with maximum torque of 234 lb.ft at 1,200rpm, though once again, *The Commercial Motor*, following its crusade for 'realistic' net ratings, quoted 94bhp and 220 lb.ft. In practice, as that journal's writer L. J. Cotton, put it in a road test report, the 'tone' was unmistakeably Bedford, though it was even smoother than the 28hp engine, which, incidentally was now beginning to be called the 214 cu in unit in some Bedford publications. Quite apart from the improved specification of the engine itself, both it and the gearbox were now mounted on three widely spaced rubber insulators, helping to cut down noise transmission.

There was a 12-in clutch and the gearbox was of a new design, with synchromesh on 2nd, 3rd and top speeds and with 2nd and 3rd ratios using helical gears. This unit was also fitted to 1951 models of O-types and other lighter models using the 28hp engine; some operators fitted it to existing models, including a few OB coaches. Despite these changes, it still had a characteristic Bedford sound, even though more subdued than the old crash gearbox of the earlier chassis. Although the gear lever acted directly on the gearbox, requiring the lever to be set forward on S-types so as to be within easy reach of the driver seated alongside the engine, its action, and that of the clutch, were light and superior from a driver's point of view to some designs still in production 45 years later.

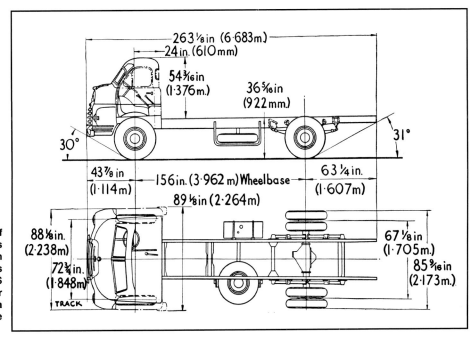

The layout and main dimensions of the SL long-wheelbase goods chassis and standard cab are shown in these drawings. The frame was straight on this model and the SS model intended mainly for tipper work, but the SA tractive unit had a cranked frame to accept the Scammell coupling gear.

Indeed, light controls were a feature of the model, the steering being particularly so despite the absence of power-assistance, a feature then in its infancy. Even though the steering was low-geared, requiring a good deal of steering wheel movement on tight turns, the S-type goods and passenger models were quite relaxing to drive.

Another new feature on a vehicle in this class was the hypoid bevel rear axle, also now fitted to O-type models in the 4-ton and 5-ton categories. The brake system, with Clayton Dewandre vacuum servo, was unusual among commercial vehicles of this class in being of hydro-mechanical form, with Lockheed hydraulic operation of the front brakes but mechanical linkage to the rear ones. The lighter M and O models had full hydraulic systems operating the brakes on both axles. In both systems there was a fail-safe provision in that failure of brakes to one axle would not put those on the other out of action.

However, possibly the most dramatic feature of the new model, both in goods and passenger form, was the appearance. The cab floor level was set high, so that only slight wheel-arch intrusion was required. The styling had a strong 'American' flavour, with bulbous front cowl and vee windscreen raked at quite a sharp angle, even though it was by no means a copy of any American model, as was to apply with the next range of bonneted trucks. The wings had a flat-topped line, though they and the cab as a whole were well rounded.

It was certainly distinctive but reactions to it varied quite sharply, from those who thought the overall effect handsome to others of a more conservative view who found it unduly aggressive after the 'friendly' style of the O and other models of the previous range. Both Bedford and Vauxhall were entering upon a decade when almost all their new products attracted strong controversy from an appearance viewpoint.

Although of forward-control layout, for the first time on a civilian Bedford model, the dimension from front bumper to back of cab was relatively long at about 5ft 8in, of which nearly 2ft was represented by the bulbous front cowl hidden from view beyond the high sill line of the windscreen. This had a practical drawback, in that vision immediately in front of the vehicle was restricted by comparison with that given on the O-series, and although

this was not a problem on the open road, it could cause difficulties in judging how much space was available when manoeuvring in tight spaces.

The SL long-wheelbase goods chassis had a 156in (13ft 0in) wheelbase, becoming SLD and SLP in dropside and platform truck forms. This wheelbase was actually 1in less than that of the OL 5-tonner, but the forward-control layout made it possible to provide a clear length within the body of 16ft, which was 2ft more than that model.

The SS short model intended primarily as a tipper (SST) had a wheelbase of 116in (9ft 8in), and an ultra-short tractor version intended for artic haulage, type SA, had a wheelbase of only 86in (7ft 2in). The S-type goods range was to remain in production until 1960, substantially unchanged in chassis design and, except in minor respects, appearance over that period, though new engine options were to be offered, as described later.

The SB passenger model also introduced late in 1950 had a wheelbase of 206in (17ft 2in), the latter intended to suit the 27ft 6in overall length limit on two-axle single-deck buses or coaches that had been in force when it was designed. In the event, this latter had been increased to 30ft with effect from 1st June 1950, before the SB was announced, but by then the initial designs were set, so early production versions of the model were of about this length, and hence 33-seat capacity was at first normal in coach form.

The SB was supplied with a similar bulbous front cowl to that on the goods models, which set bodybuilders considerable problems from a styling viewpoint, as it did not match very happily with most existing coach designs. However, Duple produced a new coach design called the Vega for the SB on its introduction, the styling of which married up with the bulbous front quite well, though even this was abandoned from 1953, and thereafter the complete frontal styling was as chosen by the bodybuilder in the case of almost all SB coaches from major British bodybuilders. In later years the standard front tended to become associated with export versions and military bus applications. Even so, SB chassis continued to leave Luton with the rounded front until much later in the course of a very long production run, and the cowl panel was promptly removed by coach bodybuilders on arrival in most cases. The SB was to long

Another artist's impression conveys the intended appearance of the SB passenger version of the Big Bedford range as at its introduction in 1950. At that stage there was still very close co-operation between Bedford and Duple, whose body design was given the name Vega, and it is clear that the intention was that the appearance would show a close relationship with the goods models, and having features quite unlike Duple's other bodywork of the time.

The SB chassis in its original 206-in wheelbase form as introduced in 1950. It incorporated a low-level section at the rear to suit coach bodywork with a luggage boot at the rear.

The frame assembly of the Big Bedford measures 324¼ inches, providing ample room and sturdy support for spacious 33-seater coachwork. The frame is cold squeeze riveted, with six cross-members, and the depth of the main section of the side-members is a full 10 inches. Side-members are arched over the rear axle, and the section to the rear is wider and at a lower level to provide space for an extra large luggage locker.
Engine accessibility is a special feature of the design. All components requiring routine maintenance can be reached by raising the hinged engine cowl to the left of the driver, and there are removable side-panels, secured by quick-release fasteners, one at each side of the cowl. The front end sheet-metal work is also secured by quick-release fasteners, so that the engine can be withdrawn for major overhaul in a minimum of time.

CHASSIS PRICE £690

outlast its goods equivalent in remaining a catalogue model until the end of Bedford production in 1986, though almost entirely for export latterly – more details of its subsequent development appear in later chapters.

With these models, Bedford had embarked on a fresh course, breaking into new markets or, to some degree, creating them. As already indicated, quite a number of existing Bedford users simply moved up for part or all of their needs. Clearly, the economics of going up from 5-ton to 7-ton capacity were tempting when the vehicle cost did not rise disproportionately, as was apt to be so if a switch

to a model from one of the traditional heavy-duty manufacturers was made.

In fairness, it has to be recorded that Bedford was not quite the first manufacturer to endeavour to capture what might be called the 'in between' market with a light 7-ton forward-control model. In 1948, Commer had introduced such a design, the QX, with what it described as an underfloor engine but was soon expressively described as the Commer 'sloper', a 4.75-litre six-cylinder overhead-valve petrol engine with its cylinders inclined at quite a steep angle to allow them to be below cab floor level.

This line-up of coaches operated by Abel's Coaches, of Wells-next-the-Sea, Norfolk, was taken soon after the arrival of an early example of the SB with Duple Vega body, MAH 428, in the Spring of 1951, and shows how the new model contrasted with existing Bedford coaches. Of the three standard OB Vista coaches visible, GNG 61, on the right of the line, dated from late 1946; FPW 26, to the left of the SB, was one of the earliest of the type, dating from early 1946, while HNG 407, second from the left, was new in 1947. The OWB on the left, JPW 462, was registered in late 1948, which implies that it was re-registered and may have been ex-military, which may account for the lack of the normal indicator box. The joker in the pack is BRE 806, of which the registration dates from early 1935, suggesting it was probably a WTL, rebuilt with OB grille and headlamps and rebodied by Mann Egerton, of Norwich, a bodybuilder more usually associated with Austin coach chassis, but here doubtless persuaded to build a body which, to some degree, was a Vista look-alike for a local concern.

This view of an SB with Duple Vega body supplied for use by Charlton Athletic Football Club in November 1951 shows off the appearance quite effectively — there was more than a hint of a contemporary air-liner's cockpit about the treatment of the cab side windows. This vehicle had its offside seats set in facing pairs with tables between them and glass quarter-lights were fitted in the roof. The sliding roof was just beginning to lose favour but had obvious possibilities here if the team was successful.

However, this did not seriously dent Bedford's dominance of the market.

To a small operator, the modest rise in first cost was an important factor, and for larger firms such as tipper operators engaged on contract work, a similar formula of buying low-cost vehicles, working them hard and writing the cost off over a relatively short life had its attractions just as had been so with the O-type tippers.

Running costs were inevitably greater than for smaller models, but petrol consumption of 9.3 mpg on an SLD with drop-side body carrying a test load of 7tons 6cwt and a total laden weight including driver and observer of 10tons 8cwt 2qr, was recorded by L. J. Cotton for *The Commercial Motor* in March 1951. This doubtless encouraged potential buyers, even if it could be beaten by heavier but much more expensive diesel models. A factor which was of increasing importance was the tendency for wage rates to rise, making the cost of employing a driver a greater part of the overall equation, so if the vehicle could carry more this helped to redress the balance. The S-type also gained by virtue of its higher legal speed and relatively lively performance on the road, and here again this, allowing more trips to be completed, could compensate for some loss of fuel economy against a slower diesel model.

Road tests by the trade press were becoming tougher, and it is interesting to note that L. J. Cotton, though praising the car-like general performance, found that it was possible to virtually fade out the brakes completely in 3 miles of an admittedly contrived test involving driving at full throttle in third gear against the brakes. He had no such reservations in regard to the SB with Duple Vega 33-seat body laden with more than the equivalent to a full passenger load tried three months later, when a different

technique of repeated sharp stops from 30mph revealed only very mild fade after 36 such stops in 35 minutes. In this case, fuel consumption on simulated coach service running at up to 40mph (realistic, despite this being illegal at the time) gave 10.85mpg, with 9.3mpg when making one stop per mile. The unladen weight was 4 tons 9 cwt, a figure less than that of many modern midibuses. The vehicle was running at 7 tons 1 cwt gross in the test.

Despite these good results, there is no clear evidence to suggest any significant recapture of operators which had already adopted diesel-engined models of other makes in the 7-ton or 33-seat class; having made the additional investment, they were reaping the reward of greater fuel economy and, often, more durable if heavier vehicles. Yet the Bedford S-type, and also the Commer 'sloper', were creating a new middle ground which was to influence the trend of British commercial vehicle design.

The situation created by the introduction of the SB on the coach market was different from that of the goods version of the S in one important respect for, to widespread surprise, the OB was withdrawn from production after November 1950, despite still selling very well up to that point. Thus Bedford ceased to offer a model in the class seating 29 passengers or less which it had dominated hitherto. Hence the thousands of operators who had standardised on Bedford coaches were virtually forced to move to the 33-seat class. It could be argued that, as with the truck models, the prospect of carrying more passengers at only modest extra first cost would, and did, tempt many OB users to switch to the SB, but in this case, the option of staying with the smaller category was no longer offered, and perhaps ironically, the most obvious competitors to the OB had dropped out of production.

W. H. Smith & Son Ltd continued to standardise on Bedford vans. Seen here at the company's garage in Newcastle-on-Tyne are two K-types dating from 1951, complete with radiator muffs in deference to the bleak north-eastern winter. Partly visible on the left is a BYC model 12-cwt of the type with wire wheels that one of the authors clearly recalls as the standard type used by Smith's in that city in the late 1930s – the sliding cab door, convenient for rapid bulk newspaper deliveries, is noteworthy.

It could be argued that this was correct reading of the market, for the small coach class diminished quite sharply in importance in the 1950s and although there were calls from time to time for its revival in production nothing very significant materialised. One chance factor may have aided the change from OB to SB to be so widely accepted, for although the Ministry of Transport's legalisation of the 30ft overall length at short notice in June 1950 caught Bedford out in the sense that the new model announced in September was initially to the 'old' 27ft 6in limit, this meant that it was not hugely larger than the OB, and for a time the new Bedford was thus still shorter than most new heavy-duty coaches entering service in 1951-2.

There did remain a significant number of operators who continued to run existing OB coaches, notably on rural bus services, quite often for far longer than might have been expected in earlier times, and the fact that they are by no means uncommon as preserved vehicles is partly due to the fact that so many survived as working vehicles into the era when preservation took off.

A new 19½-acre extension to the Luton factory was built to accommodate the extra production anticipated with the new broader range but ironically a national steel shortage held back the overall increase in commercial vehicle production to just over an extra 2,000 in 1951 compared to 1950, the total figure being 42,503, rising slightly to 43,522 in 1952. Vauxhall car production was hit more severely, dropping back to around 35,000 in those two years after touching just over 47,000 in 1950, so Bedford was again a bigger name than Vauxhall in terms of vehicle output, a situation that had also been true in most of the 1930s as well as the immediate post-war period of 1946-7.

The O-type goods range remained in production alongside the S-type into the early 1950s. This preserved OLBC 5-ton model with a special dropside body having a deep headboard in the livery of M. R. Coe, of Hockley, Essex, retains the original look of the model very effectively, save for the addition of flashing indicators to suit modern traffic conditions. Note the Ford 10-cwt van in the background on the left – the type was a strong competitor to Bedford's small van models of the period.

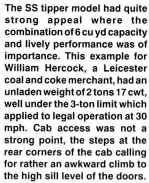

The SS tipper model had quite strong appeal where the combination of 6 cu yd capacity and lively performance was of importance. This example for William Hercock, a Leicester coal and coke merchant, had an unladen weight of 2 tons 17 cwt, well under the 3-ton limit which applied to legal operation at 30 mph. Cab access was not a strong point, the steps at the rear corners of the cab calling for rather an awkward climb to the high sill level of the doors.

Some well-known names appeared on S-type models, such as Tate & Lyle, in whose smart dark blue livery this 1953 SA with semi-trailer is seen taking part in a Lorry Driver of the Year competition. Precise manoeuvring was the skill being tested and the 300 cu in petrol engine's smooth and steady tickover would be a help to this driver, though the poor close-range vision would not.

When first announced in 1959, a bus-seated version of the standard curvaceous Duple Vega body was offered for the SB, but few seem to have entered service. Instead, Mulliners Ltd produced a bus body which was clearly an extended derivative of that built for the OB, with similar styling details at front and rear, though marrying a little awkwardly with the S-type bulbous nose. This 1951 example was operated by Express Dairies for staff transport but somewhat similar buses were produced for military use.

10 THE CA VAN, AND A NEW GENERATION OF MEDIUM TRUCKS

The major event of 1952 was the introduction of the CA van, of the same 10/12-cwt nominal capacity as the PC model it replaced. There had been previous examples of models which differed from the car model to which they were related, such as the Ford E83W and the Morris Y introduced in the late 1930s; both were fitted with off set engines. In the post-war years both Ford and Morris went to forward-control with the 400E and the J type. Bedford's CA represented a fundamental reappraisal of the needs of the small commercial vehicle.

However the Bedford CA adopted semi-forward control and, in front-end layout, could be regarded as a scaled-down version of the concept pioneered by the WT and found on the O-type, still in production at the time, even though the appearance was very different, and indeed controversial. The four-cylinder 1,507cc petrol engine was set well forward and by allowing the rear end of the cylinder block to protrude slightly into the interior space, the driver could also sit well forward, though not so far as to cause any obstruction to easy entry or exit from his seat, clearly regarded as a key feature of a vehicle where repeated delivery stops were likely. External sliding doors were provided on each side and these had spring loaded catches to allow the van to be driven with these doors open.

The three-speed gearbox had steering-column control, as on the previous PC model, but in this case the feature

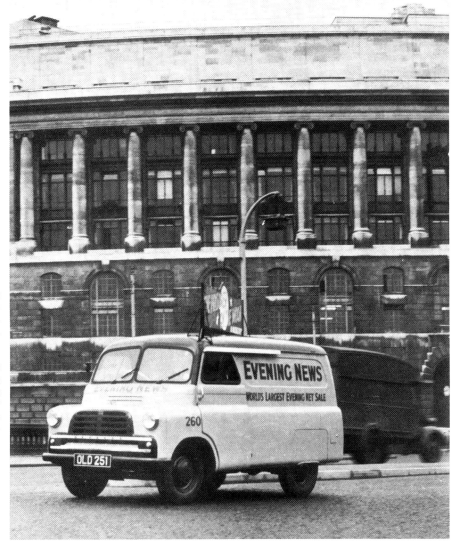

The CA van was one of Bedford's most successful products, with over 370,000 produced between 1952 and 1969. Its appearance, certainly not beautiful, was very controversial at first, but with familiarity the aptness of its stocky, somehow almost bulldog-like, look began to seem appropriate to its utilitarian character. Perhaps the most lasting memory for anyone who knew London in that period or for some years after was of the fleets of them that were used to distribute the leading evening papers, to be seen scurrying around the capital, dropping off bundles to the various news-stands via the sliding doors. This example in the yellow-painted Evening News fleet seen crossing Blackfriars Bridge dates from about 1954 and shows the original style of divided windscreen.

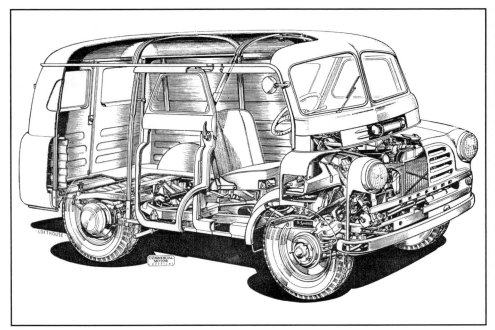

The logic of the CA design is revealed in this cutaway drawing of the model made for The Commercial Motor on its introduction. About half of the 1.5-litre engine was housed under the snub-nosed bonnet and the other half inside the body shell, this view revealing how the air-cleaner over the Zenith carburettor was tucked under the nearside of the windscreen, though hidden from view from within by the dash panel. This enabled the driving position to be set well forward, the pedals being almost directly over the independent suspension unit for the offside front wheel. Also visible is the steering-column gear-change, which worked better than most of its type, having only to cope with the three-speed gearbox, and allowed the driver to use the nearside door quite readily. The layout gave quite a roomy interior despite compact overall length of 12ft 10in.

had practical merit in that its location removed any obstruction to the driver leaving the vehicle by the nearside door, the handbrake being horizontal alongside the driving seat and low enough not to get in the way.

The mechanical design had some features in common with the contemporary Wyvern E-model car, including the engine, which although again an overhead-valve unit of typical Vauxhall pattern, was a new design adopting the fashionable 'over-square' cylinder dimensions, in other words having a bore size greater than the stroke, even though only slightly so, the figures being $3\frac{1}{8}$in and 3in respectively. It developed 40bhp at 4,000rpm, quite a modest speed for such a unit.

It was a very tractable engine, well suited to its task in the CA, giving smooth and lively mid-range performance and only becoming fussy at higher speeds, not of any consequence in normal delivery work. By modern standards, the provision of only three speeds would be criticised, but even four-speed cars of those days often had quite wide ratios and the engine's characteristics meant that it would pull strongly at quite low speeds, making frequent gear changes unnecessary.

Vauxhall had abandoned the unusual form of independent suspension using short torsion bars found on earlier models in favour of a coil-spring system adopted for the CA as well as its cars of the period, which gave quite good ride characteristics despite a short wheelbase in the original CA of 90in (7ft 6in). This helped in manoeuvrability, it being possible to turn round in a 30ft roadway without reversing or touching the kerbs. A hypoid rear axle was used and the low transmission line this enabled helped in providing a low floor level. Drum brakes were operated via a conventional hydraulic system.

The body, 6in wider, 2in higher and $3\frac{1}{2}$in longer internally than on the PC, offered a load space of 135 cu ft, an increase of 15 cu ft despite overall length reduced from 14ft 2in to 12ft 10in and an altogether handier vehicle, although external width was slightly increased,

going from 5ft 5in to 5ft 10in. It also had the virtue from the point of view of most businesses of being eye-catchingly 'different'. When first introduced, it looked particularly strange. By that date, new car designs often had built-up front mudguards incorporating the headlamps and full-width bonnets but the effect on the CA seemed odd, largely because the bonnet top was low and yet the sill line of the vee windscreen was set about a foot above it. Driving vision was not a problem because the driver sat sufficiently high and not too far back from the windscreen. In other respects the lines, basically very simple, were effective in conveying a modern image. Yet the cost when introduced was £400, to which the purchase tax of the day added £80, making it comparable to a low-cost small car of the time.

It was an almost instant success, L. J. Cotton heading his report 'The Roundsman's Joy', and sales soon soared, picking up business from competitive makes of varying designs. A line of business for which it proved almost ideally suited was newspaper delivery. In London during the period from soon after the model appeared up to the early 1970s, fleets of CA vans were to be seen scurrying around the streets, especially at the time of fierce competition between the three evening papers of those days, immortalised in the news-vendor's cry 'News, Star or Standard'. Much the same applied in other major cities, but the model appealed to a wide variety of trades.

Although the van version was the most familiar, there was also a pick-up as well as a small personnel carrier. More specialised bodywork included such varied applications as ice-cream vans, ambulances and tippers, quite apart from mobile stair units for use at airports where air liners loaded or unloaded on the tarmac. In due course it built up a following as a small motor caravan, more especially when the 102-in wheelbase version was introduced in 1959. Martin Walter invented the trade name Dormobile for such vehicles and for a time the CA was apt, inaccurately, to be called a Dormobile in casual conversations even when in van form. It remained in

Although most CA models were vans, the type was available in what was called chassis-scuttle form, and this example was bodied by Spurling, retaining the standard front-end and windscreen but having an open-backed body with hinged side doors.

production until 1969, by which time some 370,000 had been built.

At the other end of Bedford's size range was the introduction of a four-wheel-drive (4x4) model derived from the S-type and thus a successor to the wartime QL. This was the R-type, or more precisely the RL, introduced as part of an upsurge of interest in military vehicles largely related to the Korean war which was raging at that time and in which British forces were engaged.

In fact Vauxhall Motors Ltd had been asked to design a prototype 6x6 model known as the FV series 1300, one of a range of models intended to meet post-war Army requirements – others in the series were the Austin Champ FV 1800 ¼-ton 4x4 and the Humber FV1600 1-ton 4x4. These latter did go into limited production but the FV1300 never got beyond the prototype series, the project being transferred to Albion in 1952, development trials continuing until the project was cancelled in 1953. These FV series

projects were excessively complex and expensive; the cost to the taxpayer must have been staggering.

Although circumstances led to the development of military models more closely related to normal commercial types, the result was a series of Army vehicles which were to give very good service around the world. Prominent among them was the RL, put into production in April 1952 – in all, 73,135 R-type models were produced between then and 1969, when the type was replaced by the M-type. The general design could be described as similar to the S but with transmission layout to convey drive to both axles, in principle much as had been produced in the QL. This time the problem of the screaming transmission was largely overcome and the noise of the R-type was mainly that produced by the coarse tread of the military tyres.

The model became available on the civilian market in October 1953, meeting a demand for vehicles capable of cross-country operation where required. In addition to the

The pattern of Bedford producing four-wheel-drive models for military or other cross-country duty that had begun with the wartime QL was continued with the RL, perhaps better-known under the more generic R-type name. The designation suggests that initial development may have pre-dated the S-type, though clearly RL moves on logically from QL. In fact, when introduced in 1952, it inherited important elements already in large-scale production from the S-type, most notably the cab and the 300 cu in petrol engine. Although of taller build than the S to allow clearance for the driven front axle under the engine sump, the overall effect was quite well-proportioned, as conveyed in this broadside view.

Development testing of the R-type was nothing if not rigorous, as shown in these views. Note the extent to which the frame and body twisted to accommodated the movement of the axles – as usual on cross-country vehicles, the springs were relatively stiff to reduce the likelihood of repeatedly hitting the bump stops and damaging the frame.

normal military applications, other variants were produced and one of these is still apt to be in the news from time to time 40 years or so after it entered service. It comprised the famous 'Green Goddess' fire engines, mainly on RLHZ chassis, basically the RL but with modifications to suit their fire-engine role. The initial design was produced in 1953 on a variant of the S-type, the SHZ, these being normal road-going machines without the driven front wheels and thus on conventional tyres, twinned at the rear. Then the availability of the four-wheel-drive chassis led to a decision to standardise on that for later deliveries, which continued until 1956. They have a Sigmund 900 gallon-per-minute pump, emergency tanks to carry 300 gallons of water (400 gallons on the SHZ), 1,800ft of hose and 35ft extension ladders.

They were intended to deal with major emergencies – at that date there was a resurgence of interest in Civil Defence influenced by the renewed threat of the Korean war leading to a wider conflict, and doubtless the prospect of damaged roads was in mind when four-wheel drive was chosen. They were purchased for use by the Auxiliary Fire Service, although the vehicles were owned by the Home Office. The Army Fire Service also bought some of the RLHZ model, though these were painted red. In more recent years the Green Goddesses have become a back-up force that is deployed from time to time when local fire brigades are disrupted by strikes. They are well-maintained and, despite their age, have proved to be reliable performers, their 300 cu in petrol engines still capable of sustained pumping when required. The gearing chosen as suitable for the four-wheel drive makes maximum speed less than on a conventional fire engine but in other respects they have proved capable of taking over remarkably effectively from modern machines when the need arises.

The early 1950s were a time of change in regard to senior staff at Vauxhall Motors Ltd. Charles Bartlett, who had been Managing Director since 1930 and was knighted in 1944, retired in 1953 at the age of 64. He was replaced by William Ewart Hill, who had been with General Motors since 1922 but stayed with Vauxhall for only two years, giving way to Philip Copelin who remained until April 1961 when he left to run General Motors' New York office.

On the engineering side, C. E. King remained Chief Engineer until 1952, then joined the Board of the company until 1954 when he retired. Harold Drew, who had been Assistant Chief Engineer since 1929, succeeded him as Chief Engineer briefly but left for Detroit to become Chief Engineer of GM's Overseas Division, the first Englishman to hold the post. Maurice Platt was then appointed Chief Engineer at Vauxhall – he had joined the company in 1937 after being a technical journalist with *The Motor*, working on various projects, including taking over development of the Churchill tank engine from Alex Taub during the war years, but had been concerned with cars in the early post-war period. David Jones, who had joined the firm in 1934 continued to be responsible for styling though, in this field, the influence of the headquarters GM styling studio in Detroit was becoming even more strongly evident than previously.

The earlier production batches of what became known as the Green Goddesses (because of their dark green Auxiliary Fire Service livery) were built on a modified version of the S-type chassis, type SHZ, to Home Office specification. Here two, NYV 65 and 66, are seen in October 1955, having been issued to the Sheffield Fire Brigade in April 1954. Several London registration number series were wholly or largely allocated to the AFS, numbers from NYR 1 to 858 and large blocks in the NYV series being on SHZ chassis, though a minority had other types of body – there were over 1,400 SHZ vehicles in the scheme. The bodywork, also to Home Office design, was by Willowbrook on the vehicles shown – other Green Goddess bodies were by other firms well known as bus or coach bodybuilders, including Harrington, Park Royal, Plaxton, Strachans, Weymann, Whitson and Windover, plus Papworth Industries.

The four-wheel-drive RLHZ version of the Green Goddess is very similar to the two-wheel-drive SHZ in general appearance apart from the different wheels and higher build. The water tank they carry is of smaller capacity and mounted further forward, together with the hose reels on each side. Seen here is RXP 625, dating from circa 1955 but still in the Home Office stock when photographed in June 1995. The olive green livery remains, though without the red AFS emblem. The main registration series of RLHZ vehicles, mainly Green Goddess pump units, were NYV 686 upwards, plus blocks in the PGW, RGC, RXP, RYX, SXF and SYH series, over 2,000 being built. Although originally intended as part of a national fire appliance reserve for use in the event of nuclear war, they have been used in recent years to provide emergency cover of a different kind when normal fire brigades are unable to operate due to strikes.

Fire engines on other Bedford chassis were built in the 1950s. The City of Birmingham Fire Brigade chose the SB coach chassis, reduced to 12ft 6in wheelbase by Baico and other chassis engineering by Prestage Ltd, Birmingham, as a basis for this design with a Dennis pump and Wilsden body in 1951. This example, preserved by John Thompson, co-author of 'The Green Machine' which includes detailed lists of the Green Goddesses and related types, is seen when on display at the Interfire exhibition in July 1975.

Left: The SH-series fire engine chassis was also chosen for some appliances supplied to local authority fire brigades, such as this emergency tender for Croydon Fire Brigade dating from mid-1953. The registration number, LOY 999, issued in what was then Croydon County Borough's OY series, was particularly appropriate.

Below left: Late examples of some of the 'traditional' models in their final form with synchromesh gearbox acquired large radiator badges, not unlike the type used on S models, in the post-1950 period. This preserved ML 2-ton model with Sunderland registration dating from 1951 still carried the name of S. Stamp, market gardener of that city, when photographed.

Below: Although Duple continued as the main coach bodybuilder on Bedford chassis there were some notable exceptions, such as the 20 SB models with Burlingham 30-seat bodywork purchased for touring duty in 1952 by Scottish Omnibuses Ltd, then continuing to trade as SMT. They had bodywork to the Seagull style originally introduced on underfloor-engined chassis but adapted to suit front-engined models, not only the SB, as seen in the two leading vehicles in this line-up in Edinburgh, but also to rebody chassis originally fitted with half-cab bodywork, two on pre-war AEC Regal chassis making up the rear of this similar-looking quartet.

A sense of nostalgia for the Bedford OB persisted through the 1950s. One result was the Duple Sportsman body built in 'woody' estate car style, using the OLAZ 3-ton goods chassis in the same manner as applied with the WTL 3-ton model in 1935 before the WTB was introduced. The frontal styling of the body had strong Vista overtones as can be seen in this view of a 1952 demonstrator in a very 'English' scene in Kent when new. The sales response to the exposed external woodwork was poor, but vehicles with basically similar bodywork panelled in the normal way did find buyers on a limited scale, most notably with the fleet of David MacBrayne Ltd operating in the Highlands of Scotland, where small vehicles were preferred for some of the more remote services. A fleet of 22 OLAZ buses with Duple bodies of this outline was placed in service in 1952, ten seating 25, nine seating 20 and three seating fourteen as built, though the capacities were altered in later years.

Sand and gravel merchants were important customers for tippers, and the S-type followed in the footsteps of the O-type models in catering for the trade. This 1953 SS model is smartly restored in the livery of the Lea Valley Sand & Gravel fleet – the shape of the rear mudguards was a characteristic feature.

The A types brought quite a dramatic change in appearance to Bedford's medium-weight range, Here an early A-type of 1953, thought to be an A5L 5-ton long-wheelbase model, is seen with an ML 2-3-ton model of a few months earlier, both in the fleet of W. D. & H. O. Wills, the tobacco concern, outside whose No.4 factory they are standing. The A-type is carrying hogsheads of tobacco and the M-type cartons of cigarettes. Both vehicles carry tarpaulins in the rack provided over the cab. Far more commodities, even of high value, were carried in open vehicles in those days.

The A-series trucks

Transatlantic influence was certainly evident in the range of middle-weight trucks introduced in the Spring of 1953, replacing the K, M and O types that had been first introduced in 1939, and indeed had features familiar from earlier types. The new models were generally known as the A types though a policy of using a T prefix for truck models began to be applied, so designations were also sometimes quoted as TA. Sub-divisions A2, A3, A4 and A5 identified models according to weight rating, and suffix letters indicated wheelbase and body type in the manner already familiar on other models.

The A range used a cab and front-end design that was outwardly almost identical to the 'Advanced Design' cab adopted by Chevrolet for a new range of trucks introduced in the United States and related markets on 1st May 1947. To some degree, history was thus repeating itself, since the original Bedfords of 1931 were derived from a Chevrolet design, though in the new range, the mechanical design was of Bedford origin and largely derived from existing models.

The aim may have been partly to bring Bedford more closely into line with Chevrolet from the point of view of

the many parts of the world where both makes were familiar, and clearly such a policy saved Vauxhall Motors the development and tooling costs of a new cab of its own. The cab was more comfortable, with better sound and heat insulation and such details as effective dust and draught sealing, and the absence of the internal engine cowl together with the introduction of a cranked gear lever allowed the driver to exit from the cab on the nearside more readily.

On the other hand, it implied sacrifice of several advantages of the compact semi-forward-control design which had proved so successful on the Bedford range of models from 3- to 5-ton capacity for 20 years, for all the A models, like the Chevrolet, were of normal-control layout with a noticably longer bonnet than found on the O-type. The variation in layout between the K and M, on the one hand, and the O on the other no longer applied.

A new style of broader and shallower grille was adopted, having three horizontal bars. The front mudguards were built up, incorporating the headlamps, and the front skirt panel was swaged to form a deeper front bumper. On the original version the sidelamps were of square shape, built into the wings alongside the headlamps. The bonnet was hinged at the rear and provided with counterbalancing

The new cab and bonnet assembly of the A-type bore a strong resemblance to the Chevrolet 'Advanced Design' cab as first seen in 1947, restoring the situation that had applied in the early 1930s when Bedford and Chevrolet models looked very similar. Although the new cab was better finished and more comfortable than its predecessor, close-range forward vision for the driver was less good over the higher and more rounded bonnet line, making it less 'handy' in confined spaces. This A5L 5-ton model was No. 216 in the fleet of Nichols & Son (Brighton) Ltd, also responsible for the van body, which accounts for the Brighton registration NCD 100 despite the Southall, Middlesex address of Quaker Oats, on whose behalf it was operated. Signwriting such a vehicle, still done by hand in the 1950s, called for skill and a good 'eye'.

springs to make it easier to open, but the height of the new front end made anything much more than checking the water level while standing on the ground impractical.

Although close-range forward vision was not as restricted as on the S-type, it was not as good as had been the case especially on the O-type, the new bonnet top being higher and broader as well as longer than those of the previous models. This was of no consequence when travelling on the open road, but perhaps reflected the relative importance of manoeuvring in confined space as a more common problem in Britain, with older towns and narrower and less regular street layouts.

The engine was mounted about 6in further forward than hitherto, the chassis being extended forward accordingly, and the overall length was increased by between 8 and 20 inches, according to model – wheelbase lengths of most models were extended slightly from those of their predecessors. Chassis weights increased by between 2- and 4-cwt, this being due to a combination of the new cab, longer springs, wider axles and the dimensional effects quoted above.

However, another new factor with more positive implications from an operating viewpoint was the availability as a factory-fitted option of diesel engines, in

those days often called oil engines in Britain. Bedford had taken a very conservative line in this regard, no doubt influenced to some degree by American ideas, for there the low cost of petrol discouraged progress towards any alternative. Even in Britain, satisfactory diesel engines suitable for vehicles of the sizes Bedford was then producing had not been available in the early days of diesel road vehicle development.

Frank Perkins founded a factory to produce such units in Peterborough in 1932 and after building various four-cylinder designs, the Perkins P6 six-cylinder indirect-injection unit of 4.73-litre capacity was introduced in 1937. It rapidly became recognised as the most widely-used diesel engine in its class, although for a further 15-20 years the proportion of diesel to petrol remained much lower in the range under 5-ton or 26-seat capacity than was by then the case among heavier vehicles. Many sales during this period were for conversions of existing petrol-engined vehicles, and its compact size made replacement of typical six-cylinder petrol engines of the 3.5 to 4 litre class relatively simple.

Even though the Perkins P6 was the cheapest proprietary oil engine in this class, it added significant cost (about £300 in 1950) to a new vehicle so powered by comparison with the petrol equivalent and thus represented a large extra cost which took some time to recover when fuel costs were low. A few makers had begun to offer the P6 as an option, Dodge, which imported its petrol engines from the United States, doing so on a small scale from 1938, while Seddon standardised on the P6 for its entire range in the early days. After the war Commer and, for a time, Ford also offered this engine.

Bedford adopted the Perkins P6 diesel as its first official factory diesel option for the A range as an alternative to what was now called the 214 cu in petrol engine, in other words what had hitherto been called the 28hp unit. The Perkins was of significantly larger swept volume at 4.73 litres compared to 3.52 litres for the petrol unit, but the power rating, 83bhp, was almost identical, though developed at somewhat lower speed, 2,400rpm compared to the 84bhp at 3,100rpm of the 214 cu in engine.

The models in the new range were as shown alongside, quoting them in chassis form (when standard bodies were fitted, say dropside, another letter, in this case D, was substituted for Z):-

Model	Load rating	Wheelbase	Engine	Tyre size ('T'signifies twin rears)
A2Z	1¼-ton	9ft 11in	214 cu in	7.50-16
A3SZ	3-ton	9ft 11in	214 cu in	6.50-20T
A3LZ	3-ton	11ft 11in	214 cu in	6.50-20T
A4SZG	4-ton	10ft 0in	214 cu in	7.00-20T
A4SLG	4-ton	13ft 11in	214 cu in	7.00-20T
A4SSG	tractor	10ft 0in	214 cu in	7.00-20T
A5SZG	5-ton	10ft 0in	214 cu in	7.50-20T
A5LZG	5-ton	13ft 11in	214 cu in	7.50-20T
A4SZO	4-ton	10ft 0in	Perkins P6	7.00-20T
A4LZO	4-ton	13ft 11in	Perkins P6	7.00-20T
A4SSO	Tractor	10ft 0in	Perkins P6	7.00-20T
A5SZO	5-ton	10ft 0in	Perkins P6	7.50-20T
A5LZO	5-ton	13ft 11in	Perkins P6	7.50-20T

Note that suffix O signified 'Oil' and G signified 'Gasoline', the former in British style and the latter American, a curious feature perhaps reflecting the fairly strong American influence at Luton at the time, though P was already in use to signify pick-up or platform bodywork.

The A2 model of 30-cwt load-carrying capacity, was on 16-in wheels, a feature that was later to spread up the size range, in this case with 7.50-16 tyres with singles at the rear. Car-style hub caps were provided, these two changes combining to give a more modern look to the wheels than on previous models in this size range. This example dated from early 1954 for the Firestone concern, with its British headquarters on the Great West Road on London's outskirts, and had an early example of a 'reversed' registration, with numbers before the letters, Middlesex being among the earliest issuing authorities to have completed its series of letters-first combinations.

By the early 1950s, conversions of Bedford O-series models, both goods and passenger, with the Perkins P6 diesel had become quite commonplace. Many of them received the chromium-plated emblem comprising four rings and a central diamond shape that was issued by Perkins, as seen here on the offside of the grille on this preserved OS tipper with 1946 registration. The Bedford Driver's Club badge at the foot of the nearside of the grille is an authentic item but the 'Judd' plate is evidently a personal touch. Offering new Bedford models with similar engines as a factory-built option was a recognition of growing demand as the economic advantages of diesel power became more widely recognised.

conditions and driver technique. The Perkins P6 was quite a reliable performer if oil changes were carried out fairly frequently.

Inevitably, interest extended to other models in the range, and the S-type was an obvious target. In 1952, the Arlington Motor Co Ltd, well-known dealers handling several makes of coach and lorry, began offering a conversion of the Bedford S with the Leyland O.350 engine, as fitted to Leyland Comet goods models. The O.350 was a 5.76-litre six-cylinder direct-injection engine and a test carried out by *The Commercial Motor* on one in an S-type tractor chassis hauling a Scammell semi-trailer carrying 10 tons gave almost 13mpg over a 41-mile course including both traffic and main road duty. The conversion cost £700, though the operator retained the petrol engine and clearly could either sell it or use it as a spare unit for other models. The scope for such conversions was clearly limited, but it pointed the way for later developments.

The first diesel engine to be offered in the S-type models was the Perkins R6, sometimes called the R6V in vehicle form. This was, in effect, a scaled-up version of the P6, with 4in bore, 4½in stroke and 5.56-litre (340 cu in) capacity. It developed 108bhp at 2,700rpm and was thus a logical alternative to the 300 cu in petrol engine. One was fitted in an S-type 7-ton model at the Amsterdam Motor Show, exhibited by General Motors Continental NV in

The A-type trucks soon began to be added to Bedford fleets, and they were well suited to many export markets though they never became as universal a sight in Britain as the previous generation of models. This was partly because some operators had moved up to the S-type but competition was becoming more intense.

In particular, Ford, which in those days sold its goods vehicles under the Thames trade name, had introduced a new range of models, giving up the previous forward-control cab and, oddly enough, adopting a semi-forward-control layout shortly before Bedford abandoned it. Early examples still had the Ford V8 petrol engine as standard, and in Britain this did not have the level of following of Bedford's six-cylinder unit, being generally regarded as more 'thirsty' on comparable work. By 1950 the Perkins P6 was an option on these Ford models, though taken up only to a limited degree, doubtless because of the cost. However, by 1953, Ford introduced a new 3.26-litre four-cylinder overhead-valve petrol engine known as the 'Cost Cutter', of rugged design, with five-bearing crankshaft, and intended specifically for the 2- and 3-ton models. It livened up sales considerably, and Ford began to challenge Bedford in this weight range more effectively than at any time since the early 1930s, marking the renewal of a battle between the two concerns for commercial vehicle sales that was to spread wider.

Bedford's new diesel option was in tune with growing interest in overall costs, and could soon repay its greater outlay on high-mileage applications – around 15-20mpg was possible, depending on the gross weight, road

Another conversion which influenced subsequent Bedford production models was that offered for S models, particularly the SA artic tractive unit, by the Arlington Motor Co Ltd, using the Leyland O.350 diesel engine then standard in the Leyland Comet range of trucks. This preserved example dates from early 1956, judging by the registration number, but conversions of this kind were being offered by 1952, and the addition of the pair of Comet badges to flank the Bedford/Vauxhall griffin emblem was characteristic of such conversions – the 'Diesel' badge on the driver's side seems likely to have been a subsequent addition in this case, even though as used on Bedford diesel models for a time.

Another example of the SA tractive unit that had evidently received a Leyland O.350 engine, judging by the Comet badges above the grille, was this example on the fleet of the Wimpey building and contractors concern, seen hauling a Scammell drop-frame semi-trailer with Ruston-Bucyrus 10-RB excavator. The SA dated from 1951 and the picture from about 1954 – no doubt the cost of conversion was justified for a vehicle on such duty, and the petrol engine released may well have proved useful as a spare in a large organisation of this type.

The first diesel engine to be offered as a factory-installed option for the S-type range was the Perkins R6, as seen here. It had many similarities to the same maker's successful P6 unit, and on paper seemed a promising design – Bedford's publicity referred to close co-operation between engineers from the Perkins and Bedford concerns in arriving at the details of the installation – a heavier-duty 12-in clutch became standard for both diesel and petrol versions, for example. This picture shows it complete with bell housing, ready for direct attachment of the standard Bedford four-speed synchromesh gearbox. Despite its specification including what appeared to be a sturdy integral cylinder block and crankcase extending well below the crankshaft centre-line and designed to give good support to the bearings, it proved to be prone to bottom-end trouble, although this was claimed to have been overcome in the later Mark II version.

April 1953, though production did not begin until the Autumn of that year. As on the A range, such vehicles were signified by an 'O' suffix to the type letters, 'G' being used for petrol versions. In addition to the S goods range, there were also SBO and SBG passenger chassis from the same date.

In a test of an SLDO dropside 7-ton truck laden with a 6ton 17cwt 2qr test load made in the Spring of 1954, L. J. Cotton of *The Commercial Motor*, aided by representatives of Vauxhall and Perkins, covered 581 miles from Luton to Newcastle, Carlisle and back in 20 hours of running time, the average speed being 29.8mph

– fuel consumption was 12.23mpg. The diesel version of the model was subject to a legal speed limit of 20mph at that date because its licensing weight was 3tons 3cwt, but the test was realistic in ignoring this, three of the drivers running at what was described as 'normal traffic pace' of 30-35mph, though the fourth ran at up to 40mph or so – governed road speed proved to be 43mph. In practice, the R6 did not prove as reliable as its smaller stablemate, and although a revised version of the engine sought to address the problem, it was perhaps as well that plans were already afoot for the introduction of Bedford's own-make diesel engine, as described in the next chapter.

For the 1954 season, Duple radically restyled its Super Vega body for the SB, adopting a frontal design more in keeping with its other products. The windscreen sill line was lower and the chassis was modified to permit this, the front panelling supplied with the chassis being discarded completely. More controversially, the oval grille at first used bore no resemblance to that on any other Bedford model, with no more than a small badge to convey the make of chassis and one wonders what the design studios at Luton and indeed Detroit might have thought about it. This demonstrator was registered late in 1953, and it is noteworthy that the lettering on the windows reads '38 seater Bedford petrol Super Vega – coachwork by Duple' – hitherto it could be taken for granted that a Bedford would have a petrol engine. The chassis designation at that stage was SBG – the final letter signifying 'gasoline' – the wheelbase remaining at the original 17ft 2in though the overall length had become almost 29ft.

Similar in appearance, save for a less fussy side-flash treatment, were a batch of eighteen SBO coaches with 37-seat Duple bodies dating from early 1954 for the Eastern Counties Omnibus Co Ltd, of which six, including the vehicle shown, carried the Metropolitan fleetname of a Great Yarmouth operator whose business had been acquired by Eastern Counties in 1951. However, these vehicles were mainly of interest in having Gardner 4LK diesel engines rather than the Perkins R6 standard at that date. Eastern Counties, a member of the Tilling group of companies at that date forming part of the State-owned British Transport Commission empire, had standardised on Gardner engines since the late-1930s, using the very economical if noisy four-cylinder 3.8-litre 4LK in small Dennis and other buses since 1938. They are believed to have been the only Bedford chassis to enter service with Gardner engines, though it is thought probable that they were not installed on the Bedford production line. Later that year, Bristol introduced its lightweight SC bus using the 4LK together with Bedford SB axles and brake systems for use by Tilling companies and it seems likely that the two ventures were interconnected to some degree.

11 MORE NEW RANGES AND BEDFORD'S OWN DIESELS

Output of Bedford vehicles was increasing, reaching 48,354 in 1953 and 60,836 in 1954. It had been decided to transfer production of truck and related models to new premises at Dunstable, about three miles west of Luton, where there was already a parts and accessories department. A huge new plant was built as part of a £36 million expansion programme also aimed at increasing Vauxhall car output. The choice of Dunstable made that town peculiarly associated with the volume production of commercial vehicles, for one of Bedford's main competitors, Commer, based at Luton since 1906, had moved its main plant to Dunstable by 1953 – in those days Commer was part of the Rootes group whose main car factories were in Coventry – much later, alliances brought Dodge and then Renault commercial vehicle output to the Commer premises.

The first Bedford built at the new Dunstable factory rolled off the line on 2nd August 1955. The combined Vauxhall Motors floor area of 85 acres was just over double what it had been in 1937 and the workforce of 16,487 people was also almost twice what it had been then, yet the combined output of 143,567 cars and commercial vehicles that year was 240% of the 1937 figure.

The main range of models built in 1954-55 continued largely as was being produced after the introduction of the A range in 1953. Doubtless continuity of product helped in the transfer to new premises although minor revisions in specification were made from time to time during this period. The hydro-mechanical brake system of early S-types gave way to an all-hydraulic system operated via the vacuum servo by early 1954.

Soon after the Dunstable factory was opened, the SB appeared in a new longer-wheelbase form. When introduced in the autumn of 1950, it had been designed with 206in (17ft 2in) wheelbase for the 27ft 6in overall length limit that had been in force until June of that year, and early examples were of just over that length at 27ft 8in, even though the legal length limit had become 30ft by then. However, it was soon realised that it would be possible to build a slightly longer body on the chassis. By the 1952 Show, the overall length was quoted as 28ft 11¾in for the standard Duple Vega and Super Vega bodies (both at that stage having much the same appearance as the original, the Super Vega name indicating superior interior trim), with seats for 35 or 37.

The limitation on going further was the restriction on overhang. Duple followed the idea of almost yearly face-lifts then common in the car trade, introducing a fresh profile late in 1953 for the 1954 season, discarding the bulbous nose as supplied on the chassis in favour of a smooth and unbroken curve with deeper windscreen panels in curved glass, but at that stage dimensions did not alter further.

It was not until 10th August 1955 that a new 216in (18ft) wheelbase version of the SB was announced, allowing bodywork to be of the full maximum 30ft overall length of the time. The new frame was also $2\frac{5}{8}$in higher than the original design, since it had been found that bodybuilders did not use the capability of the early SB frame height of 2ft 4in to provide a relatively low floor line – arranging all seats to face forward was the priority on a coach and a floor

The S-type continued in production through the mid-1950s with no external change, though the brake system become all-hydraulic by early 1954. This SL registered later that year was placed in service by W. J. Everett Ltd, scrap metal merchants, of Kings Lynn, Bedford's photographer taking a typically effective shot conveying the atmosphere of such premises on a gloomy day in January 1956. The vehicle looked well cared-for but had the radiator partially blanked off, probably to make the cab a little less cold – heaters were still not standard.

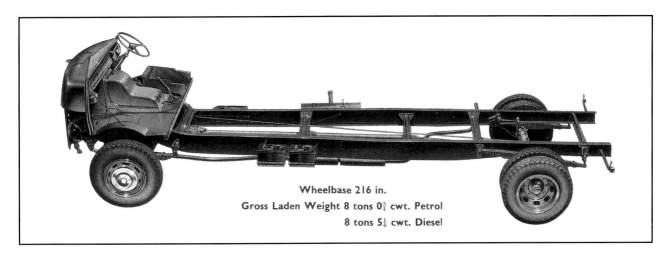

Wheelbase 216 in.
Gross Laden Weight 8 tons $0\frac{3}{4}$ cwt. Petrol
8 tons $5\frac{1}{4}$ cwt. Diesel

The SB passenger chassis appeared with wheelbase extended by 10in to 216in (18ft) from August 1955. The opportunity was taken to abandon what had been the traditional idea of a passenger vehicle chassis, with sidemembers dropped slightly between the axles, in favour of a substantially straight frame, save for a slight upward sweep over the front axle. At the rear, the frame was cut short on the basis that the bodybuilder would construct the body to be self-supporting at the rear. The front-end structure was equivalent to the cab base of the S-type goods models and, despite Duple and most other British bodybuilders providing their own front-end outline, the cowl and radiator grille continued to be fitted. In later years the external front end items were omitted and engine options altered but in essence the 216in SB chassis was to continue in production looking much as shown for over 30 years.

high enough to virtually eliminate wheel-arches within the body was favoured by all the large-scale bodybuilders.

Accordingly, the 216in-wheelbase version of the SB frame was flat from just behind the engine to the extreme rear. It now ended just behind the rear end of the rear springs, most bodies by that date being self-supporting at the rear. This had the practical advantage in manufacture that unbodied chassis were actually shorter than the previous type, occupying less space on the production line and while awaiting bodying.

Other minor changes from the original design included a lower air cleaner intake to permit a dropped windscreen line (this having been introduced to suit Duple's new

design for the 1954 season) and modified rear engine mountings for the oil-engined version. This at first continued to use the R6 engine and was thus still of type SBO, the change of wheelbase and frame not being picked up in model designations.

The modified engine mounting was an effort to reduce the transmission of noise and vibration – what had been quite satisfactory for the smooth running and quiet petrol engine had not proved satisfactory for the diesel, and indeed the engine noise level within the vehicle was to continue as one of the main shortcomings of front-engined Bedford diesel models for passenger work. In this respect, the use of full-fronted bodywork with no full-height

The longer wheelbase was barely detectable in its effect on appearance of the next generation of standard SB coach with Duple Super Vega body but the extra length was added to the body structure ahead of the entrance door, the standard seating capacity going up to 41. This example dated from late 1955, the front grille having moved on to what became known as the butterfly style.

The Burlingham "Seagull" Lightweight All-metal Luxury Coach

Years of research into the field of lightweight metal frame construction, allied to operational experience, have produced this 1956 "Seagull" model. The additional length of the new Bedford passenger chassis has enabled seating space to be provided for 41 passengers. While still retaining proved constructional methods, the scientific use of lightweight alloys achieves weight reduction to meet the demands for lower operating costs.

No sacrifice to design, styling, comfort or safety construction has been made in developing this new model.

The abridged specification will serve to show that the usual high standard of efficiency associated with "Seagull" bodies has been maintained in traditional style. A complete specification is available on request. The minimum number of extras are required to conform to the most fastidious requirements.

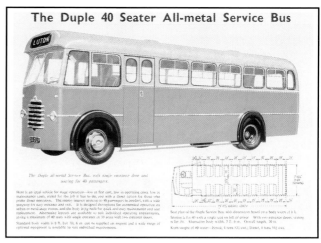

The Duple 40 Seater All-metal Service Bus

The Duple all-metal Service Bus, with single entrance door and seating for 40 passengers.

Here is an ideal vehicle for stage operation—low in first cost, low in operating costs, low in maintenance costs, styled for the job it has to do, yet with a dense option for those who prefer dense operation. The roomy interior seats up to 40 passengers in comfort, with a wide gangway for easy entrance and exit. It is designed throughout for economical operation on urban or rural stage routes, and the body is built for quick and easy maintenance and seat replacement. Alternative layouts are available to suit individual operating requirements, giving a maximum of 40 seats with single entrance, or 39 seats with two entrance doors.

Standard body, width is 8 ft, but 7ft. 6 in. can be supplied on request and a wide range of optional equipment is available to suit individual requirements.

Seat plan of the Duple Service Bus, with dimensions based on a body width of 8 ft.
Seating is for 40 with a single seat on left of driver . With two entrance doors, seating is for 39. Alternative body width, 7 ft. 6 in. Overall length, 30 ft.
Kerb weight of 40 seater—Petrol, 4 tons 12½ cwt.; Diesel, 4 tons 16½ cwt.

The Mulliner "Mighty Master" All-metal Service Bus

The Mulliner "Mighty Master" All-metal Service Bus with rear entrance door and seating for 36 passengers. To suit customers' special character and extreme overseas conditions good rails are not fitted. For use in the U.K. round rails are standard equipment.

The new Mulliner "Mighty Master" service bus combines light weight with immense strength. The body is constructed of steel sections carefully designed and shaped to counter vibration, twist and bump without fatigue while presenting a pleasing and proportional design.

Of welded construction, the body is built on the unit construction principle. This gives wide scope for variations of doorways, seating, etc., to meet individual requirements and simplifies the replacement of panels, or even complete sections, in the event of damage in service.

This body, in its various forms, has already seen extensive and varied service all over the world and has convincingly demonstrated its ability to withstand the roughest of treatment under arduous conditions.

Seat plan of the Mulliner Service Bus arranged for 29 passengers. The entrance door can be at front or rear. With front and rear entrances seating is for 36. Alternative arrangements for 41 passengers, with front or central entrance door.
Body with 2ft. 6in. or 8 ft. Overall length 30 ft. Kerb weight of 36 seater—Petrol, 4 tons. 18 cwt.; Diesel, 5 tons, 2 cwt.

Although Duple was still by far the most popular choice of body make for Bedford passenger models, a more even-handed policy became evident in the publicity material issued when the 216in wheelbase SB chassis was introduced in August 1955. Separate single-sheet leaflets were produced for each body type to accompany the chassis description, three being shown here.

The 1956 Burlingham Seagull for the SB was built to the 30-ft length and seated 41 in standard form. This was a metal-framed body, but the kerb weight quoted, 5 tons 2 cwt 3 qr for the diesel version, was only 3 qr more than the Super Vega. Petrol versions were 4 cwt 1 qr lighter.

The Duple all-metal bus body was the result of that firm's acquisition of Nudd Bros and Lockyer Ltd, of Kegworth, a business renamed as Duple Motor Bodies (Midland) Ltd and concentrating on metal-framed bodies, often for the export market. This design was offered with alternative layouts including two-door versions, the weight quoted for a diesel 40-seat model being 4 tons 16 cwt 2 qr.

Although Mulliners Ltd had sold the bus bodybuilding side of its business to Marshall in 1953, the old name, albeit in singular form, continued to be used for a time, as in this leaflet from the 1956 season set. In a sense, this body also had a touch of Duple in its genealogy, the rear-end clearly showing its roots to have been in the Mark II bus body introduced by Duple for the OB in 1946. In this case the weight in diesel form was given as 5 tons 2 cwt.

bulkhead behind the engine for models such as the SB made noise suppression more difficult than for the old-style half-cab coach on traditional heavy-duty chassis. The fashion trends of the time thus created a fresh design problem; there was limited co-operation between the chassis and body designers from different concerns at the time, even when both were concerned in a volume-produced model. The level of understanding of noise suppression techniques at that period was another limitation, hitherto not called into play so strongly when quiet six-cylinder petrol engines were involved and coaches rarely travelled at much more than 40mph.

The tyre size continued to be 8.25-20 but the diesel model now had slightly heavier-duty tyres of 12-ply rating instead of 10ply. The SBG petrol-engined chassis was priced at £855 and the SBO at £1,248, the prices for a complete 41-seat Duple Super Vega being £3,140 and £3,583 respectively. It is noteworthy how, even with the diesel version, the price of the volume-produced chassis represented only just over a third of the total vehicle price, a ratio much the same as had applied with the WTB in 1936, though inflation and a larger vehicle had increased the actual figures roughly fourfold over that period of about 20 years.

By this stage, although close general co-operation between Bedford and Duple continued, illustrated by

Duple's use of body type names beginning with the letter V for its designs for the successive Vauxhall-built Bedford coach models – Vista, Vega, etc – Bedford was beginning to give rather greater publicity help in the marketing of SB models having other makes of bodywork, producing sales leaflets to a standardised pattern for the Burlingham Seagull coach and the Mulliners bus as well as Duple products.

On the A-type goods range, a practical design change was the reversion to separate sidelamps on the tops of the front wings, first appearing at the end of 1954 on 1955 models. They were of quite large size and mounted on 'stalks', thus acting as useful markers for the front corners, something of a tacit admission that close-range vision from the driving seat was not a strong feature of the A-type. The bonnet top panel now had a prominent central rib.

When 1955 closed, the total output of Bedford commercial vehicles during the year, 64,773, as well as being the biggest achieved up to then, continued to be more than any other British make. The combined Vauxhall car and Bedford commercial vehicle output, 142,149, was also a record.

Gradually, the numbers of A-type 5-ton goods models in service grew, this scene in a Sheffield railway goods yard in January 1958 showing examples in the fleet of Burnett & Hallamshire Fuel Ltd being loaded with coal sacks, once a familiar sight when most houses relied on open fires for heating. Most of the vehicles visible dated from early 1954, though the third in line was registered at about the end of that year, late enough to have the high-mounted sidelamps, and there was also one earlier O-type in sight.

For a time in the mid-1950s, Spurling ventured into the small bus business with a rather basic metal-framed design using various models in the A-type range. That shown in the centre picture was on an A3L 3-ton petrol-engined chassis and was described on the windscreen as a 22-seater, but very small lettering added 'inc. driver', rather betraying Spurling's unfamiliarity with the bus world – there was also a similar-looking 15-passenger model on the A2. Not many were sold for public use in Britain, though the diminutive Colwyn Bay Urban District Council fleet took delivery of three 21-seaters in 1954. Most went to contractors or for export, and the view at the foot of the page shows a 21-seat example dating from mid-1955 for Laing, the contractors, this being on an A4 chassis, probably to gain the benefit of a longer wheelbase. Such vehicles were not common in Britain, it being more usual for contractors to use old buses or coaches, or to hire vehicles.

The 5-ton tipper market was one in which Bedford continued to figure strongly, and this 1954 A5S model was operated by Vivian Young Ltd of Brimscombe in Devon. Reconciling traditional styles of lettering and lined-out livery with such a front end design was not easy – clearly the contractor wished to have his name readily visible from the front, and the swage line down the ridge of the bonnet hardly lent itself to such use, but the overall look of a purposeful vehicle was not affected. It had a petrol engine – the general adoption of diesels for such vehicles took several more years to become accepted practice. The nearside sidelamp was just visible from the driver's seat, helping in placing the vehicle in confined spaces.

The SB passenger chassis was often used for other purposes where roomy bodywork was required. This petrol-engined example dating from 1954 was a mobile library for Hertfordshire County Council, with a suitably 'tidy' registration, TJH 800, issued by that authority. The body was of coachbuilt design but incorporated the front-end supplied on the chassis. In this case, a step ring was provided on the front wheel as well as a step block on the mudguard to aid entry to the cab. Note the two electric demisters attached by suction cups on the inside of the windscreen panel – these were once quite common in the days before demisting ducts and cab heating systems became standard factory equipment.

British Waterways was an apt-to-be forgotten part of the nationalised transport system when road transport was concerned, but it had its own vehicles for collection and delivery work. This A4S 8-ton artic placed in service in the winter of 1955-6 was being unloaded at the huge Trent Lane Wharf in Nottingham.

By the mid-1950s, the use of diesel engines was extending to smaller vehicle types, and by 1955 Ford was making quite a big impact with its new 4D four-cylinder direct-injection engine in vehicles up to the 3-ton class, it having become clear that the Cost Cutter petrol engine was but a stepping stone in their development. It was noisy, and the sound of laundry vans and the like so powered became a familiar one in housing estates all over Britain.

Awareness of them clearly penetrated Vauxhall's boardroom, for the Perkins P4 engine, a four-cylinder model with the same 3½in bore and 5in stroke and general design as the P6, became available in the smaller A-type models from mid-1956. More fundamentally, work on Bedford's own diesels was well advanced though not yet

Bedford vehicles were by no means always treated with loving care. This A4L dating from early 1956 of the Scottish Farmers Dairy Co (Glasgow) Ltd had collected quite a few dents in not much over two years of use when photographed in May 1958.

The Perkins P4 four-cylinder diesel engine became available in the smaller A-type models from mid-1956. After exclusively six-cylinder engines in Bedford models, other than small vans, ever since the marque first appeared in 1931, it was strange to hear what were very obviously 'fours' hard at work under Bedford bonnets. The period of availability of this unit was brief, lasting only until the end of the following year.

cylinder diesel vehicles of Bedford as well as Ford makes being driven quite hard became all too familiar. By that date the A2 chassis was rated at 25/30 cwt and the A3 at 2/3 tons, though this was to change later in 1956, when separate 25- and 35-cwt models appeared, the 2/3-ton version became a 2-ton model and a new long-wheelbase 3-ton model was introduced.

An interesting development was the introduction of power-assisted steering as an option on all 'Big Bedford' models, using a hydraulic ram built into the steering linkage, a suitable high-pressure pump being mounted on the engine. A leaflet issued in August 1956 referred to both trucks and passenger models though it is clear from the sketches of a contemporary SB with Vega body that coaches were particularly in mind. At that stage, operators were cautious about such ideas, and not many seem to have been sold. This was hardly surprising, as the SB had possibly the lightest steering among contemporary coaches of similar seating capacity, even without power assistance, though admittedly it was low-geared, and hence the case for power assistance was not strong at that stage in coach development.

Bedford's own diesel

The growing interest in diesel vehicles inevitably led to the volume truck makers developing their own engines. Even if Bedford was slightly behind Ford in getting its unit on to the market, from its introduction at the beginning of 1957, the Bedford 300 cu in diesel engine soon became the general home-market choice in most Bedford goods models upwards from the 4-ton category, and in the SB. Petrol-engined models within this category, and indeed down to about the 2-ton mark, conversely fell in numbers over the

ready for production – in typical GM style, proving work was being carried out on quite a large scale.

The swept volume of the P4 was 3,150cc (192 cu in) and 55bhp was developed at 2,400rpm, well down from even the derated 76bhp of the lowest-rated version of the 214 cu in petrol engine standard in these models. So they were inevitably less lively, and hence the clatter of four-

Of much wider and longer-lasting significance was the first Bedford diesel engine, the 300 cu in six-cylinder unit, which was made available in new C and D ranges of 4-, 5- and 6-ton models at the beginning of 1957, as described in subsequent pages, and which also soon became the standard diesel for the SB. It was intended to follow the characteristic Bedford and indeed General Motors philosophy in offering the advantages of an efficient and up-to-date power unit at lower cost than had previously been possible. It remained the standard Bedford diesel engine for the main part of the range until 1962, and remained in production for certain models for some years subsequently. Early examples of the 300 cu in unit were not without their troubles, notably a tendency for a fibre timing gear to strip, cylinder head studs which broke, usually due to corrosion, and blown head gaskets. They were fast-revving by diesel standards and certainly not quiet, but with the main weaknesses overcome helped to popularise this form of power unit among operators that had previously considered it beyond the scope of a concern without specialist facilities.

Another ceremonial send-off from the production line, this time including the Mayor as well as management and workers. 'No.1 Bedford diesel' was an example of the new D range of bonneted models which replaced the A series at the beginning of 1957. Although basically similar to their predecessors, the models from 4 tons upwards were distinguished by additional chromium strips above the grille. Note the 'Diesel' emblem below the nearside headlamp. There was good reason for the air of celebration, for it was not long before Bedford diesels became the normal choice for most models in the range, strengthening the firm's competitive position.

next few years to the point of becoming a small minority of output for British users, though they remained more common for a time in some export markets where diesels had yet to become widely accepted.

Design and development work had been going on for several years. A large-scale test programme included extended test-bench running and what was proclaimed as a million miles of road running in over 30 prototype vehicles, some of which were included in Vauxhall's own fleet of vehicles serving the factories.

As the name suggested, this first Bedford diesel, introduced as part of an extensively revised chassis range, was of similar dimensions to, and developed from, the 300 cu in petrol engine. It had the same $3^7/_8$in bore and $4^1/_4$in stroke, and hence 4.927-litre capacity. In fact, the design of the petrol unit was uprated, with a new cylinder block and crankshaft and other items such as the rocker gear, oil pump and full-flow filter in the lubrication system, to meet the diesel's requirements, these units then being standardised to simplify the production of both types using common parts and thus adding to the petrol engine's already good durability. In the development of the Bedford diesel engine, the Ricardo concern acted as consultants, reviving an association which dated back to the 1920s, when Harry Ricardo had advised on the design of the petrol engine in the Vauxhall 14/40 car.

The gross power rating was quoted as 97bhp at 2,800rpm, and maximum gross torque at 217 lb.ft at 1,400rm, in both cases without fan or dynamo and with test-bench exhaust system, though a more realistic net figure was 89bhp at 2,600rpm. It was of direct-injection form, using toroidal combustion chambers, as by then the accepted practice on larger engines made by Leyland, AEC and others.

Overall, this first venture into the diesel engine world included many features intended to give long life and reliability. Yet, inevitably the pressure to build down to a price in a very competitive market led to some features that resulted in some lack of refinement. The use of pressed covers for items such as the valve gear, timing case and side plates did little to contain the high noise level inherent in most diesels, and gave the engine rather a harsh tone. The simple pneumatic governor made idling speed apt to vary and the method of mounting tended to convey a fair amount of the resulting vibration to the cab or vehicle interior, particularly noticeable in a coach. This smoothed out somewhat as the speed rose, but the fast-revving engine, by diesel standards, made the noise level towards the top end of the vehicle's speed range quite high, a matter that was to become more important when the first parts of the British motorway network opened in 1959.

As it happened, the threat to fuel supplies that occurred in 1957 in the aftermath of the Suez crisis, and the increases in cost that followed, helped to heighten awareness of fuel economy, so the arrival of Bedford's own diesel was fortuitously timed. On the other hand, these events

Yet another engine option introduced to the top end of the Bedford range early in 1957 was the Leyland O.350 as seen here, now available as an 'official' choice, fitted on the production line. Initially it was offered as an alternative to the Perkins R6 which by then had progressed to the Mark 2 in the S and SB. Thus began a nine-year spell when Leyland engines were fitted to quite sizeable numbers of Bedford models.

contributed to a disruption of world trade and the annual output of Bedford vehicles dropped slightly for a year or two.

Arlington's venture of offering the Leyland O.350 engine in an S-type tractor from 1952 clearly stirred up 'official' interest in this combination. A note in the booklet dated January 1957 issued to Bedford salesmen, mainly about the new vehicle range described in more detail below, indicated that the O.350 unit (which Bedford quoted as the Leyland 351 cu in engine) was also available for S-type 7-tonners and the 10-ton tractor, initially for the export market but was to go into production for the home market from April 1957. It was also offered from that point in the SB coach chassis.

It is particularly noteworthy that Vauxhall made the Leyland engine a production power unit at this point. Admittedly it was a little larger and more powerful, at 5.76 litres and developing 105bhp gross at 2,400rpm, than the new Bedford unit. It seems that its main function at that stage may have been to replace the Perkins R6 pending the availability of an enlarged Bedford diesel engine. However the Mark 2 version of the Perkins R6, with speed cut back to 2,400rpm as part of measures intended to overcome the bottom-end weaknesses that had emerged, was also quoted in this booklet as the standard power unit for 7-ton trucks and the 10-ton tractor. Some Bedford models continued to be produced with the R6 until 1958, though it became more rare latterly. The P6 was dropped from the new Bedford goods range after its brief availability in 4- and 5-ton models since 1953.

The C and D ranges

The major changes to Bedford's range at the beginning of 1957 left little but the CA van, the SB passenger chassis and the R-type 4x4 model undisturbed, though the S-type 7-tonners were continued with some significant new developments.

Two new main model type letters appeared, C and D, though, as with the A types, the sense of complication to the uninitiated was compounded by references to them as the TC and TD ranges. With at least two engine options for every major model as well as various special order models and production options, the range became much more complex, the aim being to tailor vehicles to users' individual needs while retaining the cost savings of volume production of main units. In fact, in a manner characteristic of Bedford, individual units were often used over quite a wide range. For example, there was a new rear axle, of 17,000 lb load rating (the use of the lb in high multiples as a unit of measure was characteristically American – to most British engineers, 7½ton would have been more expressive), used on all Bedford normal and forward-control models of 4-ton capacity upwards.

The C models were of forward-control layout and had the same cab design as the updated S-type, retaining the same outline as when the latter was introduced as the 'Big Bedford' in 1950, though its revised version was readily identifiable by a modified grille having a chrome surround, arched on the top portion and having BEDFORD lettering in chromium-plated capitals across the mesh facing on this section. Entry into the early S-type cab was a matter of a rather precarious climb via the wheel nuts or an awkward step at the rear, but was aided on both C and S types by the addition of what were called hub steps, in other words small step rings surrounding the front hubs, a feature which had been used in larger form on the R-type. The cab under-structure was also strengthened.

The C was available as the C4, C5 and C6, respectively 4-, 5 and 6-ton models. The C4 and C5 were available only in one wheelbase length, 11ft (132in), but the C6 could have the 13ft (156in) wheelbase which was already the standard for the long-wheelbase SL 7-ton model.

The D type was a new normal-control 'Middle-weight' range, the lighter D1, D2 and D3 retaining the general appearance of the previous normal-control A-type range in its 1956 form. The D4, D5 and a new 6-ton normal-control model, the D6, had a modified and more elaborate grille, the horizontal slats widening towards the bottom and surmounted by two chromium strips below the Bedford badge on the front of the bonnet. The overall effect produced a clear family resemblance to contemporary GMC trucks. Suffix letters signified wheelbase length or other comparable variants in chassis form, such as D4S or D4L for short and long 4-ton models, and D4A signified the tractor version of the 4-ton model.

The various models in this more complex range used a combination of units suitable to their weight.

By this date, it was permissible to operate goods vehicles of over 3-ton unladen weight at 30mph, and thus the need to keep the S-type models below this figure was reduced. Accordingly, they received stronger frames, cast-iron gearbox casings and other changes to make them stronger and longer-lived.

Suffix numbers began to be used to signify which engine was fitted, the initial published series being as follows:-

Suffix	Engine type	Model range
1	Bedford 300 cu in diesel	C, D and S
2	Bedford 214 cu in petrol	C and D
3	Bedford 300 cu in petrol	C, D and S
5	Perkins P4 192 cu in diesel	D
8	Leyland 351 cu in diesel	S

It is noteworthy that the Perkins R6 was not given a number in this series, vehicles so powered continuing to be designated as SSO, SLO, SAO and SBO. The use of 5 to signify the Perkins P4 was to prove quite short-lived, as explained below.

The new system conveyed an almost complete description of each model in a few digits. Thus D2S2 indicated a normal-control D2 2-ton model, short-wheelbase, with Bedford 214 cu in petrol engine, while C6L1 signified a forward-control C6 long-wheelbase model with the Bedford 300 cu in diesel engine. The suffix numbers 1, 3 or 8 were also used for the SB range, signifying the use of the engines indicated in the table above, from 1957.

The C-type took on much of the look of the S-type – the minor revisions to the grille were henceforth common to both – but the chassis incorporated axles and other mechanical units common to the normal-control range appropriate to its 4-, 5- or 6-ton load-carrying range. The engine option was the new 300 cu in diesel or the 214 cu in petrol engine, the latter now with higher (6.77 to 1) compression ratio, and gross power up to 100bhp at 3,600rpm, though the more realistic net figure was 85bhp.

The D-type models up to 3-ton capacity retained the frontal styling of the A types. This van operated by Macfarlane Lang carries the 'Diesel' emblem and this implied that it had the Perkins P4, which was the only diesel available for models up to that category until the four-cylinder Bedford engine appeared at the end of 1957. The body was coachbuilt to the operator's requirements and in this case the windscreen assembly which could be included on the chassis was not used, allowing the bodybuilder to provided a cab built out to the full width of the body.

The SB was far less familiar as a bus, especially for everyday use by the public, than as a coach in Britain, and it was not untypical that R. Edgley Cox, ever a maverick in policy terms, was behind one of the exceptions. He was General Manager of Walsall Corporation transport department and well-known for unusual choice of vehicles. Six SBO models with Perkins R6 engines and Willowbrook 39-seat bodywork were added to the fleet in 1956, one being seen here three years later.

At the end of 1957, a four-cylinder version of the Bedford diesel engine was announced for use in 25-cwt to 3-ton models – it was the first Bedford engine not to have six cylinders, apart from the car-derived engines used in small vans. This was the 200 cu in (3.285-litre) unit, having the same bore and stroke and general design characteristics as the 300 cu in six-cylinder engine and with an output of 64bhp gross, or 57bhp net at 2,800rpm. It first appeared in D-range models early in 1958. It was given the identification number '7' and superseded the Perkins P4; for example, the D2S5 short 2½-ton model was replaced by the equivalent D2S7.

Another new option introduced at the same time, though applying to larger goods models, from 4 tons upwards, was the availability of a Bedford-made two-speed rear axle. Such units widened the overall range of gear ratios to the driver available and when used to the best advantage by the driver could be used to 'split' widely spaced ratios in the gearbox, giving more fluent performance on hilly terrain.

A fleet of Bedford D6S 6-ton models with heavy-duty tipper bodywork by Anthony Hoists Ltd was supplied to Laing early in 1958 for the construction contract for the M1 motorway, completed the following year. One is seen here being loaded with spoil by a Ruston Bucyrus excavator which was preparing the ground for the diversion of a minor road that was to run under the motorway. By that date, Middlesex registrations were advancing rapidly through the 'reversed' series, this vehicle being 208 RMD.

The C- and S-type grille had the chromed surround and prominent BEDFORD lettering from the introduction of the revised range of models for 1957. The front axle now had a small step-ring to provide a slightly more convenient climb into the cab. At the top end of the C range, the differences from the S became slight, though in some cases the S had wheels with a greater offset to accommodate 9.00-20 tyres. This vehicle of the A.1. Waste Paper Co Ltd of London E.C.2 was almost new when photographed in March 1957.

From a vehicle design viewpoint, 1957 was a busy year. In addition to the developments affecting the truck range, the CA van came in for revisions. The introduction in February of the F-type Victor car, smaller than the Wyvern, meant that its 1,507cc engine, revised in detail from the unit of the same size used in the Wyvern, and a new all-synchromesh gearbox could be used for the CA. Later in the year, the wheel size for the latter changed from 16in to 15in, helping to lower the loading height a little further. Smaller wheels were a trend of the time in the car world – the F-type had 13in wheels – though quite often counterbalanced to some degree by the use of fatter tyres, and this experience was soon to lead Bedford designers to follow suit on larger models.

Early in 1958, the standard diesel engine offered for the S-type models – the short and long 7-ton trucks, 10-ton tractor and the SB passenger chassis – became the Bedford 300 cu in unit, though some examples had been built from 1957. Accordingly, the designations SS1, SL1, SA1 and SB1 began to be familiar. A minor change was the availability of twin rear tyres on the civilian R-type 4x4 model.

Although the overall goods market was still fairly depressed, another important landmark was passed on 28th May 1958 when the millionth Bedford was produced – it was an S-type 7-ton model with Bedford diesel engine. Of that total, 360,000 had been exported, and although annual figures fluctuated according to market conditions, the contribution of Bedford vehicles to the country's balance of payments and to the transport systems of countries in many parts of the world was immense. In quite a number of years, more were sold abroad than at home.

Changes in legislation made it possible to use small van models as a basis for minibuses permitted to carry fare-paying passengers. Among the first, introduced at the 1958 Show, was this design based on the CA, the conversion being carried out by Martin Walter Ltd, of Folkestone, the firm which adopted the name Dormobile for its similar camper van which led the uninitiated to call any CA a 'Dormobile'. The PSV conversion was basic in the extreme, with longitudinal seats for five on each side plus one more-fortunate passenger who was permitted to sit in the front nearside seat. Note the semi-translucent glass-fibre top, used to gain a little more height than the standard body. Very few were used for the rural services Parliament had in mind, but some were used for private hire work for small parties travelling locally, for which the price complete of £725 was attractive.

The concept of Civil Defence used in the 1939-45 war was revived as a result of post-war political tension, heightened in the mid-1950s by the realisation that an H-bomb would inflict damage over a 20-mile radius, probably overwhelming local fire brigades and other services. The idea of the Mobile Column, comprising perhaps 60 vehicle sof various types, based away from target areas but ready to move in where needed resulted, and the big build-up of Green Goddess and related vehicles was geared to the creation of such columns. By 1958, the creation of 40 Mobile Fire Columns was planned, and a surplus of men in the Armed Forces due to the National Service scheme still in operation led to them being involved. These pictures show a training exercise being mounted from the training centre at Moreton in Marsh in June of that year.

Right: One of the key elements of the Mobile Columns, and an important function of the Green Goddess fire pumps, was water supply, not only for fire-fighting but for drinking. The pipe structure being erected over the road was high enouth to allow a double-deck bus to pass beneath it. Some of the RLHZ chassis were supplied with standard cabs and special pipe-carrier bodies, as seen here. The Vauxhall Victor F-series car was probably that of the Vauxhall Motors photographer – the engine from this model was used in the contemporary Bedford CA van. The motor bike, in this case a BSA 350, and Land Rovers in these pictures all belonged to the same overall AFS fleet.

Bedfords in the Mobile Columns

Left: Here a dispatch rider, his Matchless machine parked on its stand, directs the mobile control vehicle towards the location of the supposed incident. The batch of 34 mobile control units on S-type chassis to which this vehicle belonged was registered NYR 801 to 834, readily identifiable by the red and white chequered band and the similarly marked 'astrodome'. These vans carried VHF radio telegraphy units and in some cases a ten-line telephone switchboard, NYR 827 being allocated to the Home Office Fire Service Training Centre at Moreton.

Here Green Goddess RXP 593, a 4x4 vehicle allocated to the Training Centre at Moreton, is seen on the same exercise, with four of the lightweight portable pumps carried, two on each Goddess. These had Coventry Climax 1-litre engines largely made in aluminium alloy, similar in general design to those used in Hillman Imp cars and, in a highly-tuned form, in some racing cars of the period.

Prototypes for the new TJ range were tested over several thousand miles in Spain, including this climb in the Sierra Navada mountains. Leading is a J3 4-ton model, with a J5 6-tonner following. The view shows the difference in grille design between the smaller and heavier models, the former also being given a lower build by the adoption of 16-in wheels for the first time on models of this size.

The TJ types

Yet another new normal-control range appeared in time for the Commercial Motor Show in November 1958. This was the TJ type and, as before, the individual models were known by type letters omitting the 'T', the main range running from J1 to J6, the latter now extending the load rating up to 7 tons, with the usual pattern of length and engine option suffix codes for each. By this period the model numbers had become slightly out of step with the load ratings, so though J1 was available in 25cwt and 35cwt forms, J2 was a 3-ton model, J3 a 4-tonner, J4 a 5-tonner (also a tractor unit for an 8-ton artic) J5 a 6-tonner and J6 a 7-tonner. In essentials, this was an update of the D range introduced at the beginning of 1957, now using an all-Bedford range of engines and hence, in turn, derived from the A range dating from spring 1953.

The key new features included use of 16-in wheels on models up to the J3, giving them a lower build than the heavier variants as well other quite extensive design consequences, and there was a also a new front-end design. The new bonnet had more of a sloping profile and the cab a deeper curved-glass windscreen extending lower than the previous vee screens. There were two front grille and mudguard styles, the models up to the J3 having vertical grille slats and 'eyebrows' over the headlamps, the latter in line with a contemporary car fashion trend. The heavier models had horizontal grille slats and did not have the eyebrow effect. The sidelamps moved down into the wings again, but on many vehicles flasher units were now fitted on top of the wing.

After the repeated upheavals of the previous five years in this group of models, the TJ was to prove much more long-lived, indeed surviving beyond the end of Bedford as a General Motors concern in 1987, even if at a much reduced output level, being taken up by AWD and then as one of the Bedford models produced for export by Marshall SPV from 1992, though using Perkins engines.

Up to this point, road wheels of 16in diameter were regarded as basically a 'car' size, and indeed had been current on the CA van until a few months previously, though in a lighter form. They had been used at the lighter end of the A range from its introduction in 1953, but then only for the A2 model, at that stage rated at 25cwt and, as usual with vehicles of such weight capacity, using single rear wheels, in that case with 7.50-16 tyres. Traditionally, the 20-in rim diameter was accepted internationally as usual for most commercial vehicles from the J3 size class right up to eight-wheelers and double-deck buses.

Extensive development work had been carried out jointly by Bedford and several tyre makers to produce heavier-duty wheels and tyres of 16-in rim size but suitable for vehicles up to the 4-ton class and for use in twin form at the rear. Tyres of 7.50-16 size continued to be used for the 25-cwt, now J1, and the 35-cwt J1 had these at the front but 8.25-16 singles at the rear, while the 3-ton J2 model was now on 7.50-16 (8-ply) all round, with twins at the rear, while the 4-ton J3 model had 7.50-16 (10-ply) – there were various options, though all used 16in rims, and in later years the sizes standardised for the various weight ratings altered slightly, but the overall pattern continued.

It is clear that Bedford anticipated some customer resistance to such a change, and indeed extensive test running had been carried out, including several thousand miles over rough roads in Spain, to confirm satisfactory service. In addition to the obvious lower loading height, there were useful weight savings, tighter turning circles and lower stresses on the transmission. On the 4-ton model, the heavy-duty hypoid rear axle was replaced by a simpler and lighter spiral bevel unit with savings in weight and cost. Indeed, reduced manufacturing cost in several respects was clearly a substantial factor behind the change.

Even so, the reduced unsprung weight brought benefits in ride and handling – somewhat surprisingly. In addition it had been found during the test running that the smaller-diameter tyres lasted longer as well as being cheaper to replace. On the other hand, smaller wheels left less room for brakes and the weight saving in the 13-in-diameter units used with the 16-in wheels was apt to prove double-edged when the question of energy absorption was considered, although this became clearer on some later applications.

The new bonnet design, apart from the face-lift aspect, was designed to improve close-range forward vision, it having been accepted that the A and D series had represented a retrograde step in that respect, and on the lighter models this was yet another aspect to gain from the smaller wheels, giving a more car-like effect.

All models had alternative diesel or petrol engines, models J1 to J3 having the four-cylinder 200 cu in diesel or the six-cylinder 214 cu in petrol engine, the latter being basically the old 28hp unit as first seen in 1938, updated in detail and by then developing 85bhp and thus giving much livelier performance than the 57bhp diesel, though at greater fuel cost. The J4 and J4 could also have the 'old' 214 cu in petrol engine, or either diesel or petrol 300 cu in units, the latter pair being the only choice in the J6. Four-speed gearboxes, with synchromesh on all but first and reverse, were standard but there were alternative sets of

The TJ had quite a glamorous appearance, heightened in this case by the addition of chromium-plated front hub caps. This fuel oil delivery tanker on a J6 chassis for W. Barnett & Sons Ltd of Luton was being handed over on 4th August 1959 at local premises of Shaw & Kilburn Ltd, one of the best known Vauxhall and Bedford dealers, with headquarters in London. This view shows how the lower and more sloping bonnet line and deeper windscreen improved close-range driver vision compared to previous models, even on the larger models retaining 20-in wheels. The sidelamps were now back in the wings, just above bumper level, but the flashing indicators took over the role of markers on top of the wing line.

The longer-wheelbase CAL version of the CA introduced in 1959 increased the model's appeal, the wider sliding doors helping in situations such as this. The model had also been given a mild face-lift with larger one-piece curved-glass windscreen and modified grille.

ratios, the principle being that the wide-ratio version was used where the performance need required it and the close-ratio box where there was a bit more surplus torque from the engine. The latter was certainly not what would be understood by 'close ratio' in a sports-car sense, with a typically Bedford low (6.5 to 1) bottom gear to satisfy the General Motors criterion that vehicles must be able to climb 1 in 4 fully laden, and hence leaving a broad spread to be covered by three upward changes to reach the 1 to 1 of top gear. On hilly terrain, this was apt to make it necessary to stay in a lower gear than was ideal for lengthy periods.

Many of the wheelbase lengths were as used from 1953 on the A range, but the 4-ton J3 was available only as a 13ft 5in model, this having been specifically developed with the needs of the distributive trades in mind, giving a 14ft body length. This market had been identified as particularly important. The J6 model was offered in J6L form with 14ft 11in wheelbase and J6S with 12ft 11in; the latter was designed to suit operators of 6 cu yd tippers who preferred a normal-control layout to give a reasonably low front axle loading when laden and sufficient rear traction when unladen.

The sheer volume of Bedford's output gave it remarkably broad insight into the needs of the various classes of customer, and it is significant that photographs in the company's archives were classified by trades – effective publicity was always a strong point. There was a degree of

professionalism about the whole operation that was probably unrivalled in Britain, even if the strongly commercial approach and constant search for the most economical specification occasionally led to innovations that did not always prove satisfactory in the often tough world in which Bedford vehicles had to operate. Low-priced vehicles tend to be at the mercy of unskilled drivers and indifferent maintenance in ways that do not apply to more expensive models where the greater first cost leads to more care in protecting the initial investment.

The CA 10/12-cwt van appeared in new versions in 1959. A curved windscreen and redesigned grille brought the appearance into line with contemporary trends and then, a little later in the year, an alternative longer version with 102-in (8ft 6in) wheelbase – 1ft longer than the original – was added to the range. This not only increased load space by 20% but allowed the sliding doors, always a key feature, to give a wider opening. It soon became popular as well as giving greater scope for alternative types of bodywork.

Towards the end of 1959, the S-type became available as a tractive unit for 12-ton loads, using the Leyland O.350 engine, in this case as the standard power unit. There was also a new longer 168-in (14ft) wheelbase version of the S-type 7-ton model. Output shot up that year, reaching 90,674, a new record, of which 51,731 were for the home market and 38,943 for export. It had been an impressive decade, yet new triumphs were yet to come.

Above: By the end of the 1950s, a fairly typical modern Bedford fleet was apt to look like the line-up of vehicles owned by E. H. Jones (Slough) Ltd, wholesale fruit and potato merchants, seen above. When photographed in December 1958, none of those visible was more than four years old. Nearest the camera were a pair of CA vans delivered earlier that year and thus of the early style, then six bonneted models from the D and J ranges and, at the end, a diesel forward-control truck from the C or S range.

Centre: The search for a successor to the OB continued and this Duple body design seating 29 and called the Super Vista was built in modest numbers on C4Z2 4-ton forward-control goods chassis with 214 cu in petrol engine, the latter essentially the same '28hp' unit found in the OB. This example was displayed at the 1958 Commercial Motor Show at Earls Court. In much the same way as with the SB, the standard front cowl was discarded and a version of the Super Vega butterfly-grille front incorporated in the body, though the profile differed. Similar bodies were built on the slightly heavier-duty C5Z1 with 300 cu in diesel engine, MacBrayne being a prominent user.

Left: The CAL made a slightly more practical minibus compared to the shorter early CA, and this 1960 example, again with Martin Walter body is seen running as the Glenbrittle Bus Service in 1961.

Exports had always been important for Bedford, and as the 1960s began, the numbers grew to the extent that they exceeded home sales for several years. Holland, traditionally friendly to Britain, an attitude heightened by wartime experiences, was a receptive market for most British makes, so this TJ operating for Coca-Cola in that country was very representative – a Vauxhall taxi is also visible in the background. The 16-in wheels used on TJ models of up to 4-ton capacity helped to allow a low loading height, important to distributive trades and aided by suitably designed bodywork as seen here. The 'eyebrows' over the headlamps of these lighter TJ models were a fashionable feature of some contemporary car designs.

The SB was by far Bedford's largest selling passenger model in terms of total output and it is apt to be forgotten that this was increasingly due to exports, which remained strong right through to the 1980s despite the model being largely superseded for the home market from the mid-1960s. This scene at Bridgetown, Barbados, dates from November 1959; a newly-arrived SB, complete with Marshall-Mulliner body, stands on the quay with the slings still under the wheels. Sturdy metal-framed bodywork of similar character was being supplied to many countries, Marshall having specialised in this market since taking over the bus side of the Mulliners Ltd business, though in later years locally-built bodywork tended to be favoured. However, simple and relatively robust bus chassis remained in demand from countries with no commercial vehicle industries of their own and this was where the SB scored.

12 THE TK – BEDFORD'S MOST SUCCESSFUL MODEL

Once again, a new decade was marked by the introduction of an important new Bedford model range. Up to the autumn of 1960, the forward-control S and C ranges remained in production, continuing the general appearance and layout established in 1950. Ford had mounted a strong challenge in this size range with its Thames Trader model introduced in 1957, this having the Ford 6D engine, a six-cylinder equivalent to the 4D and of 5.4-litre capacity. It had a cab more in keeping with the styling trends of the time, though generally similar to the Bedford S in layout, in requiring an awkward climb, via a step-ring, to gain access from ground level. By 1959 there was also a coach version, model 570E, which was making the first serious challenge to Bedford's position in the low-priced coach chassis market, being directly comparable to the SB.

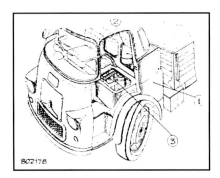

Yet by 1958 Bedford engineers were already well advanced with a new design that was destined to restore Bedford's firm grip on this sector of the market. The observant were given a clue in a patent, No. 802,178, taken out by Vauxhall Motors Ltd, of which a summary appeared in *The Commercial Motor* in its issue of 12th December 1958. It described the cab layout that was to be used for the new TK (though of course not quoted as such), even though the styling in the accompanying sketch was more rounded than was adopted for production.

The first production chassis came off the line at Dunstable on 4th August 1960 and on 6th September the initial Bedford TK range, twelve models of from 3 to 7½ tons and tractive units of up to 12-ton rating, was announced publicly. Immediately, it gained strong praise from the technical press, though even the most far-seeing could hardly have guessed the extent and long-lasting nature of its success. Output of TK models passed the half-million mark in the late 1970s, a record total for any British truck model, and it remained in production until 1984. Even in 1996, TK models still earning their keep remain quite a familiar sight, even if no longer as common as they used to be.

Over the years, Bedford models have represented a blend of American and British ideas. The initial models of 1931 looked almost identical to their Chevrolet forbears. Then, in 1933, the WT of P. Stepney Acres's inspired design set both Bedford and a large part of the British commercial vehicle industry on a fresh line of development. The S of 1950 adressed the general British preference for forward-control on trucks of the 7-ton class in very

This annotated drawing appeared in early TK brochures, pinpointing the model's main new features.

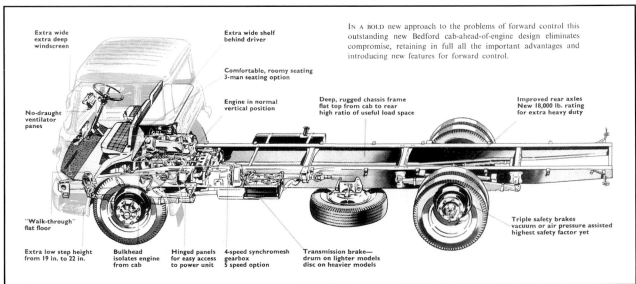

Extra wide extra deep windscreen

Extra wide shelf behind driver

IN A BOLD new approach to the problems of forward control this outstanding new Bedford cab-ahead-of-engine design eliminates compromise, retaining in full all the important advantages and introducing new features for forward control.

Comfortable, roomy seating 3-man seating option

No-draught ventilator panes

Engine in normal vertical position

Deep, rugged chassis frame flat top from cab to rear high ratio of useful load space

Improved rear axles New 18,000 lb. rating for extra heavy duty

"Walk-through" flat floor

Triple safety brakes vacuum or air pressure assisted highest safety factor yet

Extra low step height from 19 in. to 22 in.

Bulkhead isolates engine from cab

Hinged panels for easy access to power unit

4-speed synchromesh gearbox 5 speed option

Transmission brake— drum on lighter models disc on heavier models

Perhaps the most typical TK variants were the original 16in-wheel models, the KD 3- and 4-ton group and the KE 5-ton model, the latter being seen in this artist's drawing in the brochure. Although the usual skill had been used to show the design in a good light, there was an attractive functional tidiness about the appearance, living up to the motto that what looks right generally is right. What is more, it stood the test of time, remaining in production without significant change in form for a quarter of a century.

American-looking styling, while the normal-control A models reverted to the concept of Chevrolet look-alikes, later modified to some practical advantage in the TJ.

Despite a growing tendency for both car and commercial vehicle design to be more and more international in outlook, not least within General Motors, the TK was characteristically British, give or take a few minor styling details, even though an awareness of transatlantic ideas lay behind it. Maurice Platt had been Chief Engineer of Vauxhall Motors Ltd since 1953, remaining so until 1963, but he was primarily a car man. John Alden, who had served an apprenticeship with the MG concern, had been with Vauxhall since 1938, concentrating on commercial

vehicles from 1944. He became Commercial Vehicle Engineer in 1956 and Assistant Chief Engineer in 1959. The TK, a major contribution to commercial vehicle design, was Alden's concept, though in his rather characteristically dour way, he was apt to shrug it off.

There were clear parallels between the WT of 1933 and the TK of 27 years later; the main mechanical units in both cases were inherited from existing models and the advance each represented was related to clever use of their layout in the chassis. The basic idea central to the TK design was that though the engine was in roughly its traditional place directly over the front axle, the cab was set forward sufficiently to allow the driving position to be ahead of it.

'Up, up and away.' The ease of access by comparison with most forward-control models was a valuable selling point. In practice, it wasn't quite as easy as implied, as the forward position of the step left the driver slightly unbalanced at the first stage of climbing in – note the need for the steadying left hand – but the need to clamber up on top of the wing as with the S type had gone and there was no impediment to using the kerb-side door, an important asset when delivering on a busy street.

The smile of the driver posing for this picture might be self-conscious, but engine access for normal maintenance was quite reasonable and indeed sheltered. For bigger jobs, the cab could be removed completely – Bedford claimed 'in about 30 minutes' but that did imply suitable lifting equipment, and although it was made as simple as possible, with straightforward disconnection of the steering column at a flexible joint and of plug-in wiring, it was not comparable to a tilt cab.

The double-skinned pressing forming the cover over the engine carried the seats for the driver and passenger – incidentally, the latter could be wide enough to carry two if needed, a useful point in, say, a removal van.

The rear of the cab was formed to provide an internal shelf and, externally, hinged side covers allowed surprisingly good access to the engine for normal servicing, sheltered by the overhanging part of the cab. The overall cab length from front bumper to the rear panel, 5ft 11³/₈in, was not particularly short by forward-control standards, and about 3in longer than the S-type, itself not very compact – it is interesting to note that it was just 11 ³/₈in shorter than the O-type front-end, which inherited the compact semi-forward-control layout established by the WT. Even so, the new layout represented a major step forward in practicality and good working conditions for the driver.

When the TK was introduced, there was growing interest in the concept of the tilt-cab, designed to hinge forward to give unobstructed access to the engine, and the form of the TK led some contemporary observers to expect that it would be of that type. The tilt cab was far from new, and by that time well-established in the United States. The earliest known to the authors was the Sterling, made in Milwaukee, which had a tilt cab model as early as 1935. In that case the cab tilted rearwards (or could be lifted clear

by removing the mounting pins if the body did not allow tilting) but a forward-tilting version was offered from 1937. White had a tilt-cab range from 1949 and Ford introduced its C-series tilt-cab range in 1957, although it remained an American-market model, not built in any of Ford's European factories. However, such a design would have been more costly to produce and the TK achieved many of the advantages in a simpler concept.

Driver entry to the TK was easy, via steps ahead of the front mudguards, and it was a simple matter for the driver to enter or leave from either side of the vehicle. The gear-lever, quite short, was mounted close to the nearside of the driver's seat and the handbrake was horizontal on the offside, so neither got in the way of entry or exit. Vision from the driving seat was the best on any Bedford truck yet; the driver was seated behind a deep and broad curved-glass windscreen which had wipers with arms and blades long enough to clear most of its forward-facing area. Larger rear-view mirrors were another feature that would be taken for granted nowadays but at that date were still rare, and indeed more expensive makes were often well behind the standards set by Bedford in such matters – convenient car-style switches formed another example. The driving position was fairly upright but proved comfortable, no doubt partly because of the good response of the controls, with light and responsive steering.

Yet possibly the most important benefit to the driver was the degree to which noise was reduced and the cab interior began to become 'civilised' – having the engine set below and behind the driving position helped, and there were fewer paths for noise to be conveyed to the interior. Even with the Bedford 300 cu in diesel, hardly a quiet engine in itself, noise levels were low enough to permit conversation in the cab, impossible with most diesel trucks of the time unless one shouted. Heat and fumes were also conspicuous by their absence. A further benefit of car and truck manufacture by the same concern was the way in which car standards penetrated into the commercial vehicle business, with stylish facia in a style in favour at the time and the cheerful and attractive style of tartan seat trim adopted, then very fashionable. External styling was simple, in a restrained yet distinctive way that proved not to date as quickly as the initially-striking S. Overall, there was an unmistakable sense of self-confidence about the TK's overall design, amply justified by the test of time.

The range of models had a similar pattern to the TJ in using wheels of 16-in diameter up to the 5-ton class and, in general, 20-in above, although the 6-ton chassis could be supplied on 17in wheels. The smaller models had a choice of the four-cylinder 200 cu in diesel or the 214 cu in six-cylinder petrol (the latter soon becoming quite rare except for specialised applications such as horse boxes), while the larger ones mostly had the 300 cu in diesel, with the 300 cu in petrol also available. Five-speed gearboxes were a new option and two-speed rear axles were available for models of over 6-ton capacity.

The brake systems on oil-engined models now had an air-pressure servo instead of the vacuum unit still used for

It was not long before TK models became a familiar sight all over Britain. Here, the dust flies as a load of bricks slide off this 7-ton model with unusually long tipping body in Lawnmarket, Edinburgh in October 1961. The vehicle was operated by Leslie Dunbar, a local contractor. The photographer composed his picture well in showing Vauxhall Motors products, with an almost-new PA series car passing and a 1958 CA at the kerb. The latter is a passenger example, but of the personnel-carrier type for use on carrying staff and not members of the public, for which purpose one of the more elaborate conversions shown on previous pages was needed.

petrol models – actuation with either was via a hydraulic system. A more controversial feature was the revival of a transmission handbrake, it being considered that modern axles and propeller shafts were no longer liable to the failures that had caused the idea to fall out of favour in the 1920s. Indeed it was pointed out that transmission handbrakes were fitted to over half the trucks built throughout the world at that date – a figure doubtless considerably influenced by American practice.

A more subtle yet important change was the use of a 50:50 front to rear braking ratio despite the heavier loading on the rear axle of almost all goods vehicles, to take better account of the load transfer effect.

In the usual way, the individual model numbers omitted the initial T, and in this case the various weight ratings were conveyed by letters, the KC being the 3-ton and 4-ton group; the KD the 5-ton models, all of the foregoing on 16-in wheels; KE, 6-ton; KF, 7-ton and KG a heavy-duty version which could be rated at up to 7½-ton. There were the usual body suffix letters and engine type numbers. Thus the forward-control 7-ton model with 300 cu in diesel, standard cab and dropside body was type KFLD1.

Such a vehicle, priced at £1,330 basic complete, was road tested by John F. Moon of *The Commercial Motor*, the report appearing in the issue of 28th October 1960, only a few weeks after the model was introduced. One of the authors worked as part of John Moon's team in his first full-time journalist job beginning a year or so later, and can vouch for Moon's unshakable integrity. He believed in writing the unvarnished truth about any vehicle he tested

and was not intimidated by ructions at boardroom level if he felt harsh words were justified. So his headline 'At last – a driver's lorry' was praise indeed, as was the comment that the TK was the biggest step forward in improving driving conditions made by any British manufacturer in recent years. His confident prediction, "There is no doubt in my mind that the Bedford TK series will prove to be one of the most popular ranges ever to have been introduced in this country" carried a great deal of weight, as well as being amply proved in later years.

The popularity of the TK with drivers was partly due to the thought given to the cab interior. It was 'civilised' and well up to good contemporary car practice in such details as the minor switchgear while the short gear lever gave a hint of a sportscar look. The tartan-style upholstery was characteristic and gave what would nowadays be described as a 1960s look when that decade had barely begun.

The TK's merits were particularly evident in urban conditions. Here boxes were being delivered to the old Covent Garden fruit and vegetable market in central London in 1963.

Even so, he made some criticisms, such as the fact that this nominal 7-ton model could be loaded only to 6 tons 11¼ cwt if it was to keep within the recommended gross weight of 10 tons 5½ cwt. The two-speed axle fitted as an optional extra was criticised as sluggish in response, though it was mentioned in the report that a more effective mechanism had been developed. The gear change, with a system of rod linkage to the gearbox was described as feeling a little vague, though decidedly more convenient than that of the S-type. The test vehicle returned between 12.15 and 15.6 mpg when tested laden, the lower figure on a run along the M1 motorway, opened the previous year, at an average speed of 48.5 mph.

Sales success of the TK was immediate and strong, and not merely among users of the S and C ranges it directly replaced, for the ease of cab access made it attractive for such duty as general delivery work wherever a vehicle of 3-tons up was justified, hitherto apt to be the province of normal-control models. Although only introduced in the autumn, it helped to push Bedford's output over the 100,000 for the first time, the total for that year being 103,493.

A less significant introduction in terms of volume but certainly fun was the development of the ½-ton pick-up idea into the introduction of the J0, also in autumn 1960, which was an ultra-light version of the TJ and using that

model's cab and bonnet, with a chassis having 6.70-15 tyres plus the 2,651cc six-cylinder petrol engine and three-speed all-synchromesh gearbox of the latest version of the PA-series Vauxhall Velox and Cresta cars. It made a lively and yet practical vehicle, more rugged than the average car-derived pick-up. Later it switched to the 3,294cc engine from the PC version of the Cresta introduced for 1965, making it even faster. Apart from the appeal to upmarket farmers and the like for which the model was largely intended, it was not long before it found favour with the gypsy community, and for several years it was quite usual to see a J0 among the characteristic groups of caravans by the roadside.

Deliveries of the S and C ranges of goods models ceased early in 1961, leaving only the SB passenger chassis of that family of models to continue – the success of the TK did lead some people to expect a passenger version but the layout did not lend itself to bus or coach use. The only model to continue with the S-style cab was the R type 4x4 model, which remained in limited-scale production.

In April 1961, William Swallow, later Sir William, became Managing Director of Vauxhall Motors Ltd, continuing in that post until the end of 1965. He was to be the last British MD until 1996, and indeed as indicated above, there already seemed to be a resurgence of ideas that

Two TK cattle transporters in the fleet of Glover & Uglow Ltd of Callington, Cornwall, are seen in the nearby town of Launceston, about to load store and dairy cattle for delivery to several farms. The vehicles represent both the lighter and heavier end of the range, the different wheel size being evident even from the high position chosen by the photographer, doubtless influenced by the view of the castle even on a rather misty day in October 1963. Note the extra fuel tanks to allow use on long journeys without the need to refuel.

The only forward-control model to continue in production with the previous generation of cab design was the R-type 4x4, represented her by an example in the fleet of Bolton Corporation highways department. Note the O-type just visible in the background, owned by brewers Walkers of Warrington, delivering to 'The Nelson' pub on another gloomy day.

There was no lack of variety of bodywork on Bedford chassis. Here quite a roomy yet well-proportioned ambulance body is seen on a long-wheelbase CA chassis dating from 1960.

Another ambulance in a rather larger size class was this J1 with body by Levers Garages Ltd of Farnworth, Bolton, supplied to Lancashire County Council early in 1961. Glass-fibre was beginning to make it easier to make quite elaborate shapes, in this case merging the rounded front-end of the body with the TJ front-end quite effectively. This vehicle had the 214 cu in petrol engine, in other words basically the long-familiar 28hp 3.5-litre six-cylinder unit, quiet running and smooth yet capable of lively performance when needed.

Converting the bonneted J2S 3-ton tipper chassis to forward-control may seem a convoluted way of producing a small bus model, yet this design was to fill a gap in the Bedford passenger range for many years. Duple (Midland) originally devised this style of sturdy metal-framed body for operation on rough roads in Africa, but it later became adapted as a small bus seating about 19 to 21 or even a coach – this one was displayed as a 15-seat coach at the Commercial Motor Show in September 1960. A similar vehicle in left-hand drive form was supplied to the British Embassy in Moscow. The J2S or the longer-wheelbase J2L came to be accepted as the basis for coaches in the 19-seat class with either the 214 cu in petrol or the four-cylinder diesel engine.

It was decided to respond to the call for a production coach in the 29-seat class with a new model called the VAS and, again, there was a nostalgic note in the choice of Bella Vista as Duple's name for its standard body for it – this was the smallest in a new 'Bella' series of body styles. Here a prototype is seen on Vauxhall Motors trade plates negotiating a Bedfordshire lane.

stemmed from British sources in both Vauxhall and Bedford products from around 1960, continuing fairly strongly through the decade, though of course work on most of these had begun some years before they went into production. In 1963, John Alden became Chief Engineer.

A significant development, even if taken up only in fairly small numbers at first, was the availability of the Perkins Four99 diesel engine for the CA vans from mid-1961 – it was a four-cylinder unit of similar 1.6-litre size to the petrol engine, but quite fast-revving for a diesel of that period and thus giving 42bhp compared to the petrol unit's 59bhp. Diesels of that size range were still uncommon and the CA remained mainly a petrol-engined model.

The VAS coach chassis

Later that summer, a new smaller coach chassis appeared, called the VAS. It seemed to be a response to the repeated calls from some people in the operating industry for a vehicle in the size range of the OB. Over the years since the latter's demise in 1950, passenger bodywork had been fitted to various Bedford goods chassis to produce vehicles smaller than the SB. There had been almost a Vista look-alike, though originally built in a curious 'woody' estate-car style, on the OLB; passenger bodywork on some A models and a rather curious passenger conversion of the J2S, altering it to forward-control as a 19-seater, originally intended for use in Africa. None of these had sold in large

The VAS chassis had quite strong resemblances to the SB in its general layout but followed the trend of the lighter end of the TJ and TK goods ranges in the adoption of 16-in wheels, being itself designed to run at 6¼ tons gross. The chassis was supplied with the S-type front grille though none of the major British bodybuilders used it for their standard models.

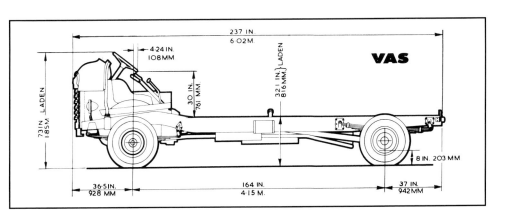

numbers, yet the idea of the appeal of a modern-day smallish Bedford coach had persisted. This link with a favourite older model was underlined by the VAS model's usual 29-seat capacity in coach form and Duple's choice of Bella Vista as the model name for the bodywork, of new style, the corresponding type for the SB being Bella Vega.

The chassis, with forward control, was of very similar general layout to the SB, but with a much shorter wheelbase of 164in (13ft 8in) and using 16-in wheels, the tyre size being 7.50-16. The maximum gross laden weight was 6 tons 5 cwt, compared to 8 tons 5 cwt for the SB at that stage – back in 1950, the latter had begun at a gross weight of 7 tons 5 cwt. The chassis was short-tailed in much the same way as the SB but the overall length with body was usually about 23ft 9in (approximately 7.25 metres).

The choice of engines for the VAS was the 300 cu in diesel, in which case the chassis type designation was VAS1 or the 214 cu in petrol (VAS2), the latter again fitting into the 'OB revival' pattern in being essentially the old 28hp unit, though the majority of those built had the diesel. Four-speed gearboxes were standard, the petrol version having the wide-ratio version, which was the original synchromesh gearbox of 1950, with its ultra-low 7.059 to 1 bottom gear – one wonders how often it was actually needed – but the diesel had the so-called close ratio box with its slightly less depressing set of ratios.

The brakes were generally of similar pattern to those of contemporary goods models, with air or vacuum servo. The handbrake, a separate drum unit, in this case on the front of the axle casing, acted through the final drive and differential. The chassis was supplied with the same 1950-style grille and round-nosed front cowl as the SB and, in Britain at least, this was immediately discarded by all major bodybuilders as soon as they started work on the chassis. There was provision for the cowls from both models to be returned to Dunstable, but they were liable to become damaged in the process and generally ended by being scrapped.

There was a fair degree of interest in the VAS, though probably less than those calling for its introduction had suggested. Over time, it took on a niche market appeal as being the only true bus or coach chassis of that size available in Britain until the advent of the midibus era.

More significant in a broader context was the announcement by September 1961 of slightly larger versions of the Bedford diesel engines, an increase of bore size from $3\frac{7}{8}$in to $4\frac{1}{16}$in pushing the respective swept volume sizes of the four and six cylinder units to roundly 220 and 330 cu in respectively, these being the names by which the new units were known. Thus the main engines used in the strongly competitive truck and coach ranges by Ford and Bedford were of the same nominal size, a fact which doubtless had a bearing on their introduction. The capacity of the new units in metric measure was 3.613 and 5.420 litres respectively, and the normal quoted power ratings 70 and 105bhp, both at 2,800rpm.

In its issue of 2nd November 1962, *The Commercial Motor* reported on a comparative road test between petrol and diesel versions of the SB, the former an SB3 with the 300 petrol engine and the latter an SB5 with the new 330 engine. They both had Duple bodies though the petrol vehicle, borrowed from the Salopia fleet and evidently about a year old, had the earlier Super Vega style rather than the Bella Vega by then current. The unladen weights were 4 tons 18 cwt and 5 tons 4 cwt respectively, figures that nowadays seem almost incredibly light for vehicles having coach seats for 41 passengers, though both were laden to 8 tons 4¼ cwt for the test. It was written by John Moon, the actual testing being shared between him and Tony Wilding, in those days his assistant as Technical Editor.

Not surprisingly, the diesel came out greatly superior in fuel economy, returning 19.2 mpg as against the 9.7 mpg of the petrol vehicle in normal road running, and 12.3 mpg compared to 7.4 mpg over a full-throttle run on the motorway. The test was not perhaps quite fair in that the diesel coach had the five-speed gearbox but even so it is perhaps a little surprising that the performance figures

The VAS sold steadily, if not dramatically by Bedford standards. By the time this photograph of a VAS1 recently added to the Barton Transport Ltd fleet was taken in Nottingham in July 1965, the 1,000 mark had been passed, including about 400 exports. The Duple Bella Vista body was the style most associated with the model in Britain though here the wheel trims normally fitted were absent, emphasising the small wheel size. Eventually, 6,552 VAS models were built over a period lasting a quarter century, the model being still in production, mainly for export, when the Bedford business was shut down by GM in 1986.

The petrol-engined SB3 continued to be favoured by Salopia Saloon Coaches Ltd, of Whitchurch, Shropshire. The example seen here in Snowdonia, No. 161 in the fleet, was one of eighteen with Duple Super Vega bodywork to the style then current which were placed in service in the Spring of 1961. Coaches on SB chassis with petrol engines and Duple bodywork had been added to the fleet every year since 1951, a policy decision to standardise on the type having been taken in 1955. Salopia, which had become one of the leading operators of extended tours in the Midlands, worked on the basis of replacing coaches after quite a short life. The 1961 fleet had all been sold off by January 1964, and meanwhile a dozen more SB3 had been added to the fleet in 1962 and a further fifteen in 1963, with fourteen more coming into service in February 1964.

were all in favour of the diesel, though some only marginally – on paper the petrol engine was more powerful, at 114bhp net compared to 98bhp for the diesel.

John also pronounced in favour of the diesel on noise grounds, which was much more surprising save perhaps flat-out on the motorway, for Vauxhall and Bedford petrol engines of that era were not at their best right at the top end of the speed range – Alan Townsin has to express disagreement with his respected former colleague in this judgement, based on wide experience of journeys in, and occasionally driving, both types. This applied especially for touring work (the main activity in the Salopia fleet), where the almost literally silent idling and quiet running at modest speeds of the petrol engine, not mentioned in the test report, contrasted with the generally rough and quite noisy behaviour of the diesel, often prone to unpleasant surging at idle due to the limitations of the pneumatic governor.

Despite its higher running costs, the petrol SB still represented 35% of sales of SB chassis for home market customers in the first nine months of 1962, the corresponding export figure being 43%. Rather surprisingly, these were the highest proportions since 1958, when the petrol figure had been 71% on the home market, and 47% for overseas sales – at that earlier date diesels were only just beginning to become established among SB users in Britain, quite a few of whom had not

then gone over to diesels of any make. The petrol SB chassis was £130 cheaper in first cost, but that difference was soon made up in lower running costs, even in those days of cheap fuel.

The suffix numbers signifying engine types current from the 1962 season, including two further additions to the list mentioned in the next chapter, ran as follows:-

Suffix	Engine type	Model range
1	Bedford 300 cu in diesel 6-cyl	TJ, TK and VAS
2	Bedford 214 cu in petrol 6-cyl	TJ, TK and VAS
3	Bedford 300 cu in petrol 6-cyl	TJ, TK and SB
5	Bedford 330 cu in diesel 6-cyl	TJ, TK and SB
7	Bedford 200 cu in diesel 4-cyl	TJ
10	Bedford 220 cu in diesel 4-cyl	TJ. TK
13	Leyland 370 cu in diesel 6-cyl	TK, SB
14	Leyland 400 cu in diesel 6-cyl	TK and VAL

Note that 5, originally signifying the Perkins P4, as quoted in the list as used in 1957, was by this period used for the Bedford 330 cu in diesel, built in large numbers.

Another development of early 1962 and relating to the CA van range was the reappearance, for the first time since pre-war days, of a four-speed gearbox on a Bedford van of this size range. It became available as a consequence of being offered on the improved FB series of Vauxhall Victor cars then recently introduced.

The above view shows one of the pre-production VAL14 chassis ready for delivery to the bodybuilders in the Spring of 1962, with temporary driver's seat, front dash assembly and spare wheel mounting. At that date a vehicle of 36-ft (11-metre) length, an increase of 6ft over the previous limit, had only been permissible for operation in Britain since the previous summer and the impression of great length was emphasised by the small wheels.

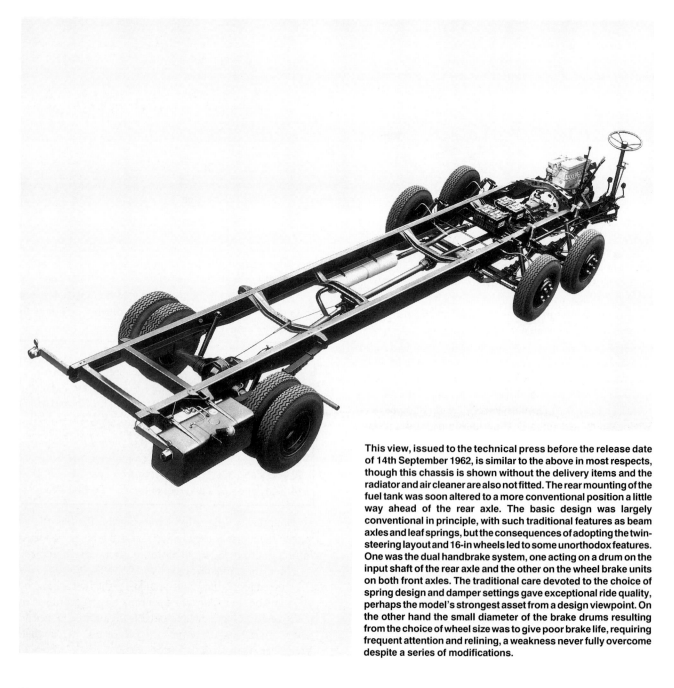

This view, issued to the technical press before the release date of 14th September 1962, is similar to the above in most respects, though this chassis is shown without the delivery items and the radiator and air cleaner are also not fitted. The rear mounting of the fuel tank was soon altered to a more conventional position a little way ahead of the rear axle. The basic design was largely conventional in principle, with such traditional features as beam axles and leaf springs, but the consequences of adopting the twin-steering layout and 16-in wheels led to some unorthodox features. One was the dual handbrake system, one acting on a drum on the input shaft of the rear axle and the other on the wheel brake units on both front axles. The traditional care devoted to the choice of spring design and damper settings gave exceptional ride quality, perhaps the model's strongest asset from a design viewpoint. On the other hand the small diameter of the brake drums resulting from the choice of wheel size was to give poor brake life, requiring frequent attention and relining, a weakness never fully overcome despite a series of modifications.

13 THE VAL TWIN-STEERING COACH

In July 1961, the maximum permissible length for a bus or coach to be operated in Britain was increased from 30ft to 36ft (just under 11 metres) and the width from 8ft to 8ft 2½in, the latter being 2.5 metres. So great an increase in length generally implied a fresh design, although some makers of heavy-duty models of roughly similar size for export were able to introduce home-market models using existing units fairly quickly, most notably AEC and Leyland, both of which had 36ft underfloor-engined single-deckers at the Scottish Show later that year.

Such a course of action was not open to the Bedford design team, for the SB was its largest passenger model and already, at 30ft, near the limit to which it could be stretched in the design sense, while the goods range at that date could contribute little in the way of units that seemed suitable for use on a 36ft-long model. A separate chassis continued to be favoured partly because of the nature of the

existing market in Britain, with specialist coach or bus bodybuilders equipped to work in that way, but also for export since there was growing resistance to the acceptance of complete vehicles in the developing countries.

The aim, as with all previous Bedford models, was to offer a vehicle significantly cheaper than could be built by the traditional heavy-duty vehicle makers, yet which offered a package that would appeal especially to Bedford's traditional type of customer – in the passenger vehicle business this was largely the independent coach operator. The resulting VAL chassis announced in September 1962 was priced at £1,775, about £1,000 less than any other 36ft model sold in Britain. The most popular body, the 52-seat Duple Vega Major, added more than double to this, at £3,625, and the body price for other 36ft models was broadly similar so the complete vehicle basic price of £5,400 was rather less dramatically below that of heavier-

Development work on the VAL was initially carried out on a vehicle with petrol engine and hence of type VAL3, known internally as 'No.1 Lash up' and received a Duple body which was itself a prototype for the production Vega Major design. This body was then transferred to a chassis from the pre-production VAL14 series as seen here, registered in 1962 as 457 DYK. It was still devoid of identity badges or emblems, though the style of body would have been instantly recognisable as a longer version of existing 'Bella' types. At that date, some Bedford prototype vehicles were being registered in London, as in this case.

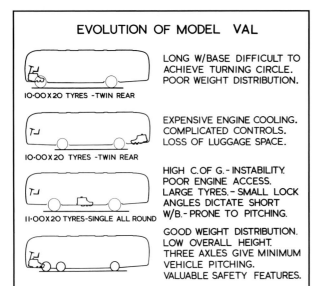

EVOLUTION OF MODEL VAL

LONG W/BASE DIFFICULT TO ACHIEVE TURNING CIRCLE. POOR WEIGHT DISTRIBUTION.

10·00 x 20 TYRES - TWIN REAR

EXPENSIVE ENGINE COOLING. COMPLICATED CONTROLS. LOSS OF LUGGAGE SPACE.

10·00 x 20 TYRES - TWIN REAR

HIGH C. OF G. - INSTABILITY. POOR ENGINE ACCESS. LARGE TYRES. - SMALL LOCK ANGLES DICTATE SHORT W/B. - PRONE TO PITCHING.

11·00 x 20 TYRES - SINGLE ALL ROUND

GOOD WEIGHT DISTRIBUTION. LOW OVERALL HEIGHT. THREE AXLES GIVE MINIMUM VEHICLE PITCHING. VALUABLE SAFETY FEATURES.

These diagrams were used to illustrate a paper on the development of the VAL presented by Alex Williamson. Although the third option shown was, except for its use of large tyres and singles at the rear, that most widely adopted for 11-metre coaches in Europe as well as Britain in the 1960s, it is noteworthy that at that stage the Vauxhall engineers rejected it. The representation of engine and gearbox was clearly diagrammatic and the suggestion of a vertical engine in that same third option was hence probably accidental. Yet it is an intriguing thought that, in effect, this diagram pointed the way to Bedford's series of coach chassis of this layout beginning with the YRQ in 1970. The 'prone to pitching' comment seems particularly surprising from a Vauxhall engineer, as in fact vehicles of this layout are rarely troubled in this way and Vauxhall expertise on suspension design was always recognised as outstanding.

duty competitors such as AEC and Leyland.

Various possibilities were examined, as outlined in a paper presented at a meeting of the American Society of Automotive Engineers in Detroit in January 1965 by Alex Williamson, who had been in charge of commercial vehicle engineering at the time under John Alden, whose title in 1961-63 was Chief Products Engineer.

The most obvious initial approach was to consider producing a longer vehicle broadly similar to the SB, but this implied a long wheelbase and with tyres of at least 9.00-20 radial-ply type needed (10.00-20 for export) there were problems in meeting the turning circle requirements. It was also found that although the tyre loading might have been satisfactory with a full load of passengers and their luggage in a rear boot, with the luggage removed the front tyres would become overloaded.

A rear-engined layout, either with angle drive, as used on General Motors coaches built in the United States, or longitudinal rear engine as being used by Mercedes-Benz, was also examined but was considered too costly for the market envisaged, implying more complex controls and a more difficult engine cooling problem, as well as being more suited to a vehicle of integral construction.

Another option considered was an amidships underfloor engine, the paper referring to a contemporary Berliet coach, using four larger, 11.00-20, single tyres with a short wheelbase arranged to give equal loading on them, but again turning circle problems arose because of the large tyres, and the high floor line to avoid undue wheel-arch intrusion was also put forward as a drawback – engine access was also thought to be poor and such a layout prone to pitching. These are interesting criticisms in view of the policy adopted in later years and there is no direct reference in the paper to such a model with twin rear tyres, as chosen by the leading British users of this layout.

The twin-steering layout inevitably made the front end of the VAL chassis more involved, though the steering linkage was further complicated by the adoption of power-assisted steering, then still rare in Britain. The system adopted used an external ram, as was usual on early designs – the front of the unit can be seen in this view just behind the temporary headlamp mounting, the rear being just ahead of the front spring anchorage for the leading axle. The chassis is incomplete, lacking the cab floorplate and accelerator assembly. Various details indicate that this was an early prototype chassis, possibly the first with the Leyland engine as adopted for production.

This view shows a slightly later pre-production chassis, almost certainly one of those completed in the Spring or Summer of 1962. Detail features had been tidied up though some which looked rather crude to engineers brought up in more traditional concerns were to continue into production – the gear lever linkage being a case in point. A noteworthy item visible in this view is the slimmer leaf spring by then fitted on the second axle – the use of a 'softer' spring than on the leading axle played a part in the good ride quality achieved. There were both cable and hydraulic pipe connections to the front brakes, the former for one of the handbrake systems. The floor height was dictated by the need to clear the engine rear cross-member, from which the rear of the engine was suspended by links in the standard Leyland manner. Another consideration was the provision of enough luggage capacity, which tended to be barely adequate even with several side lockers.

However, the trend towards smaller wheels evident across both car and truck models was already well established in Vauxhall's engineering department. The attractions of what had been achieved with 16-in wheels in both TJ and TK ranges up to the 4- or 5-ton load-carrying category was fresh in the minds of John Alden and his team, Yet the front-axle weight problem of any 36ft front or mid-engined design pointed to a need for larger rather than smaller tyres....that is, until the possibilities of having two steering axles began to be considered.

Although hitherto no such model, passenger or goods, had been included in the Bedford range, what were apt to be called 'Chinese Six' chassis, with two axles at the front and one at the rear, had been included among the models offered by several British makers of heavy-duty goods vehicles since the mid-1930s. One of them, Leyland, had also built a 30-ft-long passenger model, the Gnu, of this layout in 1937-39 even though only a handful were sold, along with a couple of similar underfloor-engined Pandas. All of these had 20-in wheels but applying the idea with 16-in wheels provided solutions to several problems.

By using two steering axles each rated at 6,000lb, and a 13,500lb rear axle with twin tyres, it was possible to adopt the 8.25-16 size all round, taking advantage of the capabilities of the Michelin X steel radial-ply tyre. The gross weight permitted for the complete vehicle, designated VAL, was 23,000lb, or just over 10¼ tons. Looking back from today, that seems a very low figure, for many of today's coaches weigh well over that unladen, and it seems remarkable to be reminded that complete early VAL coaches mostly weighed between about 6 tons 7½ cwt and just over 7 tons. With this tyre size, there was no problem in using quite a long 231in (19ft 3in) total wheelbase, measured between the foremost and rearmost axles, the turning circle being just over 70ft for a bodied vehicle between walls.

It is noteworthy in view of the small wheels that although lip-service was paid in publicity to low floor level, in fact the laden frame height was quoted as 29.7in, only an inch less than the SB and almost a foot higher than was being achieved on several low-floor double-deckers of that period – once again, minimal wheel-arch intrusion was helpful to the market for which it was mainly intended.

Weight consciousness

There was immense consciousness of the importance of weight saving in the drawing office. It was standard practice to calculate weight and the position of the centre of gravity of every component as well as assemblies as they were designed, and further exercises were carried out with actual parts in prototype or production form. No doubt this stemmed in part from the extent to which Bedford's success had been related to pushing up the weight-carrying capacity of models while keeping within the 2½-ton and then 3-ton unladen weight limits up to which operation at 30mph had been legal (and in practice designed to go a good deal faster). Even when that artificial barrier no longer applied, there was acute realisation that excess weight had to be hauled around and, indeed, implied that other components were heavier than would otherwise have been necessary.

In this sense, the approach was very professional, and one cannot help thinking that more of such discipline would not come amiss in some of today's vehicle design establishments, especially among coaches. On the other hand, problems could arise in carrying such a design approach to its limits, as indeed was to emerge with the VAL.

It is particularly interesting to discover that the first

The Leyland O.400 engine, seen as mounted in the VAL frame. When one vehicle maker uses another's engine, there is apt to be a certain coyness about the matter, but here the publicity material was quite explicit and the engine itself carried the normal 'Leyland Diesel' and 'Power Plus' plates. It was basically as being built for Leyland Comet goods models but incorporated features to meet installation requirements in the VAL chassis, most notably the exhaust manifold on the nearside. This view shows a Simms in-line fuel pump with mechanical governor.

VAL prototype, described as a lash-up and certainly not a vehicle meant to be put into production, was petrol-engined. Just why this was so, when the diesel versions of the SB had become the majority choice, is not clear, though it may have been on the basis that the petrol unit was the most powerful in-house engine at the time. It was nominally a VAL3, with the 300 cu in petrol engine, a Bedford close-ratio gearbox, 5.8 to 1 rear axle ratio and vacuum-hydraulic brakes.

Its general behaviour was regarded favourably, subject to relatively minor changes, when it was tested early in 1962, but the limited performance was not considered acceptable, with a top speed of 54mph on level ground and acceleration appreciably slower than the SB in any of its current forms. By early February, the body was returned to Duple and it was planned to rebuild the chassis to virtually the production specification, with Leyland engine, Clark gearbox, air-hydralic brakes and modified frame and suspension with revised wheelbase. It was planned to return it to Duple to have the body, modified to suit, remounted.

Three pre-production 'design check' chassis were built, as follows:–

VAL14.62/1 chassis completed 4th May 1962, and fitted with Weymann metal-framed 49-seat coach body. This vehicle was used for a 2,000-mile rough track test.

VAL14.62/2 chassis completed 30th May 1962, and fitted with Duple 52-seat coach body removed from VAL14.61/1 – evidently the chassis quoted in the previous paragraph, but by then fitted with a Leyland engine.

VAL14.62/3 LD was completed 27th July 1962, this being used to have a two-speed axle design checked. It was then sent to Plaxton to have a right-hand drive body, modified for the left-hand drive chassis, fitted.

By the standards of 1962, the choice of an engine that could develop 125bhp as a net output seemed quite adequate for a coach not intended to weigh more than 10¼ tons fully laden. No such engine existed in Bedford's own range at that date, and although Leyland engines had been used in some previous Bedford model variants, the choice of a bought-out engine for a model which was to be so much in the public eye was particularly significant. There was a fairly general willingness in that period to allow engines developed by one vehicle maker to be used in chassis built by another, but this case was a significant decision by both the makers involved.

The unit chosen was the Leyland O.400, an enlarged version of the O.350 unit used in some earlier Bedford models, the bore size being 4.22in and the stroke 4.75in, giving a swept volume of 6.54 litres or 399 cu in. As indicated in the table at the end of the previous chapter, this was given the number 14 in Bedford's engine suffix series, so the full designation of the model was VAL14. An intermediate size of Leyland engine of similar design, the O.370, was used in some Bedford models of this period, and had the Bedford engine suffix number 13.

For the VAL application the governed speed was allowed to run up to 2,600rpm, although this did not increase the quoted output – basically the same engine was being used in some versions of the Leyland Comet, and in a horizontal version by that date fitted to late-model Tiger Cub underfloor-engined bus chassis, rated at the same 125bhp net, but governed to 2,400rpm. In both cases maximum torque was 300 lb.ft at 1,600rpm, and this was a clearer indication of the engine's nature. At that date, the engines in the 9½-litre class used in most 36ft models were not giving much more power but the torque figures were above 400 lb.ft, both peak power and torque being developed at lower speeds.

Leyland went to some trouble to develop a version of

The driving position of the VAL – a prototype with Duple body is shown here – was based on a more upright steering column than that of the SB, but was comfortable, with quite a good view forward, even if space to enter or leave it was limited on early examples. The power-assisted steering was lighter than the non-assisted systems still standard on much more expensive models. Other controls worked well in normal use, save that the gear-change action was apt to be obstructive at times. The handbrake lever alongside it applied the brakes on the front wheels while the pull-up control alongside the steering column operated the transmission brake. The standard speedometer as used on other Bedford models was fitted – it incorporated a fuel gauge but no other instruments were supplied. A moquette cover was added to the engine cowl by the bodybuilder, but was not very effective in reducing the transmission of engine noise, apt to worsen when the flexible covers around the gear lever and handbrake split as was apt to happen after two or three years.

the O.400 engine to suit Bedford's needs, arranging it to have both inlet and exhaust on the nearside whereas other O.400 units had the exhaust on the opposite side, quite a major variation. Doubtless it was reasoned that the VAL was aimed at a different market to Leyland's own 36ft coach model, the Leopard, which at that date used the 9.8-litre O.600 engine in horizontal form, and what was expected to be a substantial demand for the O.400 engine in this form doubtless appealed.

Another aspect of willingness to source major items from outside the factory was the choice of gearbox. This was a Clark design, of American origin, though by then being made in Wolverhampton by the Turner Manufacturing Co Ltd. It was a five-speed unit, with overdrive fifth gear and direct fourth, with synchromesh on all but first and reverse. It had relatively wide ratios not untypical of Bedford, except for the overdrive, giving an uneven progression which meant that once a gradient became too steep for the direct fourth gear, speed had to drop to the maximum of 27mph or so possible in third. The gear change action was also apt to be fairly heavy and quite notchy, not as good in this respect as on Vauxhall-made gearboxes.

Motorway expectations

There was a growing expectation in regard to speed capability in relation to coaches, largely because of the motorway network beginning to spread in Britain. The M1, opened in 1959 as the first major motorway in Britain and passing between Dunstable and Luton on its way from the outskirts of London towards Birmingham, underlined the point, though it took a decade or so for the full implications to be understood by the coach industry. For a few years there was no limit to permissible speed for any vehicle on British motorways, yet on all other roads coaches had still been subject to the overall limit of 30mph

until 1961, when this latter limit went up to 40mph.

This latter had little practical effect other than to legalise the sort of speed a responsible driver of almost any coach had been adopting as a cruising speed on most roads outside towns for decades previously, unless the police happened to be about. Even so, the new situation meant that specific maximum speed capability began to be of interest. With the standard 5.3 to 1 rear axle ratio, the VAL14 was capable of 58mph at governed engine speed in overdrive fifth – in practice a little more than that could be seen on the speedometer – as well as meeting the 1 in 4 restart capability in bottom gear. A two-speed axle option was available, pushing the top speed a little higher, but on either version the engine noise at anything over about 40mph was intrusive and at anywhere near the maximum could only be described as excessively loud for anyone seated in the first few rows of seats.

In terms of chassis design, the decision to work on the basis of a twin-steering vehicle on 16-in wheels meant that although some features were unorthodox, others could be similar or identical to those on existing models, often in a lighter category. The front axle beams were new and gave a wheel track measurement 7½in wider than the SB, the latter designed for its original 7ft 6in overall width. The swivels, hubs and brakes were largely as used on smaller models with, initially, 12-in diameter drums and 3-in shoe width; at the rear there were 13-in drums and 4.2-in shoe width. There were also two separate handbrake systems, one operating a drum on the input shaft of the rear axle, much as on the VAS (this being regarded more as a parking brake, save in emergencies) and the other linked to the wheel brakes but, unusually, on both front axles. This latter was to meet a Construction and Use regulation requirement for a vehicle of this layout but the combination had obvious benefits in providing back-up systems.

The total frictional area per ton was said to be higher than on some more expensive two-axle models with larger brake units but some experts pointed to a comparison of the swept area of the drums as a better yardstick, in which the VAL did not show up so well. The small brakes proved prone to rapid wear, some operators finding that adjustment was needed after each longish trip and relining a frequent need. A related problem was a tendency for the adjustment of the brakes to back off and Hants & Dorset Motor Services Ltd, operating several VAL coaches, introduced a locking device. There was a series of design revisions and later examples performed better but the need for more frequent attention than required on more conventional coaches was a known weakness.

On the other hand, the suspension was generally agreed to give ride quality superior to that of almost all of the VAL's competitors, including far more expensive models, even though the combination of rigid axles and leaf springs was entirely orthodox. Vauxhall engineers had been skilled at this since the 1930s, and the secret here seems to have been related to the use of springs carefully matched to the loads actually carried by the axles. The springs for the first and second steering axles were of different stiffness, and one of the authors, present at the original press launch, recalls watching a coach negotiating a rough surface at the company's proving ground, in those days at Chaul End, and it could be seen quite clearly that the two front axles were oscillating at different frequencies and the coach body simply rode above them almost undisturbed.

Another advanced feature was power-assisted steering, still very rare on British bus or coach chassis at that date. This made the VAL even lighter than a typical SB to steer and although the initial impression was of slight vagueness, once one got used to the feel, with not much castor action, it was acceptable on most types of road. It was still quite low-geared, even so, with 6¾ turns from lock to lock. The steering column angle was much more upright than on the SB or VAS, helping to give room for up to 52 fairly tightly spaced coach seats. Correct wheel alignment was particularly important with the two steering axles but even if this was correct, some vehicles seemed prone to develop heavy shoulder wear of the tyres, usually on one of the second axle wheels.

The front-end layout was so arranged that the passenger entrance was ahead of the leading axle, which was set back to the extent that the engine, gearbox and driving position were also entirely ahead of it. There was enough room for passengers to enter the vehicle interior alongside the engine cover in a way also used in some of the pre-war Leyland Gnu twin-steer models, although the first such arrangement is thought to have been that of the Maudslay SF40 two-axle model of 1935. By 1961, the Yeates concern had produced a conversion of the SB chassis with set-back front axle and more upright steering column, and it may well have been this that inspired subsequent Bedford models with similar layout.

So unusual a chassis seemed to attract particular

The first of the series of pre-production VAL chassis built in 1962, quoted internally as VAL14.62/1, was sent to Weymann's for bodying after completion in May of that year. It was registered 472 DYK, quite closely following the Duple prototype. The 49-seat body, christened the Topaz design, was of lightweight metal-framed construction. The vehicle was then used for 2,068 miles of running on the rough track at Chaul End, being seen there by the press party at the launch of the model. Vauxhall engineers reported that two luggage compartment struts failed after 1,051 miles and the roof panel above the entrance door suffered a fracture after 1,269 miles. Several pop rivets were seen to be working loose but otherwise no body repairs were necessary. Cosmetically freshened up, it was then sent to the demonstration park at the Commercial Motor Show in September 1962, as seen here. The MCW organisation, in which Weymann was a partner, was seeking to broaden its share of the coach business, a body called the Amethyst on SB chassis also being built, but response to their controversial appearance was poor, and the matter was not pursued.

Another of the pre-production prototype chassis received a Plaxton body, using that concern's wide-window 'Panorama' concept. As seen here, the chassis of this vehicle, registered in Bedfordshire as 477 CTM, appears to be of production specification, including the fuel tank position ahead of the rear axle, though at an earlier stage chassis VAL14.62/3 was in left-hand drive form. It is noteworthy that Plaxton took the model code VAL and adopted it as a body type name, with small 'Val' script lettering appearing on the waistline just behind the driver's side window, in addition to the use of 'Plaxtons VAL' publicity lettering. In fact, surprisingly, Plaxton seems to have had second thoughts on its body styling for the model, exhibiting another quite different multi-windowed design on VAL chassis on its stand at Earls Court, though it seems that demand for this Panorama-based design was such that it was it that went into production, becoming a popular choice.

attention from bodybuilders and although the Duple Vega Major was the most familiar design, a point underlined by its choice for a Dinky Supertoy model, several others were built, some in sizeable numbers, most notably Plaxton, but Harrington and Yeates were others and MCW departed from its usual market by producing bodywork used for one of the prototypes, though not put into production. Six-wheeled vehicles, and especially passenger models, have a visual fascination and with the polished aluminium wheel trims by then in vogue, the effect as one passed could be quite striking. There were also a few buses, most notably the ten examples, with special Strachans bodies to pass under a low bridge, built for the North Western Road Car Co Ltd, and some special-purpose applications such as

mobile showrooms and a caravan transporter but these were rarities.

Overall, the VAL was a fascinating technological design and remarkable value in relation to its quite complex specification. Its ride quality bears comparison with all but the very best of today's coaches, even if the sense of refinement experienced by the passenger was let down by excessive noise at speed. The model sold in quite substantial numbers by the standards of its heavyweight competitors yet, judged with the benefit of hindsight, it was hardly a success in commercial terms, certainly in relation to General Motors' standards. It had been planned, optimistically by any criterion, on the basis that output might be up to 2,000 per annum, but despite the lively

The VAL's distinctive design tended to encourage body designers – this was Yeates's first example, built for Whippet Coaches Ltd of Hilton, Huntingdonshire, registered 390 GEW and seen at Brighton in April 1963 competing in the British Coach Rally. It was an extended version of the Yeates Fiesta body, seating 52 and, according to the lettering on the side, weighing a quite remarkable 5 tons 13cwt 2qr. There were nine VAL coaches at that rally, of which six, including that alongside the Whippet coach, were of the Plaxton Panorama style, much as shown in the upper photograph on this page. Plaxton's importance was growing quite rapidly through the 1960s.

Though the claim that the VAL was low-built did not stand up to comparisons with genuine low-floor models of the day, its small wheels and front engine did allow a lower floor line and general build than the mid-underfloor-engined single-deck models then in general use. Among very few VAL buses were the ten built in 1964 for the North Western Road Car Co Ltd of Stockport for use on a route which passed under a low bridge carrying the Bridgewater Canal near Dunham Woodhouses in Cheshire. Their Strachan's 52-seat bodywork had an arched roof cross-section to suit the contours of the bridge. One that had been pressed into relief duty on a Blackpool express service is seen here parked at that resort between AEC and Bristol underfloor-engined models.

interest shown on its introduction this was never approached and in later years sales tailed off appreciably. When production stopped after nine years, about 2,350 had been built.

Sales were doubtless hit when the word went round about the troublesome brake system, such word-of-mouth reports always being difficult to overcome. In fact, six or seven changes to the brake specification were made, including a switch to 13-in drums, improving matters to a level just about acceptable to a suitably organised operator. A further change, to 17-in wheels to permit the use of 14-in brake drums, was under consideration latterly but by then a more radical change in policy, resulting in the VAL replacement being of underfloor-engined layout, was afoot.

A wider goods range

By comparison with this, one of the most dramatic episodes in the whole Bedford vehicle design story, other events of the period from 1962 to the latter part of 1964 seem rather mundane, though the TK range was steadily making more and more friends among goods vehicle operators. In fact more TK models, significantly extending the range, were

introduced at the same 1962 Show, almost forgotten alongside the glamorous VAL and yet perhaps more significant in terms of the further extension of an already successful range. There was a new 8-ton model, the KH, also using the Leyland O.400 engine, available as the KHL long-wheelbase, KHT tipper or KHA heavy-duty tractor.

Over the years, there were many six-wheel conversions of standard Bedford chassis but among the developments of 1963-64 was the introduction of an approved 10/12-ton six-wheeler produced as a joint effort with Reynolds Boughton, specialists in such work, based on the 7-ton TK.

There were also further minor developments in the CA, now with 1,595cc engine, but the big news on the van front in the late summer of 1964 was the reintroduction of a smaller van, roughly comparable in the market it covered to the HC, based on the Vauxhall Ten car, that had been built between 1938 and 1948. The basis this time was the new Viva HA car with 1,057cc engine introduced by Vauxhall in 1963, the first car in this class to appear from the firm since the Ten, and quite closely related to a new version of the Opel Kadet – co-operation between Vauxhall and Opel as fellow General Motors subsidiaries in Britain and Germany was growing.

The Bedford-Hawson Easy Access Van, introduced at the 1962 Show, was based on a J1 chassis of 119-in (9ft 11in) wheelbase modified to semi-forward control, with the steering column shortened and set at a more upright angle than standard, giving 350 cu ft of load space. It was available in 25- or 35-cwt form with four-cylinder 200 cu in diesel or six-cylinder 214 cu in petrol engine and had a glass-fibre front end with a short sloping full-width bonnet but retaining the TJ-class identity in the grille design. It could be seen as an answer to Commer's Walk-Thru van design and was well-suited to local delivery work.

Less dramatic than the VAL but another application of the Leyland O.400 engine which, in its long-term implications, was of fully comparable importance was the KH 8-ton model also introduced at the 1962 Show. Bedford was gradually extending its range further up the weight range. A characteristic feature was the crash bar assembly attached to the front bumper. The addition of fog and spot lamps and plated hub cap suggests that this example, seen in company with a BMC and an earlier Bedford, may have been an owner-driver vehicle.

Six-wheel conversions of Bedford models were nothing new, but the TK range brought such vehicles into a more substantial category, paving the way for factory-built six-wheelers that were to follow a little later. Collecting cases of Guinness shipped from Dublin at Liverpool docks was the duty of this TK 10-ton model with Boyes third-axle conversion operated by Guinness Exports Ltd, based in Liverpool, in March 1962. At that time the Liverpool local taxation department, responsible for issuing registration numbers under the system then in use, had decided to use reversed two-letter series after having begun its three-letter combinations. This vehicle received 20 KB, an issue that would be treasured today. The red ensign flying from the stern of the ship was a more common sight in those days than today.

As conveyed in the illustration overleaf, the HA had square-cut lines, briefly fashionable in the car world, but had up-to-date mechanical features such as an all-synchromesh four-speed gearbox, the gear-change having reverted to the sensible place for such a vehicle, on the floor, and rack-and-pinion steering. The controls were particularly light – indeed it could be argued that the steering was over-light and the handling not very good. Even so, it was light in weight, giving good petrol economy, and easy to drive, so van versions, with suspension to suit alternative 6- or 8-cwt loads, made quite an attractive proposition, the rather box-like body giving a useful 70 cu ft of load space.

It sold well, and when the Viva moved on to a slightly more curvaceous body from 1966, the HA van continued outwardly unchanged, this continuing to be so with later generations right through the 1970s in much the same manner and for even longer than had applied with various of the smaller Bedford van designs in the 1930s. As with them, the mechanical design altered from time to time, taking advantage of alterations in the car models using similar units.

The Bedford-Boughton KGTC six-wheel conversion carried out by Reynolds-Boughton on the KG with Leyland O.370 engine included a double-drive rear axle. Here a 1964 demonstrator fitted with an NCK-Rapier mobile concrete mixer body makes a delivery. These conversions were factory-approved, as were Bedford-York 6x2 conversions of J6, KF and KG models.

The HA model introduced in 1964 and based on the Vauxhall Viva car announced the previous year brought Bedford back into the light van class for the first time since the early post-war period. It was also offered with Martin Walter conversion on the 8-cwt version as the Bedford Beagle estate car seen here.

The CA continued in production, still basically much as conceived in 1952 though improved in detail – by 1964 it had a 1,595cc engine as used in contemporary Vauxhall Victor cars. Martin Walter offered a range of specialised versions. Seen here in CAL long-wheelbase form is the Utilabrake Series II, as being built in 1965. It could carry a total of twelve people including the driver and was widely used as a personnel carrier for transport of staff but did not meet the PSV regulations applicable if fare-paying passengers were to be carried. There were also Workobus versions with wooden seating and the Utilacon name was still applied to a version with folding seats for seven passengers.

14 THE LATE 1960s – BROADENING THE RANGE

By 1965, the Bedford range covered most weight-carrying requirements between 6 cwt and 8 tons, extended to 12 tons and a little beyond for artics, for which the heavy-duty KHA14 tractive unit was rated at up to 41,000 lb (18.3 tons) gross. On the passenger side, most requirements between 12 and 52 seats were covered.

Over the next few years, further models were added, filling in various gaps and, on the goods side, extending the capabilities to heavier loads. Before describing these, it may be helpful to try to convey something of the company's methods, as conveyed in a recent discussion with Leo Taylor, who joined the firm as a draughtsman in 1961. He found himself to be in a minority among others at a similar level in being seriously interested in commercial vehicles, and in particular buses, rather than cars, and within a year was involved in the design of the VAM model described later in this chapter, leading to promotion, he then becoming one of the company's Commercial Vehicle Chassis project engineers.

The growth of the company meant that the Engineering Research Building opened in 1938 had been outgrown, and a new Engineering and Design Centre in Luton came into use in 1964. Within the company, the word 'design' related to styling. Elsewhere among British commercial vehicle makers, those responsible for structural or mechanical design were usually called designers, but at Vauxhall were known as project or design engineers.

Within the Commercial Vehicle Chassis section there were eleven design engineers in the 1960s, reporting to

Alex Williamson, the Commercial Vehicle Engineer, who in turn reported to John Alden. In parallel groups also reporting to Alex were the Commercial Engine and Commercial Body engineers. Each team was divided into the 'B' men starting the approved projects, bringing in the 'C' men who handled what were regarded as Current projects as the job neared completion, finally handing over when the vehicle was safely in production. The 'C' men then took over responsibility for later changes and developments of these models.

These engineers directed the efforts of 50-60 chassis design draughtsmen who were allocated work appropriate to their grade and not normally specialising on any particular system though engineers could ask for an individual particularly familiar with the subject. Ultimate design responsibility rested with the engineer. There were four separate drawing offices for engineers, bodies (car, van and cab), passenger car mechanical and commercial vehicle chassis.

There were also development and test groups, whose functions included supervising prototype build, carrying out the agreed test programme and carrying out development work. They acted as an audit group on design and a further audit was carried out by the Production (as opposed to Product) Engineering Department in the form of a pilot build programme, identifying production snags.

Even when Vauxhall Motors designed all its own products, whether cars or Bedford commercial vehicles, including almost always the units used within them, there

The HA represented the light end of what was becoming a wider range of models. Although by no means revolutionary when introduced in 1964, it was destined to remain in regular production until 1983, and indeed a handful were produced as late as 1985. Its simple design and the internal space given by its square-cut lines gave it strong appeal to users to whom these virtues were more important than stylish looks or advanced mechanical features. At first offered in 6- or 8-cwt versions, its payload range was later extended upwards – this 10-cwt example, model HAV, differed from the HAE 6-cwt mainly in regard to a sturdier rear axle and heavier-duty tyres.

was a strong pattern of co-ordination at an operational level from General Motors headquarters. This was quite apart from that in which major new projects, and their financial implications, were subject to rigorous GM assessment and approval. Part numbers were issued in large blocks, of a few thousand or so, from GM for use by Vauxhall, and these were used simply as required in an unclassified system, in which one number might cover a simple bracket and the next a major assembly, unit, or even a complete vehicle to a particular specification.

There were standardised drawing methods, again as laid down by GM, and as a qualified draughtsman who had been doing aircraft design work, Leo found what seemed undue fussiness about details such as the precise shape of arrow-heads tiresome in his early months with the firm. Yet the methods helped to ensure a high degree of professionalism about the whole procedure. Although low cost was always important, great care was taken to ensure that each item was designed and produced to the highest standards – in many ways, design for volume production is a more onerous task than for vehicles built in small numbers. Even a minor fault becomes serious if thousands of vehicles are involved and, equally, any waste or unnecessary expense is multiplied accordingly, so the elaborate design procedure had logic on its side.

Measurements were always quoted in inches, and weights in lb, right up to the largest items, in typical American fashion, and the terms used and spelling also tended to be transatlantic – for example what to most British vehicle engineers was the sump was described as the oil-pan. The work of the draughtsmen (even they were 'draftsmen', internally) was examined in great detail by checkers, including the weight and centre of gravity calculations mentioned previously, which could be quite complex in those days before computer-aided design.

Normally, dimensions were quoted only to two places of decimals, but holes in frame side-members were usually punched, with generous clearances; there was no attempt to use fitted bolts as found on some of the more expensive chassis. Frames were assembled mostly with $7/_{16}$ in rivets in 0.468in diameter holes, giving a nominal 30 thousands of an inch clearance and hence in theory a decidedly slack fit until the rivet was hydraulically cold squeezed, though in practice a degree of misalignment of the holes in the parts thus joined was not uncommon.

Pairs of side-members were placed upside down on the track at Dunstable and the cross-members, spring hangers and various brackets riveted in place, the squareness depending on the alignment of the track clamps. Springs, axles and propeller shafts were fitted as it moved forward while upside down, and then the partly assembled chassis would be turned the right way up for the pipework to be fitted in a stationary location before moving to the final assembly track for wheels, power unit and cab to be fitted. Two gallons of fuel were added, the engine (already run for an hour and power tested) was started and the chassis was driven across some shakedown rollers so any surplus fastenings would fall off, and then on to rollers to test the brakes. Any faults noted during the various stages of build would be dealt with in the rectification section and the chassis then had a refresher blow over of black paint before passing to final inspection – when cleared it would be driven to the sales park. Sample vehicles would be taken for a road test and full audit inspection.

Chassis came down the Dunstable production line in accordance with production plans based on current demand, the sequence often being mixed and thus a short J2 tipper chassis might be followed by a VAL twin-steering coach

The first stage of the assembly line in the Dunstable factory was known as the upside-down track as the frame itself and then the springs and axles were assembled in this position before each frame with these items in place was turned over mechanically so as to allow other items to be added on a further track. A rear axle can be seen being lowered into place from an overhead crane near the centre of the picture while the chassis nearer the camera was closer to the completion of this stage.

Above: When the chassis began its run down the main assembly line, the first task was to fit numerous smaller items like fuel and brake pipes before larger items such as the engine and cab were added. These views date from December 1967.

Below: Despite the mass-production methods, Bedford's manufacturing system could accommodate specialised models such as the TJ model with four-wheel drive, based on the J5S. This example with 1964 Portsmouth registration owned by the Southern Electricity Board is seen in use erecting electricity supply poles. The model was regarded as among the most useful medium-sized 4x4 models ever made, some examples putting in 20 or more years service.

and then maybe a TK or two. In general each passed through the sequence of assembly stages without disturbance to the flow, though special stations were built into the line in which the more complex VAL, or a little later the line-built six-wheel goods models when they became available, could spend more time to install the extra axle and more complex brake systems etc without interrupting the output of the other simpler models. By that period, chassis numbers were issued on a production line basis, and not classified by type as had been the case in earlier years.

Yet if the manufacturing methods were those of mass production, the amount of importance and care put into design, both in its engineering and functional/styling sense was clear from the sheer size of the Engineering and Design Centre. In addition to large drawing offices, there were metallurgical and chemical laboratories, a machine shop, metal- and wood-working shops, trim and paint shops. The number of staff working there totalled up to 2,000, more than some quite well-known firms at the more 'bespoke' end of the commercial-vehicle-building business employed altogether. Many of these were on car-related work and many others were not directly involved in design in any of its branches, but even allowing for people who were fitters or typists, say, it was a remarkable team, all engaged in improving the firm's products.

Yeates had been producing a conversion of the SB, with setback front axle and more upright steering column which preceded any of the 'official' Bedford models with similar front-end layout and indeed, in effect, 'spawned' the VAM. Harold Wilson Ltd of Stainforth, near Doncaster, trading as Premier, entered examples with the Yeates Fiesta body in the Blackpool coach rally in both 1961 and 1962, the latter vehicle, based on an SB5, being seen here – they were normally used on a local service, for which the layout allowed pay-as-you-enter operation. The body measured 31ft 2in overall and seated 44 passengers. Though approved, the conversion was not entirely satisfactory, the result not proving very durable, creating problems for Vauxhall Motors. However, the potential of the concept was recognised and this led to the development of a model built from new to similar layout.

The VAM coach chassis

The third model in the trio of passenger models with VA prefix introduced in the earlier 1960s was the two-axle VAM, nominally occupying the mid position between VAS and VAL, although the three were quite separate designs and not the varying-length versions of a common pattern suggested by the designations.

Initially, the VAM was intended as a replacement for the SB, and indeed it was still being described as the latter's successor when information on the new model was released to the press in June 1965. It was said at the time

The first prototype VAM chassis was built on the basis that it should retain as many SB parts as practicable, including axles, brakes and steering gear. This view shows its frame shape, also derived from the SB, wider at the rear than the front. The steering and brakes immediately proved unsatisfactory, and extensive redesign resulted for the production version. Meanwhile, a shorter version of the VAL was considered as a possibility but ruled out partly on cost grounds.

that the SB, of which some 28,777 had been built by then since production began in October 1950, almost equally divided between home and export sales – 14,050 and 14,727 respectively – was continuing in production "for the time being". Up to then, 904 of the VAL model had been built since production began in August 1962, of which 128 had been exported, while the VAS total was 1,152 (including 454 export) since August 1961, and thus by contemporary Bedford standards, neither were big sellers, output of both having run at about 300 per year up. In the event, the SB, which had averaged over 1,900 chassis per year up to then, was to outlast all three of the then new-generation models. Production of VAM chassis began two months later.

As well as being of medium length, it was decided it should have a layout allowing the entrance to be ahead of the front axle, directly opposite the driver. Indeed the layout ahead of the front axle, including the driving position, had much in common with the VAL. However, it resulted from the initiative of W. S. Yeates Ltd, an old-established coach dealer based in Loughborough, which had gone into bodybuilding after the war and modified some SB chassis to have a set-back front axle with entrance in the front overhang in the manner pioneered by the Maudsley SF40. The Yeates conversions, though attractive in terms of layout, were proving troublesome and caused some concern at Luton, leading to a decision to produce a vehicle of this pattern as a Bedford production model. Initially it was to be based on the SB, using as many of its units as possible. The plan was to keep the length down to 30ft and seating capacity to 41, but the reduced wheelbase was found to result in a front axle overload.

Serious consideration was given to producing the vehicle as a short-wheelbase version of the VAL, with the same twin-steering layout and 16-in wheels, but using the 330cu in engine. Perhaps mercifully, this was ruled out, partly because there was no provision for a power-steering pump on that engine, but also because the vehicle would have been too expensive.

Instead the decision was taken to design a new stronger front axle, this being designed to suit 8ft bodywork only,

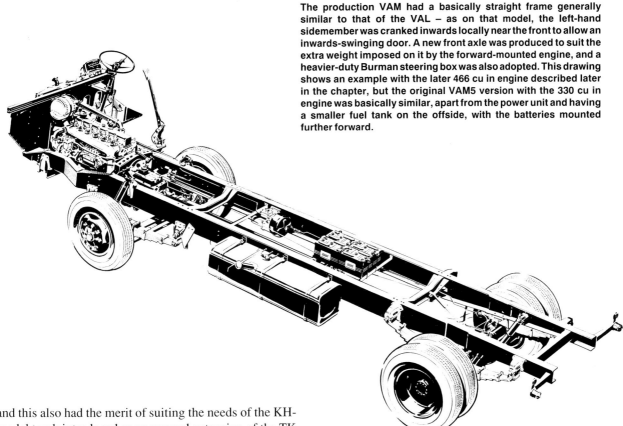

The production VAM had a basically straight frame generally similar to that of the VAL – as on that model, the left-hand sidemember was cranked inwards locally near the front to allow an inwards-swinging door. A new front axle was produced to suit the extra weight imposed on it by the forward-mounted engine, and a heavier-duty Burman steering box was also adopted. This drawing shows an example with the later 466 cu in engine described later in the chapter, but the original VAM5 version with the 330 cu in engine was basically similar, apart from the power unit and having a smaller fuel tank on the offside, with the batteries mounted further forward.

and this also had the merit of suiting the needs of the KH-model truck introduced as an upward extension of the TK range, catering for 8-ton loads. It was introduced ahead of the VAM, being in production by the Spring of 1964.

In the British bus industry, there was growing interest in what was then always called one-man operation (OMO), the driver collecting the fares from passengers as they entered the vehicle instead of them paying a conductor after taking their seats. Until the 1950s, OMO on what were called stage-carriage services was confined to small buses in Britain.

Legislation to permit the elimination of the conductor on full-sized stage-carriage single-deckers had been passed and although a rearguard action by the trade unions sought to obstruct the spread of OMO to the larger types of bus, by then it was steadily gaining ground as a means of reducing operating costs. What the Americans would have called a transit-style front-end had thus become almost universal on new full-sized single-decker buses operated by the larger fleets in Britain by the mid-1950s, almost always in conjunction with underfloor-engined layout. This had led to a similar layout for coaches becoming more popular, in some cases with dual-purpose use on bus or coach duties in mind, or eventual 'cascading' of older coaches to bus work.

Bedford's traditional market for passenger chassis had been inclined towards coaches since the 1930s. Many independent operators, accounting for most of the sales, either did not run stage-carriage services or, if they did, preferred to purchase coaches which could be used on bus work during the week and for private-hire or excursion duties at week-ends. As their routes were often rural and

sometimes quite long, this was quite logical in a functional sense, since comfortable seats and a good view of the passing countryside were of more value than the speed of loading given higher priority by mainly urban operators.

However, a new development was attracting growing interest among the larger company groups, including the nationalised companies in the Tilling and Scottish organisations, in the operation of lighter types of bus on country services. This was partly a reaction to the adoption of 11-metre single-deckers, it being felt that they were unduly large, heavy and costly for the more rural routes where the buses built to the previous shorter length limits were considered big enough and yet many of them were falling due for replacement.

Hence a design permitting the passenger entrance to be ahead of the front axle was in line with the trends of the time for both coach and bus applications. As the legal length limit at the time was 36ft, manufacturers were free to set the length of shorter models at whatever seemed an appropriate figure in relation to the general design provided that other regulations were met – maximum legal overhang was often the governing factor. The heavier-duty front axle opened up the possibility of making the VAM slightly longer than first planned. The figure quoted on its introduction was 32ft, and the standard Duple Bella Venture coach body for the model, seating up to 45 passengers, measured 32ft 4in overall. The wheelbase was

The first VAM prototype to be bodied, by Duple with its Bella Venture 45-seat body as offered on production examples, seen parked behind Vauxhall's Engineering and Design Centre building. From a coach operator's viewpoint, one of the advantages of the layout was that the external appearance was almost identical to that of contemporary upmarket underfloor-engined coaches – Duple and the other main coach bodybuilders were using the same style for larger models. The introduction of polished wheel trims fitted by bodybuilders meant that the only external sign of the chassis identity was the griffin emblem – rather unkindly nicknamed 'the chicken' within the factory.

appreciably shorter than that of the SB at 16ft 1in (193in), because of the set-back front axle.

In terms of wheel size, axle design and general construction, the VAM was more orthodox than its predecessors, using 20-in wheels and 8.25-20 tyres on both axles. The standard VAM5 model, with Bedford 330 cu in diesel engine, had a bare chassis weight of 2 tons 16 cwt 2 qr, which was ½cwt more than the VAL despite its shorter length and simpler design, as well as 6cwt more than the SB5 with the same engine. Yet even so, its lightweight credentials were confirmed by the fact that even the lightest of the 30ft underfloor-engined bus chassis on the British market at the end of 1965 weighed a ton more. Unladen weight of a VAM5 with the Clark five-speed gearbox offered as an option and complete with standard 45-seat Duple Bella Venture body was 5 tons 14 cwt 3 qr, about ½ton more than an equivalent SB5 with 41-seat body. Incidentally, the standard home-market bodies built by Duple and Plaxton for the SB measured up to 5in or so over the nominal 30ft overall from 1962, no longer being subject to the precise 30ft limit.

The frame of the VAM was straight, having a similar 10-in depth along most of its length and lowered front-end profile to that of the VAL, but set higher partly because of the larger wheels, giving a laden frame height of 2ft 8in. As before, this suited the standard styles of bodywork well, the Bella Venture body having a laden floor height of 3ft 3½in, high enough to minimise wheel arch intrusion, even more important than on an SB as there were passenger seats over both axles.

The front axle had a load rating of 4.3 tons, greater than hitherto found in any Bedford passenger model but it is significant that the 7-ton rear axle was slightly lower-rated than the unit in the SB, though this was because of its suspension, designed to give the optimum ride quality – the axle itself was as used on the SB. Suspension was traditional in method with beam axles and leaf springs, but the spring and damper settings were arrived at with the aid of a computer – something taken for granted today but a very advanced method in the mid-1960s. The computer was an experimental EMIAC analogue unit at Cranfield.

Not surprisingly, the Bedford tradition for good ride quality was maintained and when Alan Townsin road tested the Duple-bodied VAM5 whose weight is recorded above for *Bus & Coach's* January 1966 issue he described it as outstanding, though admittedly that vehicle was fully laden. However, it refuted the idea that a relatively short wheelbase was necessarily harmful in this regard. The steering was very low-geared, needing no less than 8¾ turns from lock to lock, which helped it to be quite light despite the lack of power assistance, but there was quite a strong variable-ratio effect making this lack not evident until manoeuvring in tight spaces, and he recalls that the coach proved surprisingly enjoyable to drive on a normal winding country road.

Although the report said that 'the Bedford diesel remains its noisy self', better sound-deadening made it appreciably quieter within than most SB5 coaches. With the overdrive gearbox, it would just reach 60mph, with the engine reaching over 2,900rpm due to the run-up permitted by the governor beyond the nominal limit, at that date 2,600rpm. Hence motorway travel implied continuous flat-out running – it is noteworthy that fuel consumption dropped from 15.85mpg on open-road running at not over 40mph (at that date the general limit for buses or coaches, except on motorways) to 10.6mpg from full-speed running round the Motor Industry Research Associations's high-speed circuit at Nuneaton. More significantly, it was beginning to become evident that this type of light coach was far less well suited to the new type of coach operation with long spells of high-speed running than in the days before motorways, by then spreading quite rapidly.

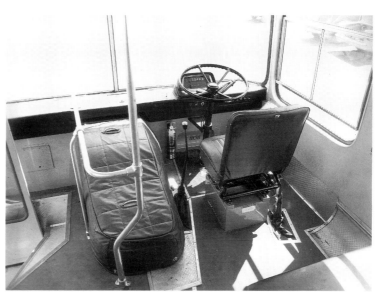

The VAM allowed a reasonably convenient entrance to be provided directly opposite the driver and hence was suitable for one-man operation. These views show the demonstrator with Pacesaver II body by Strachans, a bodybuilder then seeking to expand after moving from Acton, in the outskirts of London, to Hamble, in Hampshire. The quilted engine cover helped a little in keeping the noise level down, but the 330 cu in diesel engine was far from silent, even when idling, and the lack of other soft trim in such a vehicle was apt to make it difficult for drivers issuing tickets to hear what boarding passengers were saying.

The VAM-Strachans 45-seat demonstrator illustrated in the detail views shown above, registered in London as FXE 892C, spent a period operating on hire to Birmingham City Transport in December 1965 and January 1966. At that time there was growing interest in the use of one-man-operated single-deckers on urban services, such working of double-deckers not then being permissible, though in fact proposals to allow it had just been published and came into effect in July 1966. It took a little while for the implications to be taken into account, and for a time the Birmingham undertaking was one of several major urban fleets to express interest in a large-scale switch to single-deckers. In this case, however, the demonstrator operated on service 35 between Kings Heath and Brandwood Park, a single-deck service normally operated by two Daimler Fleetline single-deckers. Here it is seen loading at a temporary bus stop, with one of the undertaking's standard 'new look' double-deckers of the 1950-54 period in the background. In the event, though Birmingham did buy one batch of twelve of the equivalant Ford R192 models, the larger-scale swing to single-deckers did not happen, double-deck Fleetlines remaining in favour.

In addition to the VAM5 version with Bedford 330 diesel engine, the model was available as the VAM14 with Leyland O.400 6.54-litre engine, producing a model which had power in reserve in most circumstances and hence the probability of longer engine life to offset the extra cost. There was also the VAM3 with the 300 cu in petrol engine, chosen by very few users in Britain, though Salopia continued with its previous policy and took eight VAM3 and eight SB3 in 1966, this latter model having been the previous standard for the company's coach fleet since 1958. In 1967-69 the VAM3 became standard in the fleet, with yearly deliveries of twelve, ten and twelve, producing a total delivery of 42 of the type, all with Duple bodywork, as also had been standard on the SB coaches. Alan Townsin visited the firm around that time and it was an unusual experience hearing very subdued petrol-engine sounds from any of the modern coaches to be seen as they were being moved round the yard for cleaning or servicing.

This was a period when some operators followed a policy of replacing coaches, largely of Bedford or Ford make, very frequently, in some cases even annually. They fetched high enough resale prices to make this an economic proposition, bearing in mind the virtual absence of more than servicing costs and the warranty cover, and the strong sales appeal to customers of a perpetually 'new' fleet.

Probably the most famous was Whittle's of Highley, near Kidderminster, which had built up a big tours business serving the West Midlands as a whole. Batches of about 30 coaches would enter the fleet in the early months of each year and be sold a year later. In 1960-62, the fleets were a mixture of Bedford SB1 or SB5 and Ford 570E, largely with Burlingham bodywork, but the Bedford SB5 became dominant from 1963, when 30 were purchased, along with one VAL14 and one VAS1, all bodied by Duple. All were sold within a year and replaced by a new fleet of similar composition. In 1965, there were 26 SB5 and two VAL14, but in 1966 the intake switched to VAM5, of which there were 27, plus one VAL14, and in 1967, there were 26 VAM5 and four VAL14, which were still generally sold on

within the year, the only exceptions lingering on for no more than an extra month or two. Naturally the paintwork was still good, and for some years Whittle's distinctive blue and red became quite a familiar sight all over Britain as sold-off coaches often re-entered service with no more than a change of fleetname.

The VAM broadened Bedford's appeal and it was significant that for its 1967 programme, the State-owned Tilling group of companies ordered roundly 10% of its vehicle needs from Bedford, the remainder being on Bristol heavy-duty chassis. It is fair to point out, however, that Bristol had temporarily ceased production of its own light SU underfloor-engined chassis and had yet to introduce a replacement in the form of the LH. A few of these fleets had been buying small numbers of, generally, SB coaches for some years, but for 1967, the VAM, often in VAM14 form, was chosen by Crosville (ordering ten coaches), Eastern Counties (four coaches and four buses), Hants & Dorset (five buses), Lincolnshire (two coaches), Mansfield District (two coaches), Midland General (three coaches), Western National (twelve buses), West Yorkshire (four buses) and Wilts & Dorset (five coaches and two buses). In addition, VAL coaches were ordered by Cumberland (two) and Southern Vectis (four).

North of the border, Scottish Omnibuses Ltd, also State-owned, took 20 VAM5 with Alexander 45-seat bus bodies as its entire intake for 1967 – in its previous incarnation as SMT, this concern had been a customer for Bedford coaches at intervals since the 1930s, and indeed SMT Sales & Service, not included in the sale of the bus business to the State, was a major Bedford dealer, as well as building bodywork to Duple design on some OB coaches. This was the first SMT/SOL order for Bedford buses, being intended largely for rural routes in the Borders.

As with previous Bedford models, the VAM could prove very successful if put on duties suitable to its capabilities. The 'full-sized' 20-in wheels allowed larger 15¼in-diameter brake drums, which improved lining life as compared to the VAL, though fairly major changes were

There was a modest growth of interest in small coaches in the mid 1960s, and this even extended to the CA in long-wheelbase CALZ chassis form, for which Martin Walter had produced a glass-fibre body shell which was available as a four-berth caravan called the Debonair and as an 11-passenger coach with all seats facing forward and complying with PSV Regulations, as shown here. Only small numbers were built in this form.

In a rather larger class, the J2, converted to forward control, was also being used as the basis for a small coach. Plaxton produced a short version of its contemporary Embassy design, as seen here. If diesel-engined, these vehicles had the four-cylinder 220 cu in engine which made rather a harsh power unit for such use. A few had the 214 cu in petrol engine, in effect the old '28hp' unit, smoother and quite lively though with higher fuel cost.

The CA chassis was made to look quite glamorous in this drawing showing a late example, and in basic design it was still up to date in the mid-1960s, with 1,595cc push-rod overhead-valve petrol engine as standard and independent front suspension. There was a choice of a three- or four-speed all-synchromesh gearbox, two wheelbases and alternative axle ratios, plus the Perkins diesel. Ford's Transit introduced in 1965 offered a roomier design while retaining the concept of being car-like to drive and soon dominated the market, yet in some ways it was more conservative, retaining a conventional beam front axle.

made in the latter's brakes from September 1965, with more lining area, thicker front-axle linings and better heat dissipation. Some operators continued to find that brakes on Bedford passenger models were calling for more attention than on heavier types, however. It seems as if there was some lack of rigidity in the VAM brake backplates, as Hants & Dorset found that there was a need for a locking device for the adjusters, like that developed by that company for the VAL – indeed Bedford dealers offered a similar device for general sale.

Before leaving the passenger range as it then stood, it should be mentioned that it was becoming increasingly common to regard the J2 and even the CA as part of it in suitably adapted forms. At first glance it seems illogical that a normal-control model like the J2S was regularly converted to forward-control to form the basis of buses or coaches in the 19-21-seat class, but the forward-control TK, excellent design though it was, had the engine in a position that would have obstructed the gangway of a bus or coach just where this was unacceptable, between the front wheel-arches, so this had to be ruled out. Plaxton and others made suitably short versions of their contemporary coach bodies, and Duple continued to offer its metal-framed body originally intended as a rugged export bus.

The CA had proved to be on the small side for even the most basic type of minibus, a category of vehicle which had been given various concessions by changes in regulations from 1958 in the hope that it could be an answer to the growing problem of providing rural services when traffic was falling. However, Martin Walter had developed a glass-fibre body for the CAL long-wheelbase chassis intended for a number of uses, notably a roomier motor caravan than could be provided using the standard pressed steel body shell. From 1965, this was offered as a coach with comfortable forward-facing seats for eleven passengers and sold in modest numbers though one of the authors recalls the apt comment of one of his sons, then aged three, to the effect that it looked 'bit like an ice-cream van'!

The CA, in all its forms, came under devastatingly

intense competition from Ford's new Transit van introduced in October 1965. This was appreciably roomier in standard form as well as being built in a range of models capable of dealing with up to 35-cwt loads. For some applications, there was some resistance on the grounds that it was less compact, and for a year or two, most of the London evening papers' delivery fleets continued to buy the CA on the grounds that it could get through heavy traffic more readily, but the CA no longer dominated the market for that range of van size and the various derivatives, as it had since its introduction.

Further strong competition from Ford came with the introduction of its D-series truck range, replacing the Thames Trader. These could be regarded as an answer to the TK, with similar driving position but, in this case, tilt cabs were a feature. The power units were derived from the 4D and 6D from the previous range, but they were mounted in an inclined position to reduce their height, this feature having particular benefit in a tilt-cab model.

Ford was becoming an increasingly powerful competitor to Bedford in its whole range of goods and passenger models. Noteworthy among the latter was a 36ft model, the Thames 36, introduced in 1963. This was a relatively straightforward two-axle chassis using 20-in wheels, with the front axle set back, allowing the entrance to be at the front. It was updated in detail and renamed the R226 in 1965 and a shorter version directly comparable to the VAM introduced as the R192, the numbers relating to the wheelbase, both capturing a significant share of the lightweight coach market, even though Bedford remained market leader in this field.

A management change came at the end of 1965, when Sir William Swallow retired as Managing Director, his place being taken by David Hegland, the first of a succession of holders of this post who came from America – he had been associated with the overseas activities of General Motors since 1945, with spells as Managing Director of its operations in Denmark, South Africa and Australia, the last-mentioned being GM-Holden.

The TJ was becoming more of a minority choice in Britain, but there continued to be a demand from operators preferring the normal-control layout. This may have been so in this case, where the snow plough attachment made the ability to put plenty of ballast weight on the rear axle desirable to ensure adequate traction. The County Council of Durham, operators of this 6-ton short-wheelbase model, had the unenviable reputation of putting more salt per mile on the roads than any other local authority, considered necessary to combat the wintry conditions to which the area is prone.

The Forestry Commission used this KHA14 tractive unit dating from 1963 to haul a low-loading semi-trailer carrying heavy equipment from site to site. This model, with Leyland O.400 engine and maximum gross combination weight of 41,000 lb (18 tons 6cwt) had the highest gross weight rating of any model in the range before the KM range appeared at the 1966 Show.

The KM range and the 466 cu in engine

At intervals since its introduction, various models had been added to the TK range. In 1965, 30-cwt, 2- and 3-ton models were added, models KA and KB, and there was also a new tipper with 10ft wheelbase for 11½-ton gross weight.

The new heavier-duty goods models announced in time for the 1966 Commercial Motor Show formed an upward addition to that range, by then extending from KA to KH, as the KM designation and general appearance suggested, though in this case, KM was used as the class title in publicity, these heavier-duty models not being described as TK variants. This was logical in design terms

since, apart from the cab, they were completely new designs.

By that date, the maximum gross weight permitted for a two-axle goods vehicle operating on British roads was 16 tons, and the load-carrying KM models took Bedford up into this class. There were also tractor units designed to haul gross combination weights of up to 22 tons initially. The KM models retained the TK design of cab, but a heavy double-bar front bumper, dual headlamps and such items as the ten-stud wheels with larger tyres, 10.00-20 on most models, gave a distinctive and more rugged look.

The big news in terms of mechanical design was a completely new engine, the 466 cu in (7.634-litre) unit known as the '70' series, again a direct-injection in-line

The KM put Bedford into new territory with two-axle gross vehicle weights of up to 16 tons and gross combination weights of up to 22 tons. Here two examples in the insulated haulage fleet of G. H. Cutsforth Ltd of Hull are seen with an earlier TK, the taller build and deep double-bar front bumper giving quite a 'macho' look. The KM was also available in longer wheelbases than any previous Bedford goods model, as conveyed by the platform truck nearest the camera. Tastes in lettering were altering, the F-registered (1967-68) vehicle having an older style than the H-registered (1969-70) example alongside it (although the container on that truck was in the older style), the pre-suffix TK evidently having been repainted into the later style.

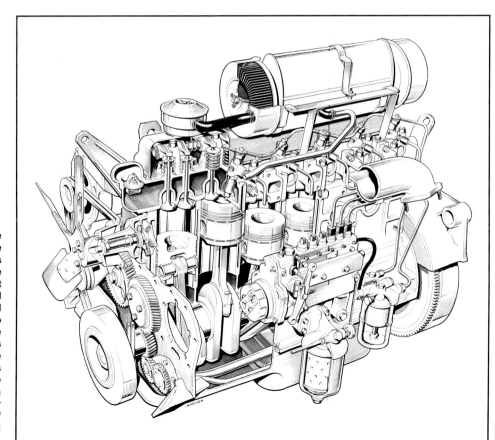

The 466 cu in (7.634-litre) engine used in the KM as well as the VAL and VAM passenger models was of up-to-date yet simple design, with toroidal direct injection, counterbalanced seven-bearing crankshaft and gear-driven timing but no cylinder liners and no separate valve guides or seats. There was a very similar smaller-bore engine, the 381 cu in, and this new family of engines was to be the basis of later units which were to power many of the larger Bedford models until the end of manufacture under GM control in 1986.

The KM range

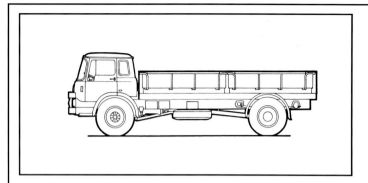

KMM 174in wheelbase GVW 16 tons

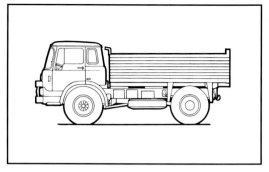

KMT 120in wheelbase GVW 14 tons

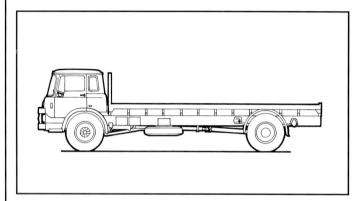

KML 208in wheelbase GVW 16 tons

KMR 132in wheelbase GVW 15 tons

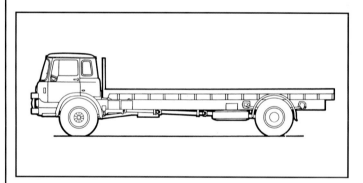

KMH 224in wheelbase GVW 16 tons

KMS 158in wheelbase GVW 16 tons

KMB 109in wheelbase GCW 22 tons

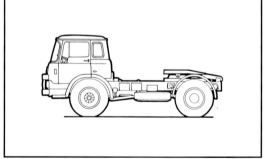

KMA 120in wheelbase GCW 22 tons

These drawings show the variants of the KM range as introduced in 1966 – the two tractor units were uprated to 24 tons GCW the following year. All had the Bedford 466 cu in six-cylinder in-line engine but in 1972 the KMR was to be selected as the basis for a 32-ton tractive unit using the Detroit Diesel 6V-71 two-stroke unit.

six-cylinder unit, with 4.562in bore and 4.75in stroke, giving 145bhp gross (136bhp net) at 2,800rpm, a high governed speed for an engine of this size though familiar on previous smaller Bedford diesels.

The general design of the 466 cu in engine was much as that of the 330 cu in unit, and the performance figures were scaled up very largely in proportion to the increase in swept volume. A concept known as 'end-to-end water flow', with a source of head gasket trouble eliminated by taking cooling water right through the block to the rear and then, via a separate connection, forward through the head without any water passing through the head-to-block joint face, had been introduced on the smaller Bedford diesels in 1964 and was used for the new engines. Their design was kept as simple as possible, with no cylinder liners (though these were to be available as a means of reconditioning when the rebore limit had been reached) and no separate valve guides or valve seats, but it was claimed that these features helped to improve cooling efficiency. A Simms in-line injection pump was used, but now with mechanical governor, improving idling.

This engine was used in all the KM models but there was also a smaller-bore ($4\frac{1}{8}$in) version of the same general design, save for using a CAV DPA rotary injection pump, the '60' series engine, of 381 cu in (6.243-litre) capacity, which developed 123bhp gross (114bhp net), again at 2,800rpm, intended to replace the Leyland O.370 or O.400 on KG and KH models. This new family of engines was to provide the basis for others used until the end of production of Bedford vehicles as part of the GM empire some nineteen years later.

For the KM, a new five-speed direct-top gearbox with synchromesh on all but first and reverse was introduced and this had more evenly-spread ratios than found on the overdrive five-speed boxes found on some earlier models, though such a unit was available as an option for the rigid models.

There was a new stronger frame, although this continued to be of riveted construction, and new axles. The 6½-ton front axle was of 52% higher capacity than the previous heaviest Bedford unit as used on the KH, designed to allow more weight to be carried at the front and intended to allow a laden weight distribution of about 40%/60% front to rear. Power-assisted steering was now standard and with tighter lock angles, the KM could turn in more limited space than the equivalent KH models. At the rear, the rating of the new axle was just over 10 tons (22,500 lb), this being a spiral bevel unit, an interesting detail being the revival of the angled casing idea found on Bedford models from 1934. A two-speed axle was optional. The rear springs had a slipper-type of rear mounting with a cam profile, giving a variable rate effect.

The brake system was of direct air-operated type with 15½in drums, these being readily detachable. There were completely duplicated circuits and on tractor units a third reservoir was added, with a load-sensing valve which reduced braking on the driven axle in light-load conditions.

There were eight models, all having the 466 cu in engine, with main features as follows:-

The KM cab interior was largely as used on existing TK models but the treadle brake pedal, directly operating the control valve, was a reminder that this model had direct air-operated brakes. By then a heater and screen-wash were standard equipment – both items taken for granted nowadays but not so in the past, even as late as 1966.

Model	Type	Wheelbase	Load rating
KMM	Truck	14ft 6in (174in)	16-ton GVW
KML	Truck	17ft 4in (208in)	16-ton GVW
KMH	Truck	18ft 8in (224in)	16-ton GVW
KMT	Tipper	10ft 0in (120in)	7 cu yd (14-ton GVW)
KMR	Tipper	11ft 0in (132in)	8 cu yd (15-ton GVW)
KMS	Tipper or truck	13ft 2in (158in)	9 cu yd (16-ton GVW)
KMB	Tractor	9ft 1in (109in)	22-ton GCW
KMA	Tractor	10ft 0in (120in)	22-ton GCW

In 1967, the KMA and KMB were uprated to permit operation at a 24-ton gross combination weight, and a deluxe cab was fitted to some variants. The KM marked another step up the weight range for Bedford, as well as bringing more concepts such as full-air brakes and 10-stud wheels hitherto associated with the traditional type of heavy-vehicle maker. It enabled Bedford to gain a stronger foothold in the sectors of the market where economics favoured the use of maximum-weight two axle models and advanced its penetration of the fast-growing articulated tractive unit business, although this was increasingly tending to favour heavier models, at that stage beyond Bedford's model range.

Introduction of the KM range also provided units which had wider application. In September 1967, the 466 cu in engine replaced the Leyland O.400 in the VAL twin-steering coach chassis, which henceforth became the VAL70. In similar manner the new VAM70, again with the 466 cu in unit, became the only diesel version of this model available, replacing both the VAM5 and VAM14, though in this case the VAM3 with petrol engine continued

Some indication of the scale on which engines were being manufactured at Dunstable in 1967 is given by this view of the cylinder block line dealing with 466 cu in engines. There are some 44 blocks stacked in the group in the foreground, for example, quite apart from those on the line and in other stacks visible in the background. A linked complex of multi-station transfer machines interspersed with single machines, washes, inspection stations and pressure test equipment carried out all the numerous machining operations with a minimum of human intervention. The plant was capable of building a total of up to 450 engines of the four diesel and two petrol types then in production per day.

The end of the main Dunstable production line at the same period, with a KM tractive unit almost ready to leave the line, followed by an R-type 4x4 model. Up to 360 commercial vehicle chassis could be built per day, this total excluding the HA and CA van models built alongside Vauxhall cars in the Luton factory. Even though the actual production rate was somewhat less, at that date the plant had the biggest output of trucks in Europe, and was producing nearly half the trucks of all makes exported from Britain.

Scottish Omnibuses Ltd had adopted 'Eastern Scottish' as its fleetname by the time a batch of 20 VAM5 models with five-speed direct-top gearboxes and Alexander 45-seat bus bodywork entered service in May-June 1967. The unladen weight was 5 tons 1 cwt 2 qr.

In June 1968, a further 20 VAM models were placed in service by the same fleet, but these were on VAM70 chassis with the 466 cu in engine and had Duple Midland bodies having semi-coach seats for 41 passengers and painted in a 'reversed' green and cream livery. For many years, the Scottish Bus Group had favoured the use of vehicles with bodywork of this character for general country service duty, when passengers were likely to be in the vehicle for some time on the long routes many of them covered. The VAM types were used mainly on services covering the largely rural Borders area.

to be available. Performance with the 466 cu in engine, as compared to the O.400-engined models, was not increased as much as might have been expected, the net output rising from 125 to 136bhp, and torque from 300 to 319 lb.ft.

In terms of passenger-appeal, the overall effect was relatively slight, the high noise level at speed remaining the main drawback of the models, the difference with the new engine being more one of tone, with more induction roar but perhaps less combustion 'clatter' than either of the smaller engines. On the other hand, higher gearing did make medium-speed running quieter, though an irritating feature was the way in which the wide gap between the 1.8 to 1 third gear and the direct fourth made it almost impossible to avoid the engine labouring for several seconds after changing up.

Comparing a VAM70 tested for *Bus & Coach's* February 1968 issue with the VAM5 with 330 cu in engine tested just over two years earlier, the most obvious change was that the new model was nearly 10mph faster, reaching 69mph largely due to being powerful enough to accept the higher gearing, and yet had enough torque to give adequate acceleration despite this. There was a useful gain in fuel economy on two-stops-per-mile running, simulating a country bus route, from 9.6mpg with the VAM5 to 11.95mpg with the VAM70, but when the higher speed was used on the motorway, the figure dropped to around 9½mpg.

The VAM70 maintained the VAM5's ability to attract

Exports continued to form a major part of production. This CALZ with extending ladder was supplied to a light and power company in Kolding, Denmark in 1966. In regard to commercial vehicles generally, Bedford was the best-selling make of truck in Denmark that year, with 29% of the market. Similar remarks applied to New Zealand, where Bedford's share was 42%; South Africa (34%) and Australia (31%). In Holland, Bedford was the best-selling imported truck, and in Norway, France, Germany and Switzerland, Bedford was the best-selling British truck.

orders from major operators, Scottish Omnibuses taking 20, this time with Duple Midland bodywork, in 1968, in the same registration batch as its initial delivery of Bristol VRT double-deckers. Further south, the Tilling group included 35 VAM70 and five VAL70 in its vehicle programme for delivery to various subsidiaries in 1968, but here there was 'a new kid on the block' in the form of the Bristol LH model with horizontal underfloor engine, usually the Leyland O.400, and naturally this 'in house' model was favoured increasingly for the group's lightweight vehicle needs. Even so, the main competition in this

market continued to come from Ford.

Thus Bedford's use of engines bought-out from Leyland ceased and all the main chassis were supplied with a range of engines entirely of Bedford make. The price of the standard VAL70, £1,910, was marginally higher than that of the VAL14 which had been £1,890, but part of this might have been due to inflation, just beginning to become a national problem. However the VAM70, at £1,626, was £70 cheaper than the VAL14 but some £290 more than the VAM5. The petrol VAM3 model was £35 up. With the 466 engine came the latest Clark five-speed overdrive gearbox as standard, but this continued to have a characteristically Bedford wide spread of ratios, save for the close-ratio overdrive. The standard tyre size also went up to 9.00-20, the steering being not quite so light as that of the VAM5.

At the same time the VAS diesel model switched from VAS1 to VAS5, thus having the 330 diesel instead of the 300 unit, the petrol model continuing as VAS2. The penny had at last dropped in regard to the unwanted 1950-style front-end sheet-metalwork, which was no longer supplied. The SB continued, largely as an export model, but also having a following in Britain, partly as a furniture van, as its layout and long-wheelbase gave more load-space than a TK, though modest numbers were still being sold for coach use in Britain – at £1,240 for the diesel SB5 chassis, it was good value where a simple vehicle was needed.

The range continued little changed through 1968, though ultra-short 7-ft (84-in) wheelbase versions of the 4- and 5-ton TK models were introduced jointly that summer with semi-trailer-makers Taskers for urban delivery work. More significant in terms of factory-built production was the KME six-wheeler, a version of the KM with 18ft 8in

A special ultra-short 7ft-wheelbase version of the TK 4- and 5-ton chassis was produced as a joint exercise with Tasker from 1968, this example bearing British Rail's then recently introduced emblem.

The RL 4x4 model continued in production through the 1960s, by which period it was the only current model retaining the style of cab first seen on the S-type in 1950. It is seen here in the version having twin rear wheels with twin-boom wrecker body by Reynolds-Boughton Engineering Services Ltd, of Amersham Common, Buckinghamshire. An example is seen parked outside the Kings Arms Hotel in Old Amersham.

Lacre, which had made its own three-wheeled road sweepers in the 1920s and 1930s, turned to Bedford chassis in later years and used the TK model by the late 1960s. This example was on a 7-ton tipper chassis with the 330 cu in diesel engine. The air intake for the engine was extended so as to draw air from a dust-free position just behind the top corner of the cab. The exhaust was also led upwards, but through the casing of the body, protruding slightly through the roof. Left-hand-drive chassis were often specified for such vehicles, as for this demonstrator. Note the variety of cars of the period parked behind – from left to right there were a Riley 1.5, an Austin 1100, a Ford Consul Classic, a Triumph Herald, a Vauxhall Viva of the HA type from which the HA van was derived, and a Ford 100E.

(224in) total wheelbase, the rearmost axle being a trailing unit. Here again, Bedford had moved into a 'big-league' corner of the market.

Overall Bedford sales had reached a fresh peak in 1965, with a total of 112,360 vehicles sold and the total exceeded 100,000 in 1960, 1964, 1965, 1966 and 1969. Yearly figures fluctuated not only in response to Bedford's success in relation to its competitors in the various types of vehicles sold but also in response to general trade conditions in the countries where they were offered and on a world basis. On 24th March 1969, Tony Benn, then a Minister in the Labour Government of the day, drove the 1½ millionth Bedford off the line, a KM export model –

49% of that total had been exported.

An urban bus project

A plan that would have broadened Bedford's involvement in urban buses that was pursued for a time in the late 1960s was one for joint involvement with Metropolitan-Cammell Weymann in an integral single-decker. Negotiations took place between the marketing department and Dick Knowles of MCW, the background being that concern's experience of building integral buses using Leyland mechanical units, under threat as Leyland began to exploit the possibilities of producing its own vehicles of this type. This policy, ultimately leading to the Leyland National, left MCW

The project for an integral bus to be jointly produced with MCW described in the text did not materialise, but there were a few instances of Bedford models of the late 1960s being used on urban services. One of the more surprising was in Basingstoke, at that date rapidly expanding as a result of being selected as one of the towns to take 'overspill' population from London. At that period, the main operator in this part of north-east Hampshire was Wilts & Dorset Motor Services Ltd, a Tilling group company, and although most of the town services were run by Bristol Lodekka double-deckers, some of a batch of six VAM70 models added to the fleet in 1968 were allocated to Basingstoke and run on local routes. The Willowbrook bodywork had two doors, the centre one marked 'exit only' and seating was provided for 40 passengers, up to 19 more being permitted to stand. Despite the 'urban-bus' nature of these features, the vehicles were ill-suited to such duty, having a high floor line, and did not remain long before being switched to more rural services.

without a partner to supply the mechanical items. At that time there was strong interest in 11-metre single-deck buses for city services, initially fostered from 1961, when vehicles of this length became legal in Britain, by the ability to run them without a conductor. At first this did not extend to double-deckers, though in fact such operation became legal from 1966, hence making this surge of interest in urban single-deckers short-lived in this country.

There had been some previous co-operation in a project for MCW (in those days itself a joint operation between Metro-Cammell in Birmingham and Weymann at Addlestone, Surrey), building light metal-framed coach bodies in Bedford chassis in the early 1960s, including one on one of the prototype VAL chassis. It had been short-lived but the link was re-activated to the extent of some design work being done on what might have been marketed as a Metro-Bedford.

The design proposed would have used the heavy-duty axles from the KM goods range with a 466 cu in engine mounted longitudinally in line at the rear, using Allison fully-automatic transmission. Bedford engineers made several trips to MCW, then concentrated at Elmdon, near Birmingham Airport, following the closure of Weymann in 1965, to direct the draughtsmen. However, it became clear that the engine installation was not really suitable. The layout would have implied considerable intrusion of the engine compartment into potential passenger space at the rear of the vehicle. Further, it was considered that the Bedford engine did not have the right image for a city bus. The two firms had quite different ideas on design, manufacture and marketing – problems that were to recur in later years with Marshall and the JJL – and the project was dropped by mutual agreement. MCW then linked up with Scania, initially producing the Metro-Scania single-decker, a much more expensive design using a transversely mounted Scania 11-litre engine and closely based on the existing Scania CR-76 bus.

The CF van

In the autumn of 1969, the CA was taken out of production after some seventeen years and 370,045 examples had been built, to be replaced by the CF, officially announced on 31st October. The missing letters signified projects which had not gone into production – on one occasion towards the end of the 1950s, a forward-control van had been almost ready when Ford beat Bedford to the post with a model of similar layout, and it was judged best not to be seen to follow.

Yet it could hardly be disguised that the CF was an answer to the Ford Transit, of similar size and not dissimilar layout and general appearance. There were two wheelbase lengths, 8ft 10in (106in), which was 4in longer than even the longer CAL version of the earlier model, and 10ft 6in (126in). The internal capacity of the shorter-wheelbase models was 185 cu ft, and the longer models gave 252 cu ft, in both cases with passenger seat in place.

The shorter model was available in versions for 15cwt, 18cwt and 22cwt, and the longer in versions for 25cwt and 35cwt, this last model having twin tyres on the rear axle, in a manner again comparable to the Transit. Tyre sizes varied from 6.30-13 to 7.00-14.

However, there were significant difference in design. Bedford retained its faith in independent front suspension, contrasting with the Transit's beam axle, and Vauxhall's usual expertise in suspension design was also evident at the rear, where single taper leaf springs were used, eliminating inter-leaf friction entirely. Another advanced feature on a vehicle of this nature and size was the rack-and-pinion steering.

The petrol engines and some other items were derived from the latest Vauxhall Victor range, the FD, which had been introduced two years earlier. In stages, this model had become a significantly larger car than the original Victor F-series first seen in 1957 and the larger of two engine sizes offered was thus suitable for even the largest CF.

The CF, as well as replacing the CA, broadened the range of weight and internal volume available within its range considerably. In earlier generations of van, 30cwt or above implied a model with basic design and mechanical features largely as used on models designed to carry 2, 3 or more tons. Now there was a 35-cwt CF model, as seen here, and although alternative engines and other items were used to cover this wider range, it benefited from using many parts common to the lighter versions down to the 14-cwt model. Even so, this top-of-the-range model had twin rear wheels and other features suitable to its gross weight, the standard petrol engine being of just under 2-litre size in this case. The van shown, run by Mackinlay McPherson Ltd, wine merchants, of Edinburgh, was an early example of the type, with H-suffix registration.

The Victor FD had introduced new four-cylinder petrol engines of 1,599cc and 1,975cc, both with overhead-camshaft driven by toothed belt, a new concept at that time. To help in reducing bonnet height on the car, they were inclined at an angle of 45° and this feature was carried over to the van. The 14 and 18cwt models used the smaller engine and could have either a three-speed or four-speed gearbox, while the bigger models had the larger engine with a four-speed gearbox.

Both these petrol engines were quite high-revving units, developing their maximum power, 64bhp and 75bhp in van form respectively, at 5,500rpm, and some of the flexibility and willingness to pull smoothly at low speed of the older push-rod design, well-suited to the CA, was lost, even though peak performance was lively in relation to the much more spacious body.

There were also diesel options, these again having Perkins engines, now the only bought-out engines in the whole Bedford range. In this case the 14, 18 and 22cwt models used the 4.108 and the 25 and 35cwt models used the then recently introduced 4.154. The model was of

The layout of the petrol engine, inclined at 45°, and the rack and pinion steering, can be seen in this drawing.

The CF was also available with a variety of bodywork. Here a 35cwt model with livestock-transporter body is seen with a 14cwt dropside truck, both registered in Fife.

semi-forward-control layout, with engine cowl projecting into the front end of the internal space. Initially the Transit had an advantage in this respect in the petrol form still most common for this size of vehicle at that stage, as its engine was a V4 unit, and thus very compact and not requiring the intrusion into the interior, but the V4 was dropped after a few years and later models were more directly comparable in this sense.

The CF was a useful vehicle and picked up quite a lot of business yet it was so obviously an answer to the Transit that it was almost impossible for it to recapture the huge market that model had built up even in its first few years, unless some strong advantage became evident. In fact the two models were quite evenly matched, each having some advantages but not of an overriding nature. Both were offered in a variety of forms, using either the pressed-steel basic shell or alternatively in versions in which other bodywork was fitted by outside coachbuilders. What was significant in both cases was how the range covered by a mass-produced van – what in America would be called a panel-van – was extended upwards in Britain from the range of up to around 12cwt right up to 35cwt, well into the type of market that hitherto had been covered by models at the lighter end of the middle-range commercial vehicle ranges, such as the J1 and in an earlier era the K 30-cwt and even earlier the WS model derived from the original Chevrolet LQ of 1929-31 which was in effect, the 'father' of the whole Bedford range.

So the 1960s drew to a close, with much achieved by Bedford and more planned for the future, but also with growing challenges on the horizon.

Right: The smaller TK models found growing favour as a basis for horsebox bodywork. The 16-in wheels allowed the floor level to be low enough to make entry up the loading ramp less hazardous and quite often the rider would share in the driving, so the compact size, responsive controls and 'civilised' cab were important merits. Such vehicles were often still petrol-engined, adding to the level of refinement for occupants, both equine and human. This one had wheel discs of the type often fitted to VAS and VAL coaches.
The lightest KA model had disc brakes as first introduced, being claimed to be the first production truck so fitted, in the UK at least, but the pads wore out in 6,000 miles or less and drum brakes were soon substituted.

Below right: Although there had been six-wheel conversions of earlier Bedford models, the 1960s was the era when they became significant in numbers, leading to approved joint projects and eventually to factory build of such vehicles. Most were of conventional layout with an additional rear axle, but this twin-steer conversion of a TK is thought to have been the first instance of a 'Chinese six' on tipper work. W. E. Snow Ltd had started its business with a REO Speed Wagon, later running Seddon and Austin vehicles.

Below: The growth in the use of Bedford six-wheeler conversions on work such as this encouraged the development of more powerful engines and heavier-duty models. This TK-based vehicle dating from 1964 in the fleet of Fred Sherwood, of Whatton, Leicestershire, doubtless had a 330 cu in engine and it is not difficult to imagine the din as it climbed out of the quarry fully laden with engine at peak revs in a low gear.

Portugal was another lively market for Bedford vehicles. This 1968 left-hand-drive VAM for use by a medical and rehabilitation centre had bodywork by Caetano, a leading bodybuilder in that country.

The following year, Caetano coach bodywork began to be sold in Britain under the name Moseley Continental Coachwork and a 1969 VAL70 is seen here. The Caetano emblem is visible just above the corner of the front bumper – this design was called the Estoril. The rather angular but neatly executed styling and elaborate form of livery appealed to operators seeking something 'different'.

The limited success of the VAL in the coach market made sales of the model for specialised needs welcome. This car transporter with drawbar trailer was used by Mondia N. V. of Antwerp, Belgium. It is seen carrying eight Opel estate cars, so their conveyance was appropriately within the General Motors family. The pattern of Opel as the centre of development for General Motor's European-built cars while the group's commercial vehicle development work for worldwide applications (other than for North America) was concentrated at Luton was gaining momentum.

Providing transport for racing pigeons was perhaps the most bizarre of roles carried out by the VAL. The vehicle dating from around 1968 was used by Charles Catterall of Blackpool. Simultaneous opening of the doors produced quite a spectacular massed take-off. The front panel and grille were as used on the contemporary Plaxton Panorama coach design.

15 THE 1970s – NEW METHODS AND QUIETER COACHES

Vauxhall Motors Ltd entered the 1970s with strong indications of self-confidence, even though it was to prove a decade of growing competition. In addition to the Engineering and Design Centre dating from 1964, the first part of the immense Millbrook proving ground had been brought into use in 1969. Chaul End, a few miles from Luton, had been used for some work of this kind for a decade or so, though later concentrating on its function as the company's research laboratories, together with noise and vibration testing.

The Millbrook site, 18 miles north of Luton, covered some 700 acres, with a wide variety of test tracks amounting to 25 miles in total, of widely varying kinds from a 3.3-mile hill route with gradients of up to 1 in 4, separate 'truck slopes', a 2-mile-circumference high--speed circuit with five traffic lanes suitable for varying speeds of up to 100mph or more, and nearly a mile of rough Belgian pave-style road. There were also a truck rough track, dust tunnel, a ride and handling course with various bends and cambers and a one-mile straight. Particularly significant was a salt trough and a track where salt spray was fed in from the sides – corrosion had been recognised as a growing problem, particularly in the car and light van

ranges, not helped by increased use of salt on wintry roads. Overall, it offered a range of test facilities on one site that were the finest of their kind in Britain and indeed ranked among the world's finest of this type.

The first new Bedford type to appear in 1970 was the M-type 4x4, which replaced the R-type. Development work in conjunction with the military authorities leading to the new model had been in hand for eight years and the most obvious new feature was the adoption of the TK cab. Despite the rugged appearance, the specification, with a choice of 300 cu in petrol or 330 cu in diesel engines and air-hydraulic brakes, was built to meet a Ministry of Defence specification which put the emphasis on strict weight limits. It was required to carry a 4-tonne payload and meet the 'medium mobility' cross-country capability which was something of an understatement, 'go-anywhere' being not too great an exaggeration. However, the requirement that it was to be air portable and ability to be lifted by a helicopter meant that tight weight control was essential.

The original designation was MK, the latter signifying a special multi-fuel version of the 330 diesel engine capable of running on Derv, petrol, AVTAG and AVTUR

The facilities at the Millbrook proving ground included these 'truck slopes', of consistent 1 in 4 and 1 in 5 gradient and long enough for hill climbing, hill-restart and handbrake performance to be thoroughly tested. Such a range of facilities was unrivalled in Britain and among the best anywhere. Seen being tested is a TM model as introduced in the mid-1970s and described in the next chapter.

An MK 4x4 with standard Marshall steel dropside body negotiating a cross-country route while on test. The model was designed to meet Fighting Vehicle Research and Development Establishment (FVRDE) specification No. 9354 as a general service vehicle for use by the Army, and was notable for its multi-fuel engine.

(these latter letters being aviation fuels), but conventional petrol or diesel engines were offered for more general use including civilian versions and the model became known simply as the M-type. As much of the R-type mechanical design was retained as possible, commonality being regarded as important – the transfer box and driven front axle were close to their limits of power transmission and carrying capacity. There was a four-speed main gearbox and two-speed transfer box, which could also be used to give two-wheel drive, but only in high ratio. There were optional 11ft 6in (138in) or 13ft (156in) wheelbases, and a civilian version with 9.00-20 cross-country tyres using

An M-type chassis with twin-tyred rear axle, as offered as an option for civilian applications. The cab and other items are removed to show the general layout, causing the unsupported inner steering column to look unduly slender. The model was to remain in production into the 1980s, still selling in quite substantial numbers.

twins at the rear was available as an option to the 12.00-20 military-type singles all round.

New model designations

At this point it is appropriate to mention a new model designation system that had begun to be introduced in 1968 as a consequence of computer scheduling. We are grateful to Leo Taylor for the explanation of the principles adopted, clearly geared to the changing needs of identifying an increasingly complex range within a busy factory, but the cause of considerable confusion to those outside the Vauxhall organisation.

Hitherto familiar designations well-known to operators were suddenly replaced by seemingly meaningless codes, examples being EJM3 instead of KDL5 or CHJ1 instead of J2S10, while among the passenger models PJK1 replaced VAS5. Helping to aggravate this confusion, some items previously identified by numbers were now denoted by letters and vice versa.

Existing model designations continued to be used to some degree for established models, certainly in conversations between technical staff, but also up to a point in sales literature and published lists of models. Some well-known type codes such as the SB never really died out even though the official designations were changed.

The new system had a seven-character code, in which each character specified a particular feature of the vehicle in question. Frequently, however, the first three letters provided sufficient identification of the main models for day to day use. Taking a VAS5 as an example, the new code in full became PJK1BZO. This was made up as follows:-

Model line	P
Engine type	J
Gross vehicle weight group	K
Wheelbase range	1
Drive line (gearbox and axle)	B
Cab type	ZO

The letters chosen for 'model line' were quite different to those used previously, some of the main ones being as follows, with previous codes where applicable:-

New code	Description	Previous code
B*	Bus and coach chassis	VAM
C	Normal control truck	J (TJ)
E	Forward control truck	K (TK, KM etc)
H	Forward control 6x2	
K	Forward control 6x4	
M	Forward control four-wheel-drive	
P	Bus and coach chassis	VAS
N	Bus and coach chassis	SB
T*	Bus and coach chassis	VAM
W	Bus and coach chassis	VAL
Y	Bus and coach chassis	(new range, see below)

Some of these soon fell out of use.
*The former VAM, continuing in production for export, was later changed from T to B, clearing the way for a new car range. E later also covered the TM, but the TL range of 1980 was given D, and those TK models that continued were switched to S. Model line W was later reallocated to the TM 4x4, the six-wheel version being given R.

The second character indicated the engine, this now being indicated by a letter. The following list includes the codes L, M, N and W referring to engines introduced subsequently and described later in the text, included here to aid reference. Note that in this and other instances the letter 'O' had an open or all-embracing meaning, sometimes convenient when referring to models or units in general terms:-

Engine letter	Description	Previous No.
O	All engines appropriate to the model line	
D	214 cu in petrol engine	2
F	300 cu in petrol engine	3
H	220 cu in diesel engine	10
J	330 cu in diesel engine	5
P	466 cu in diesel engine (derated)	
R	466 cu in diesel engine	70
L	8.2-litre diesel engine (derated to 110kW)	
M	8.2-litre diesel engine (119kW or turbo-charged to 130kW)	
N	8.2-litre diesel engine (turbo-charged to 153kW)	
W	6V-71 diesel engine	

When turbocharging became standard the basic letters were retained. B and V were later added to cover Cummins 10-litre and E290/E370 engines respectively. It is thought that some of the engine letters were re-used, and at AWD, which retained the system, P and R were used to signify Perkins engines.

The third character indicated the group of gross weight (measured in kilograms) into which the chassis in question falls. Note that some of the ranges overlap:-

GVW letter	Gross vehicle weight range	
O	Not specified	
B	Below 2300	
C	2300-3000	These weight ranges were sometimes adjusted in later years but model letters for existing models were not changed. Artic models took the letter appropriate to the basic type.
D	2700-3400	
E	3200-3900	
F	3400-4500	
G	4100-5400	
H	5000-5900	
J	5400-6400	
K	5700-7000	
L	6800-7000	
M	7300-8600	
N	8200-10000	
P	9500-10400	
Q	10000-11100	
R	10400-12700	
S	12300-13600	
T	13200-14500	
V	14100-16300	
X	18100-30000	

The fourth character was generally a number signifying the wheelbase class, though A was used for the 'extra short' category:-

Wheelbase letter	Wheelbase range
0	Not specified
1	Short
2	Medium
3	Long
4	Extra long
5	Short tipper
6	Medium tipper
7	Long tipper
8	Short tractor
9	Medium tractor
A	Extra short

The fifth character signified the gearbox and axle combination. Note that some combinations, as simply defined in the reference list, repeat:-

Drive line letter	Gearbox	Rear axle	Other
O	Not specified		
B	4-speed direct top	single-speed	
C	5-speed direct top	single-speed	
D	5-speed overdrive	single-speed	
E	4-speed direct top	two-speed	
F	5-speed direct top	two-speed	
G	5-speed overdrive	two-speed	
H	4-speed direct top	two-speed	
J	5-speed direct top	two-speed	
K	5-speed direct top	two-speed	
M	9-speed overdrive	single-speed	
N	6-speed direct top	single-speed	
Q	9-speed overdrive	single-speed	
T	9-speed direct top	single-speed	
V	6-speed overdrive	two-speed	
W	4-speed main		Winch

Body type letters	Description
OO	Not specified
CO	Cab
DO	Narrow tilt cab (for TM)
EO	Driveaway front end with mostly permanent content
FO	Wide tilt cab (for TM)
GO	Tilt cab (for TL)
HO	Sleeper tilt cab (for TM)
KO	Integral bus (JJL)
MO	Military cab (for M-type)
PO	Pick-up
ZO	Cowl or, on passenger models, temporary driveaway front end

In the above, it has to be borne in mind that this was a 'living' code system, used to identify vehicle differences in accordance with what was in production at a given time, and modified from time to time accordingly. The above attempts to cover the main codes used over the period up to 1986.

The development of the Vehicle Identification Number system led to the chassis number beginning with the above seven-character code, plus a letter indicating the year of manufacture, beginning at A to signify 1971, B for 1972 etc, plus a further letter identifying the General Motors plant of origin, W signifying Dunstable. The six-figure chassis numbers that followed were as allocated to frames as they started on the final assembly conveyer and thus were not classified as to type.

In the early 1980s, new international regulations made some changes necessary, the letters Q and O no longer being permissible, causing YMQ, as then in use, to become YMP, and the seventh character of the model designation was dropped. At the same time the letters SKF were added at the front of the complete VIN code to signify the manufacturer and country of origin. Thus such a number would have no less than eleven characters of a descriptive nature as a prefix to the six-figure serial number. As if that were not enough, also embossed on the VIN plate, there would be a series of three-digit numbers specifying what were called the Regular Production Options built into the chassis, signifying such items as 180 for heavy-duty rear suspension, or 501 for automatic transmission.

The YRQ coach chassis

The high internal noise level at speed had been the most obvious drawback to Bedford passenger models ever since the diesel versions became the general choice in the later 1950s. The underfloor engine position by then usual on more expensive models made it much easier to reduce the amount of engine noise reaching passengers. However, these had horizontal engines and Bedford, ever-mindful of costs, had decided against making a horizontal version of its engines for what was seen as a small part of overall sales and which would not have had any application for other models.

A solution to this impasse arose as a result of a combination of circumstances. One factor was the relaxation in the late 1960s of the requirement, which for many years had been part of the PSV (Conditions of Fitness) Regulations, that ground clearance under a central strip of a bus or coach should be a minimum of 10in over the front two-thirds of the wheelbase. Another was the modest height of the 466 cu in engine, helped by its short stroke dimension of 4.75in. By modifying the shape of the sump to make it as shallow as practicable, the otherwise unaltered engine could be mounted so that its valve cover projected only an inch or so above the level of the tops of the tyres. Thus, bearing in mind that the leading coach bodybuilders set the floor height so as to minimise the intrusion above this level of the wheel-arches, which had to allow for the upward movement of the wheels over bumps, it became possible to fit the engine under a gangway level little if any different to that of a typical VAM model.

The layout did have a drawback as compared to a horizontal engine in that attention to items mounted in the cylinder head required access via a floor trap, with a need for care that oily hands did not come in contact with the moquette of the passenger seats. Removing the engine also required it to be lowered further before it could be extracted from under the frame side-members. In historical terms, it was not quite the first instance of an underfloor-mounted vertical engine in a bus, as Seddon had built a small model of similar layout using a Perkins engine in 1950, but that was built only in very small numbers.

In principle, the resulting new model announced in September 1970, the YRQ, was basically a VAM70 with the 466 cu in engine moved from the front to a mid-frame position, about a third of the way back between the axles. The general design of the frame and the 16ft 1in (193in) wheelbase did not alter, nor did the front or rear overhang of completed coaches. The radiator was mounted just ahead of the engine, inclined forward slightly, and with mud flaps to protect it from road dirt thrown up by the front wheels.

Many items of the chassis design were unaltered from the VAM but the brakes were upgraded, with lining area up from 600sq in to 652sq in and a new feature was the spring-operated parking brake. In addition to its relocation, several modifications to the engine helped to make it quieter – there was a more rigid crankcase, modified fan

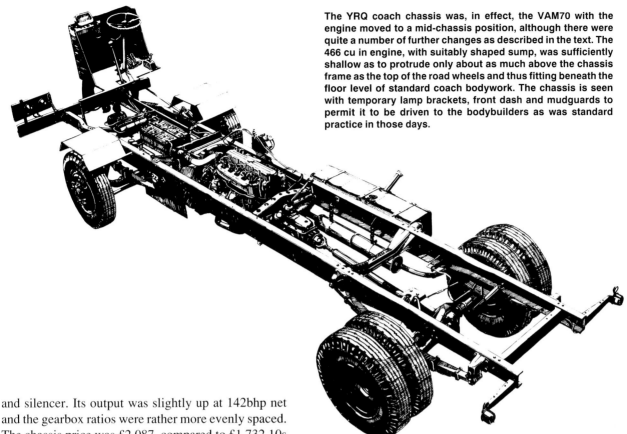

The YRQ coach chassis was, in effect, the VAM70 with the engine moved to a mid-chassis position, although there were quite a number of further changes as described in the text. The 466 cu in engine, with suitably shaped sump, was sufficiently shallow as to protrude only about as much above the chassis frame as the top of the road wheels and thus fitting beneath the floor level of standard coach bodywork. The chassis is seen with temporary lamp brackets, front dash and mudguards to permit it to be driven to the bodybuilders as was standard practice in those days.

and silencer. Its output was slightly up at 142bhp net and the gearbox ratios were rather more evenly spaced. The chassis price was £2,087, compared to £1,732 10s for the VAM70 a year earlier, but part of this reflected growing manufacturing costs. The model was offered only with the 466 engine. The VAM was withdrawn from the home market but continued to be built for export, being better suited to operation where road quality was poor and an underfloor engine unsuitable.

The reaction from the trade press was so enthusiastic that the Bedford sales department issued a booklet directly reproducing the road test reports – including the criticisms – from four of the journalists involved, Ron Cater of *Commercial Motor*; John Fielder of *Coaching Journal*; L. J. K. Setright, of *Transport Journal* and Alan Townsin, then of *Motor Transport*. All praised the quietness – John Fielder described it as "....worlds apart from its predecessor. Indeed one could imagine that the chassis had undergone some technical revolution." Setright, well known as a car as well as commercial vehicle journalist, referred to "exceptional quietness"; Ron Cater described it as among the quietest passenger vehicles he had driven, and Alan, who had been nagging about the need for noise reduction in test reports on Bedford coaches for years, said ".... at last Bedford has produced a quiet-running coach".

The last-mentioned, conscious of some rumblings from the industry on brake performance, and cautiously commenting that there was no means of assessing long-term brake behaviour in a day's testing was, even so, encouraged by the fade test he carried out at the Motor Industry Research Association test ground. A series of 28 full-pressure stops were made at one minute intervals from 30mph, something which Alan recalls he always tried to do *before* lunch – in passing, we wonder if trade press

journalists still do this kind of searching test nowadays. Instead of fading, as usually occurred to at least some degree, the retardation slightly improved during the test, reaching a very satisfactory 0.85g at the end.

The vehicle just managed to climb the admittedly very short 1 in 3 test hill and, on a second run, it proved possible to allow the vehicle to roll free for a couple of feet on this gradient and then stop it quite sharply using the spring handbrake only.

On the other hand both Ron Cater and Alan both reported experiencing some difficulty in obtaining gears cleanly in the Turner gearbox, especially second, and the latter recalls this as a characteristic fault with this box in various Bedford and other chassis. The unladen weight with Duple Viceroy body was 6tons 16cwt 1qr, about 5cwt more than a similarly-bodied VAM70, but fuel economy under most conditions was about 1mpg better.

A report made by Bill Wootten, the proprietor of W. Wootten & Sons Ltd of Lewisham, to John Alden, Vauxhall's Chief Engineer, on a pre-launch journey made in June 1970 in the Duple-bodied demonstration coach was also included in the booklet, this too being generally favourable though the call for a longer gear lever sounds as if he and his co-driver may also have experienced similar difficulty in this regard – Bill Wootten had made forthright comments on Bedford coaches at meetings of the Passenger Vehicle Operators Association, which in those days represented independent operators. It also reveals that an earlier prototype had been sent to Wootton's premises for examination and comment, indicating willingness to learn from operators' experience.

The YRQ soon attracted orders from numerous operators all over the country, the overwhelming majority being coaches for independent operators. Some 1971 business was already committed elsewhere but in 1972, it became the top-selling single-deck chassis in Britain. A survey based on PSV Circle news-sheets reported upon by Paul Heels in *The Omnibus Magazine* quoted the number of YRQ models entering service that year as 650. This was vastly better than the home sales figures of a little over 150 per year being achieved by the VAM around 1970.

Among the big touring holiday users based in the Midlands, it is significant that not only Whittle's entire 1971 intake of full-sized coaches comprised sixteen YRQ-Duple models but that Salopia also chose this combination for most of its 1971 deliveries, there being seven YRQ and four petrol-engined SB3, though in fairness three VAM70 coaches had been tried alongside eight SB3 the previous year. Significantly, both took one Ford Transit with 12-seat Deansgate conversion in this period – by then the CF was available in comparable form, but the Transit had become the accepted choice, even in Bedford-minded concerns such as Salopia.

Another regular Bedford customer, Scottish Omnibuses Ltd, which had chosen the VAM70 in 1968 but switched to the Bristol LH for its light single-deck needs in 1970, returned to Bedford with an order for ten YRQ delivered in 1971, then taking fifteen in 1972, ten in 1973, fifteen in 1974 and ten in 1975. all with Alexander bodywork, mostly seating 45 but some in 1974-5 having more spacious seating for 38. Small numbers were sold to National Bus Company subsidiaries, that State-owned organisation having taken over both the Tilling and BET bus company empires, though the Bristol LH was the more usual choice for light bus or sometimes coach applications. Another major operator of the type was Ulsterbus.

Overall, the YRQ put Bedford back into contention in the coach business with a model having what might be called star quality, popular with passengers and very capable within its limits. As motorways extended, the possibilities for coach operation involving running at or near the 70mph limit, or even above it, for extended periods were growing. One YRQ, whose operator had better be nameless, was found by Vauxhall engineers to have its governor incorrectly adjusted, to the extent that the speedometer would touch 90mph, which must have implied an engine speed of about 3,600rpm – needless to say this was reset to give a more reasonable 72mph. Aside from this type of 'fiddling', some operators were learning the hard way that running fast-revving engines continuously

A production YRQ with Plaxton Panorama Elite III body used by Vauxhall Motors as a demonstration coach. The Panorama Elite body style, first introduced at the 1968 Show, was a popular choice for the YRQ, its curved-glass side windows setting the standard for most British coach designs during the 1970s and complementing the YRQ's refined comfort. One wonders whether this trendsetting body design might have influenced both Bedford and GM stylists in the evolution of later types, notably the JJL.

The CF lent itself to passenger-carrying versions rather more readily than the CA, there being sufficient headroom in the standard body shell to avoid the need for a non-standard roof. This was the 22-cwt model which could take 11 or 12 passengers, available converted to PSV form though more usually operators catering for fare-paying passengers chose the longer 35-cwt model.

Edinburgh City Transport had become a regular user of Bedford coaches of successive types for local excursions since early post-war days, this 1971 example with Duple Viceroy body being on YRQ mid-engined chassis. They were painted in a white and black livery, quite different to the madder and white of the undertaking's buses. The Viceroy body style was the last produced by Duple before the move of the main centre of production from Hendon to the former Burlingham premises in Blackpool.

The VAL70 continued in production alongside the YRQ for a couple of years, still looking quite striking when fitted with modern styles of bodywork, as in the case of this one with an early example of the Plaxton Panorama Elite body. However the YRQ's refinement underlined the high internal noise level of the VAL as well as offering the promise of requiring less time and cost in regard to servicing, so VAL sales to UK operators fell back to around 100 in 1971.

at even the normal maximum speed was not a recipe for reliable service. In one sense, the YRQ, and the family of models having the same main features that followed from it, almost invited continuous maximum-speed driving in not making the driver as aware of how hard engines were working as in front-engined models.

There was a change of Managing Director in October 1970, when David Hegland handed over to Alexander D. Rhea, who was to remain in office until April 1974

Developments among Bedford goods models in the early 1970s were at first modest, though the introduction in 1971 of double-drive KM six-wheelers for operation at 20/22 tons gross marked another step into the heavier end of the market.

Towards the smaller end of the range, automatic transmission became available in some CF van models, having become an option with basically the same engines in the Victor. Similarly, the HA van took up the 1,256cc

The YRT chassis introduced to replace the VAL model adopted the YRQ's concept of mid-chassis mounting for its vertical 466 cu in engine, though it also incorporated heavier-duty axles and an Eaton synchromesh gearbox.

engine introduced on the Viva, which by that date had moved through HB to the HC model with a third body shell while the van stayed visually as introduced in 1964. This clearly did not worry the Post Office, which placed an order for 2,000 HA vans, the first of several big orders for this model. This was quite an important break-through, for traditionally, small Morris models had been the favoured make for the Post Office fleet since the early 1930s, using successive models of Minor, Eight and then Minor again, themselves not infrequently retaining features from earlier generations of cars.

It was very obvious that the introduction of the YRQ gave a clear hint of the forthcoming demise of the VAL coach chassis, since that supposedly top-of-the-range model had thereby become outdated, as well as now being noticeably inferior in refinement to the next model down the size scale. It was hardly surprising that sales, never as high as hoped, were falling, with only about 100 sold in Britain in 1971. By February 1972, initial mention of a new model, the YRT, was being made to more important potential purchasers.

Some observers had wondered whether the twin-steer concept might be married with a mid-engined layout, but the availability of axle units suitable for the weight of an 11-metre coach from the KM goods range made this unnecessary. Quite apart from being a more economic manufacturing proposition, this decision gave the model heavy-duty axles complete with brakes to match, the latter also marking a change for Bedford passenger models in being of the directly air-operated type. This effectively overcame the brake and tyre wear problems that had plagued the VAL; by then the latter was seen with hindsight as having carried the lightweight units concept a little too far.

It is noteworthy to recall that London Transport, interested in multi-axle vehicles as a means of achieving

As usual for Bedford passenger models, most deliveries in the 1970s continued to be coaches for independent operators, but there were significant exceptions. The United Counties Omnibus Ltd, the National Bus Company subsidiary which included the Luton area in its

territory, ordered 50 Bedford chassis for delivery in 1974, split between 28 YRQ and 22 of the new YRT model, all with Willowbrook bus bodywork. One of the first of the latter, a 53-seater, is seen ready for delivery in NBC's standard 'corporate identity' green livery – it was allocated to Aylesbury. By that date, NBC was generally standardising on Leyland National buses though some intake of other types continued. These vehicles ran into a technical problem when it was found that the standard 9 cu ft air compressor could not cope with the air-operated windscreen wipers, added to the requirements of the doors, brakes and clutch. Larger 15 cu ft compressors had to be retrofitted.

The SB continued in production, outliving its intended successor, the VAM, so far as Britain was concerned, although that type too lived on as an export model. Small numbers of SB models were still being sold to British coach operators in the early 1970s though the type would not have remained available to them had it not still been in very strong demand as an export model. This picture dated from October 1971 and showed the Plaxton body as being offered in Britain for the SB for the 1972 season. By that date the model was officially the NFM if fitted with the 300 cu in petrol engine or the NJM if it had the 330 diesel, though to most people familiar with the type these were still effectively the SB3 and SB5 respectively. It continued to sell abroad until 1986 and the end of Bedford as a GM subsidiary, a remarkable career for a type first introduced in 1950, the total number of SB chassis built being 57,129, easily the highest total for any British bus or coach model.

a low floor height, purchased a 1967 VAL for experimental purposes in 1976 and soon discovered why this vehicle, like many other VAL models, had a Telma retarder. Tests showed that without it, the brake performance could not meet LT standards. Colin Curtis, in charge of the project, struck up a good relationship with Leo Taylor and his colleagues at Vauxhall, but abandoned that course of development because of the inherent brake and wheel-alignment problems.

The YRT, as well as being both simpler and more robust in these respects, gave the capability of coping with a higher all-up weight than the VAL. Apart from the additional weight of more elaborate bodywork, some coach operators were finding that many passengers, notably American or Japanese tourists visiting Britain, were taking more luggage than had been usual in earlier times.

The VAL ceased production and was replaced by the YRT in the summer of 1972, the latter having an 18ft 6in (222in) wheelbase and being rated at up to 12¼ tons gross when introduced. The 466 engine and its installation were basically much as used in the YRQ, though detail features of the engine were revised and its quoted output became 136bhp, still at 2,800rpm, in accordance with a newly agreed net rating system. Thus Bedford now had two models with the same characteristics in terms of refinement, though the heavier-duty axles of the YRT and many other details of its specification meant that it was a good deal more than a long-wheelbase YRQ.

Other features which distinguished the YRT were a heavier-duty five speed overdrive gearbox, now made by Eaton, power-assisted steering and an air-assisted clutch. It used 9.00-20 radial-ply tyres and with a typical standard body weighed about 7¾ tons unladen, about a ton more than a typical VAL, and if running at the full laden weight, this difference could rise to 2 tons. The improved specification inevitably brought higher cost, and the YRT chassis price of £3,250 made quite a sharp contrast from the £1,775 of the original VAL14 a decade earlier, though growing inflation was beginning to seriously distort such comparisons. This was still low enough to give a competitive advantage compared to traditional heavy-duty makes and

yet in terms of much of its design apart from the engine and gearbox the YRT was itself a heavy-duty chassis.

Its wheelbase conformed to the standard for 11-metre single-deckers which formed part of the new bus grant specification, and indeed it proved possible to switch a Plaxton body built on an AEC Reliance chassis to a prototype YRT.

This was a factor which helped the production flow of major bodybuilders, among which Plaxton, producing over 1,000 bodies per year in total, had moved well in front of Duple in terms of output by this period. The Plaxton Panorama Elite body introduced in 1968 was a trendsetter, and many YRQ models were so fitted. Duple seemed to have faltered after the upheaval of moving production to the former Burlingham factory at Blackpool, though the new Dominant body design introduced in 1972 was proving a help in making up some of the lost ground.

About 625 YRT models entered service with British operators in 1973, nearly as many as there had been YRQ models put on the road in 1972. This was a great improvement on the 100 VAL models sold the previous year, and though the YRQ inevitably dropped back, the total number of Bedford models added to British coach and bus fleets that year, about 1,350, was an immense improvement on the total of just over 600 in 1970. The 1973 total included about 140 of the VAS model, which, though never a huge seller, had continued to attract a fairly steady demand on a limited scale. There were even still a few SB models, though that model had dropped below the 100 per annum mark in Britain after 1971 – thenceforth it was almost entirely an export type.

The YRT drew most of its sales from independent coach operators, Bedford's traditional stronghold, though there was some interest from the State-owned company groups. Bedford thus materially strengthened its position as the leading marque producing single-deck chassis sold in Britain, with Ford selling roughly half as many (roundly 400 of the 11-metre R1114, which was the successor to the previous R226, and 240 of the shorter R1014 which replaced the R192) and the only serious challenger in the lightweight end of the market. Ford's reaction to the

Bedford 466 cu in engine, had been to turbocharge its 330 cu in diesel, obtaining 141bhp, the first two figures of which were used at the end of the new designations. Although the turbo-charging did help to reduce noise slightly, they retained front-mounted engines and this was now a handicap in terms of passenger appeal by comparison with the new Bedfords.

The YRQ specification was brought more closely into line with that of the YRT in the 1974 model, as introduced towards the end of 1973. Direct air operation of the brakes, the Eaton gearbox, power-assisted steering and air-assisted clutch were all now standard on both models.

Taken in manufacturing group terms, the British Leyland Motor Corporation (including Bristol, half-owned but effectively under Leyland control) was bigger, especially as it made virtually all the 2,000 double-deckers supplied to British operators that year, but its single-deck sales, of a similar number in total, were split among several marques. In terms of single-deck buses, the integral-construction Leyland National had leapt into prominence, with 783 examples entering service in 1973, but these were almost all sold to National Bus Company or other major fleets. Of more significance to Bedford was the rise in sales of the Leyland Leopard underfloor-engined chassis, which had grown and was running at over 500 per year from 1972. Many of these were for NBC or Scottish bus group fleets, largely as coaches, but there were growing sales to independent coach operators, deciding that its extra cost was justified for the more intensive types of duty.

However, Bedford's revitalised and strong sales position in the coach world, amplified by continuing healthy export sales, notably of the ageless-seeming SB, represented only quite a minor part of the overall picture, with Bedford's annual output in that period running at around 100,000 vehicles of all types. Viewed from General Motors headquarters in Detroit, even this paled by comparison with overall annual output figures measured in millions of vehicles – even the annual output of Chevrolet alone had gone over 2 million cars and trucks on several occasions.

On that scale, Vauxhall/Bedford was only one part of a business increasingly seen in world terms, and the engineers at Luton, effective though they often were in responding to British market needs and those in export markets built up from a British perspective, were apt to find themselves carried along by decisions reached in Detroit. To some degree, this was inevitable as international co-operation grew and such influences as European legislation affected design. Yet the traditional Bedford approach, of making effective use of standardised units and keeping closely in touch with the needs of specific types of user still bore fruit.

One example of this resulted in the introduction in 1973 of a twin-steering goods model at almost exactly the time the VAL was bowing out. This was a version of the TK designed to meet the needs of the brewery, soft-drink and similar trades and permitting a 14½-ton gross weight while retaining the low platform height given by the use of 16-in wheels.

Enter the Detroit Diesel

However, there was growing interest, again on a world basis, in the heavier end of the goods range. At the Commercial Motor Show in September 1972, the most significant Bedford exhibit in terms of its implications for the future was a tractor unit designed for 32-ton gross train weight, considerably more than any previous Bedford. It was shown in prototype form – at the time, it seems not to have been given a model name of its own, though a similar design had been offered on the Australian market, often a trail-blazer for new vehicle types, in 1971.

It was basically a KM chassis and cab fitted with a Detroit Diesel 6V-71 engine quoted at 200bhp at 2,100rpm and giving 550 lb.ft of torque at 1,200rpm. This vee-form engine would not fit into what was basically the standard TK cab and was, therefore, mounted largely behind it, this accounting for the relatively long wheelbase for a tractive unit of 11ft (132in) – the basic chassis used was the KMR tipper variant. Pat Kennett, then *Motor Transport's* Technical Editor, remarked on how small the vehicle looked compared to most 32-tonners. The nature of the

The demand for the combination of a low loading height and a roomy platform led to the introduction of the KG twin-steering 14½-ton gross version of the TK with 466 cu in engine and 224in (18ft 8in) overall wheelbase announced in 1973, soon after the twin-steer VAL coach chassis had ceased production. It was favoured by breweries – the example shown being operated by Scottish and Newcastle Breweries – together with soft-drink makers and others in the distributive trades, always a section of the market to which Bedford paid great attention.

The 32-ton tractor looked much the same as a standard production KM model save that its wheelbase was not as short and the air intake behind the cab gave the clue that there was something unusual about the power unit. This was one of those put into service in Vauxhall's own transport fleet.

design indicates that it was more of a venture to assess the market for such a vehicle than a true production model, although a year later it was included in a buyer's guide to models available, the designation quoted – KM-ERV6 SVO5 – implying it was regarded as a 'special' from the production viewpoint. The numbers built were limited but, significantly, several were added to Vauxhall's own transport fleet.

It is noteworthy that another option in providing enough power for such a vehicle had been pursued to the stage of building a prototype. This used a pair of 466cu in engines, geared to run as a combined unit using the same principle as the prototype BT half-track vehicles built towards the end of the 1939-45 war, as described in Volume 1. In this case the frame was widened to accommodate the two engines mounted side-by-side but it proved to have insufficient rigidity and the project was abandoned.

The Detroit Diesel name had been adopted some time earlier for the range of two-stroke road vehicle diesel engines first put into large-scale production in that city by General Motors Corporation, initially under its own name, in 1938.

The two-stroke principle had attracted designers of diesel engines from quite early days. The problems of getting enough air into each cylinder to allow every downward stroke of the piston to be a firing stroke seemed less intractable than with the petrol/air mixture of a petrol engine. Thus, in theory, something not too far below twice the power should be obtainable from a given size of engine as compared to a four-stroke engine. In practice, the latter, with the alternate downward strokes used to draw air into the engine, was much more manageable and in operation

gave better fuel economy for a given output though requiring a larger and heavier engine. Most production diesels used in motor vehicles, especially of European makes, were and still are of this form.

The Detroit Diesel 6V-71 engine was already very well established in America but little known in Britain. It was relatively compact, providing an impressive 202bhp from its modest swept volume of just under 7 litres yet its vee-six layout inevitably made it wider than an in-line six-cylinder unit and although the engine itself was not tall, the air intake on top feeding into the supercharger between the cylinder banks meant that the installation would not fit under the seat panel of the TK-type cab.

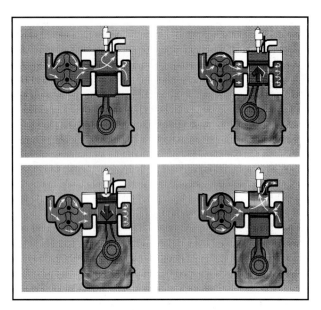

These diagrams convey how the two-stroke diesel achieves what occupies four strokes in a conventional engine in half the time. At the bottom of the piston's stroke (first diagram) air enters the cylinder very rapidly through ports in the cylinder wall that are uncovered as the piston moves down, hastened by the mechanically-driven supercharger. As the piston rises (second diagram) the air is compressed, raising its temperature so that the fuel injected near the top of the stroke will ignite, the piston then being driven downwards (diagram three). The first part of the next intake of fresh air (diagram four) pushes the exhaust out of the cylinder via the four exhaust valves before the process repeats.

The history of GM's development of its two-stroke diesel engine has a link to the background of Bedford's origins being, in terms of commercial vehicles, the British successor to Chevrolet, as outlined in Volume 1. Charles F. Kettering had risen to prominence as an innovative engineer within General Motors in the early 1920s, being responsible for the so-called 'copper-cooled' – in reality, air-cooled – petrol engine tried somewhat disastrously in its cars by Chevrolet in 1922-3. Despite this, his talent for developing fresh ideas continued to be recognised and in 1928 Alfred P. Sloan, GM's President, put Kettering in charge of research into diesel engine design; by 1930 his studies led to a decision that a two-stoke diesel engine was practical. Early designs were for some railway applications, where high specific output was an important attraction, the first being for the pioneer Burlington Zephyr diesel railcar prototype of 1934. Further development led to GM became a major manufacturer of diesel locomotives.

This artist's drawing shows why the KMR ERV6 tractor unit with the Detroit Diesel 6V-71 engine needed a longer (11ft) wheelbase than versions with the Bedford 466 cu in in-line engine. The engine was positioned behind the driver's and passengers' seats and although about half of its length was under the shelf at the rear of the cab, the remainder protruded behind the cab, so it was necessary to set the rear axle back by a similar amount to allow clearance for the front of the semi-trailer and its brake hose connections.

By the mid-1970s, the HA van had become a very familiar sight on the road, being particularly favoured by organisations such as public utilities, as in this scene showing one run by the water authority in the Liverpool area. Similar vans were being used by the Post Office and with 3,200 added to those already in use in many areas 'Postman Pat' was more likely to be making his rounds in an HA than any other type of van.

Meanwhile the smaller series of road transport engines using the same principles had appeared, over 4,000 being in use in GM rear-engined buses by 1941.

A modular system was adopted, each engine having the same cylinder dimensions of 4¼in bore and 5in stroke giving a swept volume of 71 cu in per cylinder, this figure appearing in the type numbers of the various engines. The initial road transport range consisted of three-, four- and six-cylinder engines, this last, the 6-71, having a swept volume of 426 cu in (6.981 litres) and yet developing 165bhp at 2,000rpm even in pre-war form.

In post-war years the same concept was developed by GM in vee form, still with the same '71' cylinders and hence the V6 unit, designated 6V-71, retained the same swept volume. Most of the GM 'New Look' buses had this engine, also fitted to the main competitive make, the Flxible – indeed it had become the near-universal American bus engine by the 1960s. There were also eight- and twelve-cylinder versions used in GM and other trucks.

In the United States, its use was so common that people in the transport industry were well used to the appropriate driving technique and maintenance methods. In Europe, this was not so, and one of the authors recalls the culture shock of riding from Kennedy Airport into New York in 1973 on a GM coach so powered, the engine seeming to be revving at astronomical speed for a bus power unit. In fact this was an illusion due to the two-stroke cycle, the same effect applying to the Foden two-stroke, which was the only British-designed engine operating in a similar way. In fact maximum torque, as can be seen from the figures quoted for the unit used in the KM, was developed at a not dissimilar rotational speed to that of typical British-designed diesels. Drivers used to manual-gearbox vehicles with engines like the Gardner had to learn to disbelieve what their ears appeared to convey when switching to a Detroit Diesel – a tachometer (more popularly known as a

rev counter) really became essential.

Rather similarly, the engine's features were unfamiliar to mechanics brought up on traditional-style British diesels. The Detroit Diesel has a positively-driven blower which feeds air into the cylinders through ports in the cylinder sleeves when the piston is near the bottom of its stroke and although there are four valves per cylinder all are exhaust valves. The injector combines the function normally served by the injection pump, being push-rod operated in the same manner as the valves.

Also on display at the 1972 Show were improved versions of the TK cab, with bulkhead panel reshaped to allow an improved seating position, especially for taller drivers, this applying to all models upwards from the KD, then being marketed as a model light enough not to require the driver to have an Heavy Goods Vehicle licence, and to some newly-introduced KM variants plated to 16 tons gross under recently-changed regulations. Among these was a new 12ft 4in (148in) wheelbase KMS tipper model. The 466 cu in engine, in Mark II form with minor improvements, became available in three ratings, the 136bhp version for passenger work, the 133bhp version now being used to power all standard KH and KM models, while a derated 116bhp version replaced the 381 cu in version of the same basic engine design in KG models. There was also a new 10-cwt version of the HA van.

The Post Office ordered another 3,200 HA vans early in 1973 and, soon afterwards, a significant initiative illustrating growing co-operation with Opel was a new venture under which the CF van and TK truck were exported to West Germany. News was also released of a £25 million project to increase truck-building capacity at Dunstable, and word was buzzing around the industry that this related to a full-scale move by Bedford into heavier trucks.

16 THE TM RANGE

The logic of extending Bedford's range to cover what was effectively the top end of the truck market, apart from specialised vehicles, doubtless seemed almost unanswerable when the possibility was first considered towards the end of the 1960s. The 32-ton articulated vehicle in particular had grown enormously in importance as motorways had extended during that decade. Numerous firms with subsidiary factories in development areas, set up in response to Government policy intended to combat unemployment, were using such vehicles to supply them. Vauxhall itself supplied its Ellesmere Port car factory on Merseyside, opened in 1959, with items made in Luton in this way. Although this was clearly a special case, there were numerous instances of similar regular large-scale supply, as well as the increasingly centralised deliveries of commodities to supermarket chains, using large artics.

A similar picture was evident across Europe, and the roll-on, roll-off ferry had become so familiar as to have been shortened to ro-ro in normal conversation in the international haulage industry. Railways were in decline, and by the time the model was launched in 1974, 7,000 or more 32-ton artics were entering service annually in Britain alone.

Big trucks designed to cover big distances had been a way of life in the vast space of the United States for much longer. General Motors had been building some of them and supplying its two-stroke diesels for many more, though competition, notably from the Cummins engines, was growing stronger, and the idea of opening a new outlet doubtless seemed appealing.

By the early 1970s, the American influence on Vauxhall/Bedford at management level was strong. In addition to growing numbers of American members of the Board of Directors, Bill Larson was by then in charge of commercial vehicle engineering. With their knowledge of the reliable service being given by GM-powered heavy trucks in the United States and the group's expertise in volume production, the deduction that Bedford could win a big share of the British and, in time, the European heavy truck market no doubt seemed soundly based.

Yet by 1974 the level of competition in this market had already sharpened considerably. Up to the 1960s, within Britain it was almost entirely covered by the traditional British heavy goods vehicle makers – mainly AEC, Atkinson, ERF, Foden, Guy, Leyland and Scammell. Of these, AEC, Guy and Scammell were brought into what became the British Leyland group by 1968, leaving Atkinson (which became Seddon-Atkinson following a merger), ERF and Foden to trade independently.

Then imports began to appear, with growing success, most notably Volvo and Scania among the early entrants. Mercedes-Benz had not been very successful with commercial vehicles in Britain at first, but from about 1972 began to become a much stronger competitor. Then there were others – DAF from Holland, MAN and Magirus-Deutz from Germany, Berliet and Saviem from France and Fiat from Italy, and even the possibility of Hino from Japan, soon to be selling well in Ireland. What is more, GM were not alone among the big American-controlled groups interested in this market – Ford was also gearing up to intervene and Chrysler had developed a vehicle based on a Spanish Barreiros but badged as a Dodge.

Pat Kennett, writing in the first, October 1974, issue of *Truck* magazine he founded after being the much-respected Technical Editor of *Motor Transport,* summed up the situation by saying there were already too many heavy-truck makes on the British market. He pointed out that the British 32-tonner market, at around 7,500 per year, was only big enough to give an average sale of about 360 chassis per year if divided equally between all the actual or potential participants. He predicted that in 1975 Volvo, ERF and Leyland would each sell a couple of thousand or so and the likes of DAF and Scania roughly half that, leaving little room for others. Even so, he predicted that the Bedford TM, "a good truck", would take a lot of sales from the more ambitious importers. Significantly, a TM was chosen for the non-advertising cover of that first issue.

There was certainly no lack of self-confidence at Luton. Development testing of prototypes had been going on since about 1970, and full use was made of the Millbrook test ground for a comprehensive and what was described as a disciplined test programme. A 48-page 14½in by 11in brochure, mostly printed in full colour, with title 'A Confidential Preview of the New TM range from Bedford' was produced before the general launch, describing the new range, no doubt to show potential large-scale buyers and doubtless trusted members of the technical press, who adhered to agreed release dates in those days and accordingly could produce very thorough technical descriptions.

The printer's date of this in-house brochure is June 1974, but such a production, with perspective sectioned drawings of the vehicles and the major units must have occupied a team of skilled people for months. It covered the Detroit Diesel-powered models released as Phase 1 in October of that year, the Phase 2 Bedford-engined models announced in mid-1975 and those with the eight-cylinder 8V-71 in 1976. It had cautionary notes about illustrations

The TM range was the subject of a large-scale development programme, a fleet of prototypes being tested at the Millbrook proving grounds and run for thousands of miles in various overseas locations under widely varying climatic conditions and at different altitudes. Here one of the early prototype six-wheelers with L-suffix registration of 1972-3 is seen operating with a trailer in North Africa. Note the air conditioning unit on top of the cab. This was one of the illustrations in a brochure dated June 1974 issued to selected potential users in advance of the general release date that autumn. It was pointed out that the mirrors, their brackets and the position of the griffin badge were incorrect in relation to the production specification.

of prototype vehicles, which were noted as incorrect in minor details such as mirrors or badge position in relation to the production design, yet by its very precision conveys how carefully the whole project had been thought out.

The initial range of late 1974 covered eight models, all with the vee-six Detroit Diesel 6V-71 two-stroke, by then rated at 216bhp at 2,100rpm and with maximum torque of 590 lb.ft at 1,600rpm. The engines had the characteristic features as outlined in the previous chapter, and although basically of standard Detroit Diesel design apart from minor details to suit the TM installation, were assembled in a new shop close to the main assembly line at Dunstable. A large-scale training scheme was set up to acquaint fitters with the new engine.

The vehicles released in the first phase used proprietary transmission and drive axle components; a Lipe-Rollway 14in twin-plate clutch, a Fuller RTO 609 gearbox and Eaton drive axles. These latter items were already to be found in other makes of vehicle already common in

Britain, and indeed there was a general trend towards the use of bought-out items, often of American origin in terms of design, even on trucks made by concerns with no transatlantic connections, simply because they were well-developed units already in large-scale production.

The frames were of plain channel section steel of between 9½ and 12½ in depth, still of riveted construction, though one of the pictures of a prototype in the advance brochure shows bolted construction. The front suspension was by very long two-plate taper-leaf springs – in an old Bedford tradition, they gave a softer ride than most competitors. Conventional multi-leaf springs were used at the rear, though with the variable rate slipper mounting much as used on smaller models for two-axle versions.

Full dual-circuit air brakes with spring parking brakes were standard across the range, the brake units being of substantial construction with 15½-in drums. Power-assisted steering was standard, the power cylinder being integral with the steering box.

This picture of a prototype tractor unit with the Detroit Diesel 6V-71 engine was among the initial TM range release material. The tilt cab was Bedford's first application of the idea, this view conveying how well the engine area became exposed. Even so, most routine maintenance was carried out via hinged panels at the front of the cab so tilting the cab was not intended to be needed frequently. Much thought was put into every aspect of the design and even though planned for release in three stages, in 1974, 1975 and 1976, the whole range had been very largely finalised in all but quite minor respects by 1974.

A great deal of attention was given to cab design. In line with other contemporary models, quite a tall cab was fitted, though a factor in this was the need to house the V6-71 engine, which was quite broad because of its vee layout and yet needed more depth than might have been expected because of the air intake sited above the supercharger between the two banks of cylinders. The cab was of rather angular design, with a wide rectangular grille having squared corners and a windscreen with only slight curvature, yet the

The TM instrument panel helped to convey a 'quality' look. An essential feature with the 6V-71 engine was the revolution counter, marked to convey the engine's most efficient speed range.

overall appearance and neat detailing had a 'quality' look which does not look dated over two decades later.

Cab comfort, with good seats, noise insulation, heating and ventilation, was put forward as a major selling point, quite rightly when the longer distances such vehicles were travelling is borne in mind, quite apart from the need to match the greatly improved standards in these respects which had by then been achieved by other makes. It was a tilt cab, but all routine servicing was carried out through the front panel, and strength to meet forthcoming regulations was a feature. Early production models all had what was called the 'D' cab, slightly narrower than the base on which it was mounted, but later there was also the full-width 'F' cab and also the 'H' sleeper version of that, both having a higher standard of finish.

The whole project had the benefit of the concentrated thought of the substantial team of engineers at Luton plus the immense backup of resources on tap, particularly in relation to the engine, from GM in Detroit. Inevitably, an economic level of acceptance of what was considered in Britain, and indeed most of Europe, as an unorthodox engine was bound to take time, quite apart from having to compete in a hard-fought market on the basis of down-to-earth costing and capability comparisons. In addition, Bedford had to overcome the handicap in this market of having being seen over the previous 43 years as a mass producer of smaller trucks, built to a price even if recognised as offering good value.

One of the problems of planning the introduction of a major new vehicle range which has to be set in train several

Proving of the TM range included operation in cold-climate conditions. This TM1900 drawbar outfit is seen in Norway in the early months of 1974.

The TM range was planned as an integrated whole and prototypes of versions not due to be introduced until 1975 were running in almost-final form in 1973, when this example was registered, or earlier. The TM1500 tipper with Bedford 500 engine was planned to operate at 15 tonnes (14.8 tons gross) – note the rectangular shape forming part of the door pressing, not adopted for production. In practice, British two-axle TM models ran at 16 tons gross, that being the maximum permissible gross weight for a two-axle model by that period. Though the TM cab was neatly-designed, it looked rather tall on such a model.

Alternative cab features are conveyed by these two drawings. The standard D-type cab is seen on the left, this having the upper portion slightly narrower than the base, the outer edges of which are formed to act as the third level of step when climbing up from ground level. This was well finished internally, though not quite to the level of the two full-width cabs, type F and the H-type sleeper cab with additional length to provide space for a bunk behind the seats, as shown on the right in air-conditioned form.

The TM sleeper cab had an atmosphere giving a hint of a quite high-grade executive office. The Detroit Diesel required a high engine cover separating the driver's and mate's seats. There was quite a wide range of gearbox types available for TM models, including nine- or ten-speed models for use with the 6V-71 or 8V-71 engine.

years before the crucial point when it is put on the market is that economic or political circumstances cannot be predicted. In the event, in 1973-4 a crisis in the Middle East, followed by a coal strike in Britain, resulted in a period of three-day week working in industry. Although Bedford's own production and sales held up well during the period, the episode, aggravated by increased fuel costs, created a mood of uncertainty in 1974-5, just as the TM range was new on the market.

The commercial vehicle industry tends to act as a barometer of business confidence, and thus Bedford's overall sales dropped from 109,463 in 1974 to 95,129 in 1975, most of the fall being due to a weak home market – exports, at 53,379 and thus 56% of the total, held almost steady from the 53,895 of the previous year. The proportion of Dunstable's output exported was even higher, at 70%, Bedford being top exporter of British-built trucks that year. In fact, exports were to account for more than half the output of Bedford vehicles for the next few years, re-creating a situation which had applied in 1961-63 and

Production at Dunstable continued to be concentrated largely on the TK range, particularly in regard to the home market. This pantechnicon was based on a KG chassis, the construction of the cab as part of the body concealing its identity to some degree. Marsden of Warrington was one of the leading furniture van builders and this was the largest van the concern had built at the time, having a 2,000 cu ft capacity – it also hauled a 1,200 cu ft trailer. The outfit is seen here at Dover, heading a convoy taking the props for the 'Star Wars' film to Morocco for location shooting.

again making an important contribution to the overall business as well as Britain's balance of payments – however, Vauxhall car exports were well down from what they had been in the 1960s, though holding reasonably steady in Britain save for 1975 itself.

The TM had to gain acceptance amid this rather unpromising climate. On early models, and despite claims of good noise insulation in the publicity material, too much of the Detroit Diesel's angry snarl found its way into the cab, and although earlier diesel trucks of almost all makes had been noisy things to drive, the standards that had been set by firms such as Volvo and Scania made this no longer acceptable. Driver influence was becoming a more important factor especially in heavy truck sales, partly because of sizeable numbers of owner-drivers but also because the need to recruit good drivers by larger operators, especially for trans-continental work, gave them more leverage.

Bedford's might-have-been double-decker

While the limelight was on the TM goods range, a possibility that Bedford might produce a double-decker bus using the Detroit Diesel engine arose from an approach from Van Hool-McArdle of Dublin. Van Hool & Zonen had grown immensely since its foundation in 1947, becoming the leading coach bodybuilder in Belgium by the 1960s, with a major export business to Holland, France and other countries, and a small foothold in the British market by the early 1970s. The McArdle link was planned as another step in Van Hool's process of expansion. Coras Iompair Eireann, the State-owned Irish transport organisation, had built most of its own bus bodywork, until the 1960s often based on pre-war Leyland designs and on that make of chassis. It had been agreed that the McArdle concern would take over the CIE bodyworks to build Van Hool-designed bodies for that concern, initially using Leyland Atlantean chassis. However, as a proposed second stage, CIE was interested in having vehicles built to its own specification, and as General Motors diesel locomotives were giving good service on CIE railways, it was proposed that Bedford might co-operate in the construction of a semi-integral rear-engined double-deck bus with structure of Van Hool design for operation, largely in Dublin, by CIE and using the Detroit Diesel 6V-71 engine.

Some design work was carried out, and by early 1975 studies were undertaken in regard to making the design acceptable to qualify for British new bus grant specification, including the 14ft 6in overall height – there were plans for a choice of conventional leaf springs or air suspension. Discussions were held on a plan to build two prototypes early in 1976, to be bodied that summer, the second vehicle being made ready to be exhibited at the Commercial Motor Show in October of that year.

Clearly, this would have tied in well with the availability of the 6V-71, in production by then at Dunstable for the TM, while Allison, GM's automatic transmission specialists, was the obvious supplier in that regard.

However, soundings indicated that the engine would not have been acceptable to major bus operators in the UK, and in addition the market was becoming increasingly competitive, with MCW (by then linked with Scania), Ailsa, Dennis and Foden all in, or about to join, the battle for double-deck business. Another difficulty was that Van Hool-McArdle had run into problems, and the combination of those factors led to the project being dropped. Eventually, CIE did arrive at a range of vehicles designed in Germany and built in Ireland by the Bombadier concern.

The 500 engine

Meanwhile the TM range was expanded in mid-1975 by Phase 2 of the launch, bringing in the Bedford-powered variants. These used a new engine called the 500, that being the capacity in cubic inches (500.27 cu in, to be precise, or 8.198 litres). It continued the Bedford pattern of in-line direct-injection diesels, retaining conventional European four-stroke technology. In essentials, it was a slightly enlarged version of the 466 cu in unit as built for the previous nine years, though rather unusually the bore size remained unchanged at 4.562in and it was the stroke that was increased, from 4.75in to 5.1in. This meant a new crankshaft and altered dimensions of related parts, yet the degree of change was relatively slight and the initial power output increase quite modest. As introduced for the TM range, it developed 151bhp net at a more conservative 2,500rpm than the 2,800rpm standard with the 466, and 377 lb.ft torque at 1,200rpm. The governed speed was cut back from the 2,800rpm used on the 466 cu in engine because experience had shown that durability when operating at higher gross weights would benefit, and in fact the 466 cu in engine had been similarly cut back, except for coaches and the KG (for which it had been set to 2,650rpm).

The existence of the Bedford 500 engine was first revealed in the pre-launch TM brochure of mid-1974 but it did not appear in production models until a year later. For the initial TM application its power output was 151bhp at 2,500rpm but the design had potential for development, later turbocharged versions taking the figure over 200bhp.

The TM had quite an impressive look, even with the narrower D-type cab. This example dating from 1975-6 was operated by Kent County Council, being seen here with low-loading trailer carrying a Caterpillar tractor. This cab design had conventional double windscreen wipers whereas the wider F and H types had triple arms and blades.

Reflecting the way in which Bedford was acting as the world General Motors commercial vehicle centre outside North America was this TM300 tractor unit with the Detroit Diesel 8V-71 vee-form eight-cylinder engine and air-conditioned sleeper cab. It was rated at 38 tonnes and had 'Bedford Blitz' lettering for the German market. The Opel 'lightning' badge was carried at the corner of the grille – 'Blitz' being the German word for lightning and used on Opel commercial vehicles since the 1930s. This official Vauxhall Motors picture dated from September 1975 and thus the vehicle had been built ahead of the general launch of this group of TM models the following year.

The two-axle TM models built for service in Britain were generally powered by the Bedford 500 engine, save perhaps where a drawbar trailer was being hauled, itself not common in Britain. Quite a high proportion of them had enclosed bodywork of one kind or another, the TM seeming to be thought appropriate where a fair amount of investment was being put into the body. In this case, the Penman body was of the demountable type which was gaining favour in the mid-1970s. The vehicle was operated by the Plymouth and South Devon Co-operative Society Ltd – the 'four-ring' Co-op logo had been adopted nationally by such organisations as a reaction to the spread of commercial stores using national brand names.

Clearly this provided an engine better suited to the 16-ton two-axle end of the TM range, and it was also used for quite a high proportion of the range's six-wheel and tractive-unit models operating at up to 24 tons gross – in all, nine models with the 500 engine were added to the range, these having five- or six-speed gearboxes similar to those in KM models. To existing Bedford operators, especially those familiar with the KM, the 500 engine was far less of a leap into the unknown, helping to build more momentum into the TM output. Quite often the TM chassis was chosen for more specialised types of bodywork, the two-axle TM entering a type of market where the competition quite often came from models such as the AEC Mercury rather than the traditional head-on battle with Ford. The 500 engine was also introduced for the KG, KH and KM ranges in place of the 466 cu in unit, while the 300 cu in petrol engine option for the KD, KE and KG was withdrawn for the UK market, a reflection of the virtually complete disappearance of the petrol engine from all but the light end of the truck scene, although such vehicles were still produced for export.

The arrival of the 500 engine also provided an opportunity to upgrade the power unit of the Y-series coach chassis, also in mid-1975. The YRT, though still selling well, was no longer a 'lightweight' in the old sense, and was proving to be rather underpowered by contemporary standards when operating fully laden on motorway journeys. By then, both Leyland and AEC had moved on from 9½-litre engines to 11- or even 12-litre capacity for their 11-metre coaches, and although these had somewhat heavier chassis, the difference in overall weight between such vehicles and Bedford's models was not so great as it had been in the days when the SB was the most popular coach chassis on the British market.

The YRT was succeeded by the YMT, with the 500 engine in a higher-rated 157bhp form than used for the TM range, governed speed in this application being 2,800rpm, as with the previous engine, and thus much faster-revving than the larger-capacity engines favoured by Leyland and AEC. The argument was that engines in coaches were less highly stressed than in the heavier truck applications, and also required higher road speed. The YRQ gave way to the YLQ, again with 500 engine but de-rated for this application to 138bhp. In most other respects, the YMT and YLQ retained the general specification of their predecessors and in particular the Eaton five-speed

Visually, there was nothing external to distinguish a YMT from its predecessor the YRT, the significance of the change being concentrated on the adoption of the 500 engine in place of the 466. By then, even the chassis make could rarely be identified by more than the 'Red Chicken' usually carried on the grille (though even this was not always displayed) and in the Grey-Green fleet, still largely concentrated on express services linking London with East Anglian coastal resorts, such coaches ran alongside Leyland Leopards with similar bodywork. This YMT with Duple Dominant II 53-seat body dated from 1978.

The bulk of Bedford passenger chassis supplied to British operators continued to be coaches, mainly for independent operators. Among the more interesting exceptions was Maidstone Borough Council, where the General Manager, Alan Price, not only switched to single-deckers from the mid-1970s, itself not uncommon among smaller municipal fleets, but largely standardised on the Bedford YMT, of which over 30 were operated. Several, like this example, had Duple Dominant bus bodywork with the high seating capacity of 61, achieved by the use of three-and-two seating over part of their length.

overdrive gearbox. Unladen weight of coaches was still inclined to creep up, a YMT with Plaxton Supreme 53-seat body very typical of the period and tested by *Commercial Motor* in April 1976 turning the scales at 8 tons 7 cwt 2 qr. Motorway consumption worked out at 9.71mpg, improving to 11.33mpg on a mainly main-road route, and Martin Watkins, carrying out the test, reported that the gear-change was much more precise than on the early YRQ, even though still heavy in action and with occasional difficulty in obtaining second when stationary.

Bedford continued to be the most popular individual make in the British single-deck bus and coach market, though the proportion of the market held began to fall, slightly at first. According to Paul Heel's analysis of PSV Circle reports, the number of Bedford coaches and buses entering service in Great Britain in 1975 was 886, representing just over 30% of the market, this share being almost unchanged from the previous year. Of this total, 90% was for independent operators, almost entirely coaches, and at that date Bedford still took 50% of that market – in other words, as many as all other makes put together. Over half the total that year was on YRT chassis, including

small numbers to NBC and municipal fleets, while Scottish Omnibuses took 20 for the first time.

In 1976, the total recorded dropped to 798, representing 24.6%, the fall being mainly of YRQ or YLQ models, as operators tended to favour larger vehicles, though NBC subsidiaries, mainly National Travel companies, put nearly 70 YRTs in service that year. Overall, 1976 was a good year for Bedford, as it outsold all other truck makers in the United Kingdom market.

Van developments

It was also a very busy time for new model introductions, indeed Vauxhall's busiest ever, when car and commercial vehicle types are included. The Vauxhall car business was increasingly being coordinated with that of Opel, and the immensely-successful Cavalier range first appeared at the 1975 Motor Show as a Vauxhall version of the Opel Ascona, at first built in GM's plant in Belgium, though Luton-built from August 1977.

Even more international was the Vauxhall Chevette, also launched in 1975, which was the British version of GM's T-car, sold under the Chevrolet name in the United

The Chevanne, introduced in the Autumn of 1976, was derived from the Vauxhall Chevette car and indeed this prototype example dating from earlier that year carried a Vauxhall rather than a Bedford badge. It was produced alongside the HA, being intended for a different market, with more stylish appearance, car-like handling and refinement as virtues which tended to appeal to the proprietors of businesses who did much of the driving themselves.

The Basic Transportation Vehicle was what the name implied, and resulted from a General Motors project launched in 1972. It used the 1,256cc petrol engine and most of the other mechanical units from the HA van, built into a very simple GM-designed sheet-metal chassis and superstructure made in the destination country. This example was the 'Plai Noi' (little elephant) as built in Thailand. Some versions went into production that year, including one built in Malaya, but the project tended to be undercut by more conventional (and more stylish) Japanese products.

States or Brazil, Opel in Germany and Isuzu in Japan. It used the Viva 1,256cc engine and four-speed gearbox and in September 1976 appeared in Bedford commercial-vehicle form as the Chevanne ½-ton van. This was sold alongside the HA van which offered almost twice the internal volume in its square-cut lines, but the Chevanne was a much more stylish vehicle as well as being surprisingly pleasant to drive, with precise rack-and-pinion steering, good handling qualities and effective anti-drum interior trim on the van side panels making it much quieter than most small vans. Quite apart from the type of business where appearance of delivery vans was important, it appealed in circumstances where the proprietors of businesses did a good deal of the driving. About 5,000 Chevannes were built per year until 1980, between a third and a a half of the HA van output.

Yet another outlet for the 1,256cc engine and HA mechanical units was the Basic Transportation Vehicle (BTV), another manifestation of the concept of vehicles for world markets. The idea was to supply sets of complete running gear, plus items such as radiator, fuel tank and basic electrical equipment to what would nowadays be called 'third world' countries for incorporation into a very simple GM-designed chassis frame and sheet metal cab made by the assemblers in the destination country, using local supplies. One was displayed on Bedford's stand at the 1976 Commercial Motor Show, and it was reported in Bedford Transport Magazine that among the local names given to versions of this vehicle were 'Andino' (from the Andes) in Ecuador; 'Harimau' (tiger) in Malaysia; 'Plai Noi' (little elephant) in Thailand, and 'Boafo' (helper) in Ghana. The project was the brainchild of Embree Kennedy, while with General Motors (South Africa) before becoming Bedford's Chief Engineer, and continued in production on

a very limited scale until the early 1980s, with an output of 1,060 sets in 1977 but gradually falling to 172 in 1981.

Mr Kennedy was also interested in four-wheel-drive and details of an experimental version of the CF van with this feature were also released in the Autumn of 1976, intended to cater for the needs for an 'off-road' van for organisations such as electricity and gas authorities or the construction industry. It used a transfer box manufactured by FF Developments behind the five-speed gearbox offered on some versions of the model, with a limited-slip differential. The drive to the rear wheels was basically standard but that to the front wheels was via a Morse chain and a short propeller shaft to a front differential and drive shafts to each front wheel.

Of wider interest was a new four-cylinder 2,064cc diesel engine also intended for the CF. This was described as a General Motors design but its origin was Opel and it was imported from that concern's plant in Germany where it was already fitted to CF vans built under the Blitz name. It was of indirect-injection type, with heater plugs to aid starting and it was claimed to be one of the quietest small diesels of the time. Maximum power was 60bhp at 4,400 rpm.

Other developments announced in 1976 were at the opposite end of the size range, marking the completion of the planned phased introduction of the TM. These had the Detroit Diesel engine in its eight-cylinder 8V-71 form, of similar design to the 6V71 but with an extra cylinder in each bank of the vee, taking the capacity to 9.3 litres and the output to 296 bhp net, with 784 lb ft torque, designed to cope with gross loads of up to 42 tonnes where that was legal. By that period, it had become normal to quote weights in metric form, although in practical terms the difference between a ton of 2,240lb and a tonne of 1,000kg is slight, 1 ton being equivalent to 1.017 tonne. For those models, a Spicer ten-speed gearbox with air-operated splitter was standard, though Allison automatic transmission was available.

There were also two new cabs, the full-width F-type and the H sleeper cab, recipients of British Design Council awards. The TM range at that stage included the following models offered on the British market (though some of them could only be operated at full weight when abroad), as listed below:-

Badge designation	Type number & engine	Axle layout	Design GVW tonne	Wheelbase
TM1700	EMV1 500	4x2 (short)	17	13ft 4in
	EMV2 500	4x2 (medium)	17	16ft 1in
	EMV3 500	4x2 (long)	17	17ft 2in
	EMV7 500	4x2 (tipper)	17	12ft 0in
	EWV2 6V-71	4x2 (medium)	17	16ft 1in
	EWV3 6V-71	4x2 (long)	17	17ft 2in
TM1900	EXX2 8V-71	4x2 (medium)	19	16ft 1in
	EXX3 8V-71	4x2 (long)	19	17ft 2in
TM2250	KMX2 500	6x4 (short)	22.5	12ft 3in
TM2600	KMX3 500	6x4 (medium)	26	14ft 7in
	KWX3 6V-71	6x4 (medium)	26	14ft 7in
	KXX3 8V-71	6x4 (medium)	26	14ft 7in*
	HMX3 500	6x4 (medium)	26	16ft 8in
	HWX3 6V-71	6x2 (medium)	26	16ft 8in
TM2300	EMT8 500	4x2 tractive unit	23 GCW	9ft 1in
TM2500	EMV8 500	4x2 tractive unit	25 GCW	9ft 10in
TM3250	EWV8 6V-71	4x2 tractive unit	32.52 GCW	9ft 10in
TM3800	EXX8 8V-71	4x2 tractive unit	38 GCW	10ft 3in
	EXX8 8V-71	4x2 tractive unit	38 GCW	12ft 0in
TM4200	KXX8 8V-71	6x4 tractive unit	42 GCW	13ft 0in

*Wheelbase increased to 15ft 9in with sleeper cab. At that stage the full-width and sleeper cabs were available only on 8V71 powered models. Further variants were built purely for export. Many of the load-carrying models were designed to work with drawbar trailers, increasing the overall gross weights in accordance with the specification.

Hence for 1977 the TM range was complete and the major exercise begun about eight years earlier could begin to be assessed. The sales of TM models in that year, the first with the whole range on offer, amounted to a total for home and export of 1,600. Looked at as a venture into heavy truck manufacture by a maker not previously in this field, that could be counted as something of an achievement. But by Bedford's normal output standards, it was less impressive; that year's output of TK-range models being 18,092 and even the TJ bonneted models, by then very largely an export model, totalled 13,003, while bus and coach chassis of all types totalled 1,725 (again with a large export proportion) and even the M 4x4 total was 1,943.

In terms of value, this is a somewhat unfair comparison, for a TM tractive unit with Detroit Diesel sold at twice or even three times the price of a TK. More important was the impact of this range on the market, which was not enough to seriously disturb what was a very big overall market, considered over Europe as a whole, nor as yet to justify the investment made. Sales resistance to the Detroit Diesel was proving harder to overcome than had been hoped, while the 500 cu in engine was barely big enough to be counted as a serious long-distance heavy truck unit.

Beyond all this, the financial picture was becoming more worrying. Years when Vauxhall Motors Ltd made a loss were becoming the norm rather than the exception, but 1974 and 1975 had been particularly bad, largely due to world and national conditions. There was a much smaller loss in 1976 but the former self-confidence, once so strong, especially in terms of the Bedford side of the business, was beginning to slip away. Legislation was becoming more complex, and new European brake regulations applicable to vehicles sold in Britain led to the decision to withdraw the TJ range from the home market altogether in 1976. By then the bonneted truck had almost entirely fallen out of favour and home sales of the model were not sufficient to justify the cost of the design changes needed. This was not so abroad, and especially in continents like Africa where the climate made bonneted trucks more appealing than in Europe, and the TJ was destined to outlive Bedford's days as a GM marque even if built on a much smaller scale.

The TIR symbol for sealed international traffic was an increasingly important part of the scene on British roads. This TM3250 with Detroit Diesel 6V-71 engine and standard-width 'D' cab of Dobson of Edinburgh was hauling a Crane-Fruehauf semi-trailer van.

Among early examples of the TM3800 tractor unit with 8V-71 engine to enter service with British operators were these two dating from the winter of 1976-7 operated, by Scottish and Newcastle Breweries Ltd, also with Edinburgh headquarters; one with tanker trailer and the other with curtain-sided trailer. This view shows how the wider cab was used in conjunction with a different driving position, the steering column being moved outwards, further from the vehicle centre line. Note the 'McEwan's Export' sign on the cab roof.

This TM2500 six-wheel recovery truck was operated by a contractor providing the Bedford Roadcall breakdown service and operating on trade plates. The cab was of the sleeper type, again having an illuminated sign of similar design on the cab roof but this time with flashing lights appropriate to its duties, though the windtone horns look as though they might have been chosen for visual as well as audial effect.

17 THE JLL AND OTHER PROJECTS OF THE LATE 1970s

Yet another Bedford model to be announced in 1976 was the remarkable JJL midibus, which still excites admiration for its stylish design 20 years later, as well as some mystification as to why it never became a common sight on our streets. The reasons for only four being built are a combination of factors, one of which is certainly that hackneyed phrase 'before its time', at least partly justifiable in this case. The model's history is quite complex, and this itself sowed the seeds of some of the later problems. Yet it is a fascinating story with wider implications, worth more space than the handful of vehicles built might suggest.

In the early 1970s, there was Government interest in the possible use of small buses for specialised services, notably demand-responsive 'Dial-a-ride' and 'Park and Ride' services. Manufacturers were encouraged to design or adapt suitable vehicles. The Road Research Laboratory, then known as the Transport and Road Research Laboratory, was also active in the field.

In general, most existing small passenger vehicles which met the public service vehicle requirements allowing them to be used to carry fare-paying passengers were then owned by independent operators and made available for private hire rather than employed on bus services. Very small numbers were to be found in some of the publicly-owned fleets of one kind or another, a few were used on subsidised rural services or other specialised ventures, also often subsidised on an experimental basis.

Except for those special cases, straightforward economics had virtually killed off the small bus, as Bedford's

own history showed, and it has to be remembered that the upsurge in the numbers built in the mid-1980s was a direct consequence of the prospect and then the actuality of deregulation. Most existing small buses were adaptations of vans or small goods models, the VAS being almost the sole true passenger model designed to carry fewer than 30 passengers then commercially available on the British market, yet on average not many more than 100 examples were sold annually, almost all with coach bodywork, with a roughly similar number exported.

Abroad, different circumstances sometimes led to wider use of small buses, mainly in the less-well developed countries. A European exception was Italy where, by the late 1960s, Fiat had introduced its 416 model city bus, of only 6.4-metre (21-ft) length, though sturdily built, mounted on 7.50-20 tyres and having an unladen weight of almost 5 tonnes. It had a 4.7-litre six-cylinder diesel engine mounted transversely at the rear and the entrance opposite the driver ahead of the front axle, with a claimed passenger capacity of no less than 52, of whom 40 had to stand. It seems likely that it was this design that may have inspired the development of a British equivalent.

In 1973, Vauxhall's future planning activities included consideration of a midibus but it was rejected on the grounds that the demand would be insufficient to make it economic and hence of much lower priority than a heavy-duty bus, which was being investigated as a potentially viable project.

However, that same year Marshall of Cambridge (Engineering) Ltd, which had built bus bodies as a diversification of the Marshall group's aviation interests, set about designing a small rear-engined city bus, using Leyland axles and other mechanical components from the Terrier range, at that stage including the 98-series engine of BMC origin. This choice of make was to some degree historical, in that the Marshall group included old-established Austin car and then commercial-vehicle dealerships, by then all part of the British Leyland empire, the Terrier being a design successor to Austin commercials.

In its earlier years, the Marshall bodybuilding concern had tended to concentrate on export bus bodies, the business having been begun by the acquisition in 1953 of the bus body activities of Mulliners Ltd of Birmingham when that business was acquired by Standard-Triumph. It recruited Ian Owen, from the lively bus design office of Midland Red, as Chief Engineer and Jack Davis, ex-Metro-Cammell, as Sales Manager, though the latter was later succeeded by Don Smith. From 1961, Marshall had competed very effectively for orders for single-decker

Fiat had introduced the model 416 bus seen here by the late 1960s. Although short, with 6.4 metre (21 ft) overall length, it was designed to carry some 52 passengers, mostly standing. It had a 4.7-litre six-cylinder diesel engine mounted transversely at the rear and a five-speed synchromesh gearbox.

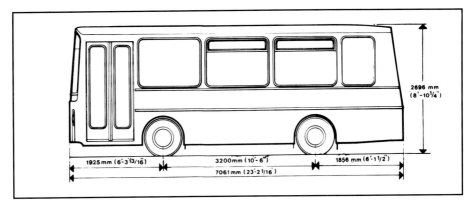

Marshall's brochure for its BB.80 bus included this outline drawing and seating plan. The side view gives a fair indication of the appearance as visualised by the designer, with quite a deep windscreen and rather angular lines in the manner found on some of the concern's other bus designs of the period. The plan views shows that there was to be a space of 0.5 metre behind the rear seat.

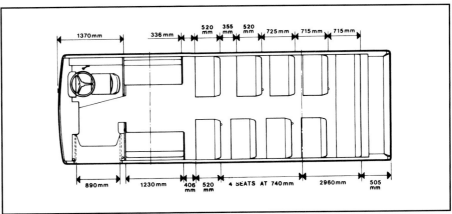

bodies, largely on Leyland Leopard or similar chassis, for the British Electric Traction group, built to BET's standard pattern. Like MCW, Marshall was another concern hit by the advent of the Leyland National single-decker, which from 1972 was being supplied to most of Marshall's former customers among former BET companies, by then part of the National Bus Company.

Ian Owen's aim was to produce a product to help in restoring Marshall's fortunes, the midibus being seen in that light. There was contact with various possible suppliers of mechanical components during the design stage and

The Marshall brochure also included this artist's impression, which also gives some idea of the intended appearance although grossly exaggerating the length and, to a lesser extent, the width.

some informal discussion on the problems with Vauxhall took place in 1973, as well as an enquiry for details of a suitable Bedford engine for the midibus project, though contact went no further at that stage.

By August 1974, a specification had been drawn up for what was called the Marshall Camuter city bus (BB.80), 23ft long, 7ft 6in wide, with 10ft 6in wheelbase and mounted on 7.50-16 tyres, which could seat 27 passengers and carry ten standing, or be arranged to have fewer seats to give room for more to stand. The engine, by then a Perkins 4.236 four-cylinder 3.9-litre diesel, was mounted transversely at the rear, with an Allison AT540 four-speed automatic gearbox. From this the drive was conveyed by a Morse chain drive, mounted at the offside rear corner of the vehicle, from the front end of which a short propellor shaft took the drive to a bevel box and thence by propellor shaft forward to the rear axle. The steel-framed body was to be of rather angular appearance, a feature characteristic of some previous Marshall bus designs. Work on a prototype to this specification began, though completed only as a part-panelled shell.

That year, a more formal approach was made to Vauxhall concerning the possibility of a joint production venture, after a similar proposal was rejected by Leyland. Bill Larson, then in charge of engineering at Luton, also rejected participation, on grounds similar to the in-house project considered the previous year.

However, in 1975, a further approach was made, this time to Embree Kennedy, who expressed interest. The climate for progress had become better by then, not least because of W. R. (Bob) Price, who had become Vauxhall's Managing Director in April 1974 – he had been with GM

The test-rig vehicle, as developed by Marshall but seen here at the Millbrook proving ground, at first glance appeared to bear little resemblance to the drawings of the BB.80 design, save for the clue to the intended side window apertures given by the unpanelled framing. The windscreen was of a style that might have been appropriate to a goods vehicle of 30 years or so earlier and the side windows fitted to the part of the body that had been enclosed were doubtless stock items from some other Marshall body. That may not have mattered too much from a chassis testing viewpoint but might well have heightened the Vauxhall styling studio's desire to make a fresh start.

This three-quarter rear view of the Marshall test vehicle shows the sharply raked rear profile. At that stage, the radiator, together with a header tank and a water pipe running from the nearside rear corner, was mounted at a high level internally, but especially with an unpanelled body the cooling would have been quite unrealistic by comparison with a completed vehicle. Note the door opening midway along the right-hand side, evidently intended for an emergency door yet the existence of similar framing on the nearside below wheel-arch level suggests that a centre-exit version with layout similar to the Fiat 416 may have been in mind.

since 1951, and was interested in possible niche markets. The outcome was that Vauxhall prepared a specification for mechanical components for a joint venture project using a Marshall body structure, the constructional work to be done by Marshalls at their works in Cambridge.

GM styling influence

By February 1976, Marshall was given an order to design and produce four prototypes, the original skeletal test vehicle being modified to take Bedford units as an initial step. However, at that stage, Vauxhall's styling department became involved – it was the first time it had had an opportunity to become involved with a complete bus, and imbued with General Motors' attitudes on the importance of styling, it was hardly surprising that the original Marshall concept was considered unsatisfactory. In fairness, drawings show that the finished vehicle was to have been a good deal more attractive than suggested by the development prototype, with

its shallow 1940s-style two-panel flat-glass windscreen, not intended to represent the final appearance.

Anyone who visited the General Motors Technical Center, completed in 1956 in a park-like 900-acre site on the outskirts of Detroit at a cost of $125 million, could not fail to be impressed with the professional approach. There, the 1,400-strong Styling Staff under the direction of the legendary Harley Earl occupied one of the three main clusters of buildings surrounding an artificial lake. In his book *My Years with General Motors*, Alfred P. Sloan, President of the Corporation from 1923 and not retiring until 1956, devotes a whole chapter to styling – indeed he might be said to have invented the word when he renamed what had been the Art and Color Section the Styling Section in the 1930s, for it does not appear in that context in contemporary dictionaries.

With this background, strong GM influence on the Vauxhall designers was inevitable, and it is not difficult to

The original Marshall BB.80 design got as far as this version with Bedford badge, evidently following the original intended styling in most respects and by no means without merit even if not considered acceptable for a vehicle to be sold as a complete Bedford vehicle.

quite widely copied subsequently was the positioning of the destination display behind the curved glass of the deep windscreen. The length was increased slightly to 24ft 8in and the wheelbase to 11ft 2¼in. The height of the first step from the ground was 13.4in (340mm) and the second step to gangway level 8.5in (215mm), though there was also an internal step to the rear three rows of seats. Unladen weight was quoted as just over 4½tons.

Mechanical units were switched to Bedford components, notably the 330 cu in diesel engine and axles from the lighter end of the TK series, the 7.50-16 wheel size being retained. The Allison AT540 automatic gearbox, already a GM group product, also remained, as did the layout of the transmission. Brakes were operated by an air-hydraulic system and suspension was by conventional leaf springs. At the Commercial Motor Show in September 1976, the full-sized styling model and the power train assembly were displayed, the vehicle being given the JJL name in accordance with Bedford practice, the initial J being a new bus series letter, the second one appropriate to the 330 engine and L signifying the intended 6800-7000kg gross weight range.

There was a cut-back in Government subsidies that year and among the casualties was one to develop demand-responsive bus services. The Show exhibit had attracted much general interest but insubstantial evidence of any strong demand, and work on the project was suspended later that month by Vauxhall Motors pending a re-assessment of its prospects for commercial success.

During the following months, a study was made of the potential market, even more of a crystal-ball exercise than that for a new model intended to take over the same role as an existing one. It was considered that it might be possible to sell about 200 to British operators annually, plus 50 for export, assuming there would be a left-hand drive variant (relatively easy to produce for such a vehicle).

see some resemblences in the resulting Vauxhall Motors design under the direction of Wayne Cherry for what became the JJL to such vehicles as a motor caravan designed a few years earlier in the GM studio, although the latter had front-wheel drive using a Pontiac V8 car engine. The JJL front-end profile was more curvaceous than the Marshall BB80, though a detail which was retained and

Instead, the Vauxhall styling studio got the bit within its teeth and spent considerable time on its own design, coming up with this full-size model, which was exhibited at the 1976 Commercial Motor Show and was adopted as the basis for the completed JJL vehicles.

After a pause while the potential demand was reviewed, construction of the JJL prototypes resumed at Marshall's premises in Cambridge in the spring of 1977. This view shows a fairly early stage, with the rear of the frame temporarily supported to ensure that the structure remained square as the weight of the Bedford 330 cu in engine, Allison automatic gearbox and other parts of the drive train was imposed as they were installed. A drawing of the framing is hung from the waistrail for reference as Vauxhall and Marshall staff discuss progress. The enclosed Morse chain drive on the right of the drive train was perhaps the most unorthodox part of the mechanical design but proved trouble-free in service.

Here two body shells were in course of being panelled and the finished shape becomes more readily evident. The atmosphere in the Cambridge workshops was very different to that at Dunstable, or even in Vauxhall's experimental department, and the different approach of concerns geared on the one hand to 'bespoke' construction of vehicles in relatively small numbers and on the other to planning for mass production was not easy to reconcile.

Work on the prototypes resumed in the Spring of 1977. As this proceeded, the problems of reconciling the methods of two quite different types of firm began to become apparent. Vauxhall was a big concern in its own right and geared to volume production methods, quite apart from being the main British branch of the world's largest company of any kind, with many of its procedures co-ordinated from GM headquarters in Detroit, 3,000 miles away. It was inevitable that its methods were measured, verging on the bureaucratic – copies of letters or inter-office memos were apt to be sent to a dozen people within the firm.

Marshall, with an annual output of bodies counted in hundreds at its output peak, was at most in the middle rank among British bus bodybuilders and, like most such concerns, had a flexible approach to design, being very used to coping with variations agreed often at short notice with minimal formality. The concept of all designs being precisely defined and recorded to the last detail before being released for production was foreign in such a climate, as it would have been in the British bus

bodybuilding industry generally. Being able to produce variations to meet individual operators' requirements was part of the stock in trade of such firms, and as repair was often apt to be on a 'cut and fit' basis, precise recording of every detail was not attempted.

So the stage was set for difficulties. An example was a piece of $^3/_8$ in steel plate that happened to be lying around the workshop and used to make a bracket, to the horror of a Vauxhall representative who pointed out that there was no record of the grade of material. Also causing unease was the practice of drilling holes for engine and transmission items using hand-held drills through the fixing holes in the components themselves, with the attendant risk of misalignment and inconsistency. In a more general way, there were problems of unwillingness to await approval for a proposed item before going ahead with it, or departing from what had been agreed. Distance between Luton and Cambridge was part of the problem, since even a brief discussion would imply a total of three hours travelling time, and people might not be free from other duties to make the trip for several days.

One of the JJL prototypes ready to leave the Marshall workshop; on the left, a double-decker is just visible – Marshall had turned to building double-deck bodywork, produced on a variety of chassis, for which demand was increasing quite sharply in the late 1970s.

The airfield at Cambridge, which Marshall's premises adjoin, provided an appropriately glamorous view for this picture of a newly-completed JJL.

Even so, the work proceeded and the four prototypes gradually took shape, being completed in 1978. Testing of the first one, JJL1RKO9008, began at Millbrook, and in August that year, 9009 was sent to be shown to the General Motors board, 9010 appeared at the Commercial Motor Show at Earls Court in October, while 9011 was chosen for use as a sales demonstrator. Again, an active sales exercise was carried out over the following Winter and Spring, resulting in the receipt of some tentative orders – for example, by April 1979 the National Bus Company was proposing to take eight, no doubt for one of its evaluation exercises – it was quoted a probable price of £24,500 or so. There were also a few cases of proposed use of the model for non-PSV duties where its elegant outline appealed, such as for mobile bank branches or as a motor-cycle transporter for Barry Sheen, in those days world champion rider.

Even so, the total number of vehicles for which there were specific enquiries was only about 150. By July 1979, the first three sets of Bedford parts for production vehicles were ready to go to Marshalls, and the award of a Design Council commendation was a welcome recognition of the design's merit.

Yet fresh concerns were arising – testing had revealed that the 12-in brakes used with the small wheels reached high temperatures when put through a simulated urban bus schedule of four stops per mile, leading to cracking of the linings and short life – in other words a revival of the VAL problems, capable of being solved but implying further cost and delay. There were indications of new competitors, not comparable in technology or styling but less inherently costly, notably Leyland with its own Terrier derivative, retaining its front engine, and sold under the revived Cub name, and Alexander, producing a vehicle based on the Ford A-type, the latter far from successful, though that was not known at the time.

Analysis of the potential market as judged at that date revealed further worrying factors. Existing mini or midi buses in service with major operators in the United Kingdom in 1978 amounted to 259, out of a total combined fleet of 47,108 buses. Selling even 150 per year of what was to be a higher-priced vehicle than existing small buses would imply doubling the nations's existing fleet of such buses within two years, which seemed decidedly optimistic on the evidence at that date. What was more, even assuming so big an initial rate of sale was feasible, the large new fleet of buses with a planned life of about ten years would imply no replacement business for something approaching such a period.

There were further hesitations, including fresh evaluation of the possibilities of expanding output by offering a chassis version for other bodybuilders to complete as well as a left-hand version. The project stuttered on until 1980, when it was decided to abandon it.

The four JJL models completed were registered at various dates between their completion in 1978 and 1981. The final design was not significantly altered from that of the full-sized styling model of 1976, though the grille slots at the front fed air to the front-mounted radiator. This was JJL1RKO9010, the vehicle that was displayed at the 1978 Show, seen after being registered EKX 648T, the legal owner being Vauxhall Motors Ltd and the unladen weight quoted as 4880kg. It had been used largely for brake testing and then became a demonstrator, being loaned to Maidstone Borough Council in February 1981, purchased in June 1982 and joining two others by then in the fleet. Together with the other two, it passed on long-term loan to Brighton Borough Transport in October 1983. The project had been dropped by Vauxhall Motors in 1980 and the vehicles were sold off via Marshall, which never lost interest in the possibilities. In September 1996, just as we go to press, the first two production examples of a slightly longer vehicle of similar layout called the Marshall Minibus have entered service with Chester City Transport – they have Cummins B-series four-cylinder 3.9-litre turbocharged engines and Allison automatic transmission.

In 1981, the four vehicles were sold off via Marshalls, not being badged as Bedfords, on the basis that although spares for standard units would be available, no provision of special parts would be made via the Bedford spares organisation. All four passed through the hands of the Maidstone municipal fleet, where the General Manager, Alan Price, had already broken with convention by purchasing a fleet largely based on Bedford YMT chassis to replace double-deckers on the town's services. The demonstrator, 9011, was initially hired in May 1981, registered as HKX 553V. Then 9008 (UKX 335X) and 9009 (AVS 903T) were purchased by Maidstone in October 1981, When 9011 was damaged in an accident, it was returned to Marshall but Maidstone then decided to purchase 9010 (EKX 648T).

When 9011 was repaired it was sold to an independent operator, Rowland & Goodwin, of St Leonards. Brighton Borough Council had the three Maidstone buses on long-term loan from October 1983, operating them on a shuttle service from Brighton station. There they came under the charge of Paul Crowther, who had worked on the JJL project at Vauxhall, and reported that the non-standard item on which doubts had been expressed because of the lack of further spares, the Morse chain drive, had worked perfectly, the six spares held still being unused. The

Rowland & Goodwin vehicle passed to Bournemouth Transport and was then purchased by AWD, 'inheritor' of the Bedford business, with the possibility of reviving the project in mind, but despite it being shown to several operators and bodybuilders, the idea was not pursued further.

The irony is that only a few years after the project was abandoned, the adoption of the deregulation policy by the Government led the National Bus Company in particular to order vast fleets of minibuses. Yet even then, these were at first minimum-cost Ford Transit 16-seaters, much cheaper than the JJL had been despite several years of inflation, so it by no means followed that any orders for the JJL would have materialised had it gone into production and remained available. In design terms and even if needing some further development in matter such as brakes at the point at which it was abandoned, the JJL comes much nearer to vehicles like the Dennis Dart belonging to a generation a full decade after its days of hope.

Meanwhile, back at the production lines...

While the JJL story was unfolding, mainstream activities continued with less drama and more success. It is easy to overlook the role played by the small Bedford vans, or

Although largely unremarked, the HA van continued to sell well, and indeed in 1978, when the entire JJL output of four vehicles was produced, HA output amounted to 16,319, a remarkable figure for a model then fourteen years old. Here one owned by Chloride Industrial Batteries Ltd is seen, the driver evidently checking the performance of a battery in a Ransomes fork-lift truck. By that period, the HA conformed to the practice on larger models in that the 'badge designation', in this case HA130, related to gross weight.

W. H. Smith & Sons Ltd, large-scale Bedford users since the days of maroon WS models in the early 1930s, continued to favour the make, by the late 1970s in orange and brown livery with the then new logo. Here a CF350 with Wilsdon box van body returns to the company's Birmingham depot after a news run in that city. It is all too easy to discount the unglamorous van side of Bedford's business, yet output of CF models in 1978, at 46,277, almost exactly matched the combined output of the TK, TJ, TM and M truck models plus all bus and coach chassis that year, 46,790.

more correctly vans and related models, in Vauxhall's fortunes, apt to be regarded as the unglamorous side of the car business or dismissed as not 'real' commercial vehicles. Yet over many years output of vans generally outnumbered that of trucks and even in the late 1970s was running at over 50,000 per year, with a peak in 1978 of 68,804. Among these, the CF always suffered by being in the shadow of the Ford Transit, yet annual output was above 35,000 in the 1977-80 period, again with a peak in 1978 of 46,277.

Broadly speaking, there were very similar annual totals of CF models to the combined figures for all truck models, again using this term in a generic way and including the coach and bus chassis, in the late 1970s and indeed on into the 1980s, when both totals were in decline. Even a top of the range CF was of relatively low value compared to even a typical TK, but the degree of standardisation meant that the vans could be turned out very economically, with original development costs long since repaid and only much more modest costs for later changes or additional variants, for example for changes to the gearboxes fitted to the various models (made by ZF on

the heavier-duty models) and a mild face-lift in 1976. On the other hand, this was a fiercely competitive market – but then that applied increasingly to the whole automobile industry.

Rather similarly, the TK, relatively little changed from its 1960 launch in essentials, continued to be the best-selling truck range, with yearly figures of 18,000 or so in the late 1970s, including the KM, now counted as a TK variant, which it always was in designation terms. The TJ, by then a purely export model, was not all that far behind, at well over 10,000 per year to the end of the decade.

Badge designations

There seemed to be growing understanding that the internal type designations for Bedford models had become too complex for general use in the outside world. A 'badge designation' system similar to that used for the TM range, with the main type letters and then an approximate gross weight guide (in kilogrammes divided by ten), gradually came into use in publicity by the mid-1970s, the main categories being as listed overleaf.

The TK range continued to maintain a solid share of the market, remaining the most numerous Bedford truck model in the late 1970s, especially on the home market. The KM model was still distinguishable by the heavy-duty two-bar bumper and quadruple headlamps but was now marketed as part of the TK range instead of as a model in its own right as in its earlier years. This tipper of 148in wheelbase was basically of type ERV with the 466 cu in engine, switching to EMV with the 500 cu in unit but was being marketed as type TK1630, signifying its 16.3 tonne gross rating.

Badge designation	Model	Internal code prefix*	Badge designation	Model	Internal code prefix*
TJ340	J1	COD	TK1630	KF tractor	EOQ
TJ610	J2	COJ	TK1930	KG tractor	EOR
TJ700	J3	COL			
TJ850	J4	COM	M1120	M 4x4	MOR
TJ940	J5	CON			
TJ1100	J6	COQ	TK860	KD 6x2	EOM
			TK1000	KE 6x2	EON
TK570	KB	EOG			
TK750	KC	EOL	TK1260	KG twin-steer	EOR
TK860	KD	EOM			
TK1000	KE	EON			
TK1260	KG	EOR	* Note that these code prefix examples quote the second letter		
TK1470	KH	EOT	as O – on actual vehicles the letter would be as appropriate to the		
TK1630	KM	EOV	engine fitted, eg CDD for 214 petrol or CHD for 220 diesel, etc.		

By 1976, there was growing emphasis on the models not requiring an HGV driving licence for the British market, mainly the TK750, though the TK860 could also be used if 'downrated' to 7.49 tonne, in cases where the 330 diesel engine was thought preferable.

In line with Bedford practice for many years, close interest was taken in matching the customer's needs, if need be with specialised bodywork. Bedford sales staff were armed with lists of bodybuilders of particular categories – there were no less than 23 names of makers of bulk discharge bodywork for grain, foodstuff or granules and 58 for metal dropside or platform bodies, for example. The TK was still an effective model in the sense of doing the job for which it was intended, even if styling details revealed that it was far from new, and up against stiff competition from the Ford D-type, mildly face-lifted in 1978.

One step down the range size was the KH, sharing the 10-stud wheels of the KM but with two headlamps and a single-bar bumper. This variant became badged as TK1470, the example shown being in the Tate & Lyle fleet.

Output of TK models rose to 22,649 in 1978, not as high as it had been in the 1960s, but a peak during the late 1970s. A related and significant landmark was reached that year with the production of the 500,000th TK, actually produced at GM's assembly plant in Portugal from a kit of parts sent out from Dunstable. Overseas assembly played quite a prominent part in reaching that total, which was a record for any British truck model. The total production of Bedford trucks since 1931 reached two million that year, again a record for any British truck make, while the total of Bedford vans reached one million, thus bringing the overall total to three million. The old slogan 'You see them everywhere' was as valid as ever and no-one could have guessed that this immensely strong position could be brought to an end in less than a decade.

Meanwhile, in 1977 the TM range received an important boost with the introduction of a 4x4 version, using the 500 cu in engine and the D-type version of the TM cab, to be available in military or civilian versions. The model was the first production application of a 202bhp turbo-charged version of the 500 engine, now increasingly being referred to as the 8.2-litre in a swing to the acceptance of metric units. The principle of turbo-charging as a means of increasing output of diesel engines in particular had been recognised for some time, Thornycroft having introduced some models so powered in the 1950s while Ford had been offering a turbocharged version of its 330 cu in engine since 1968. Bedford engineers had been developing a turbocharged version of the 500 since that engine was first introduced, and it seems clear that its structure had been designed to suit, though it was not to be offered more widely in this form until 1981.

The military TM could carry an 8-tonne payload and was given a good send-off with an initial Ministry of Defence order for 2,000. It was produced alongside the M-type 4x4, which continued with the 330 cu in engine (or the 300 cu in petrol unit), catering for a lower weight range and remained in production at a rate of around 2,000 per

The saviour for the TM range proved to be the 4x4 version and the large orders from the Ministry of Defence it attracted. This was a heavier-duty vehicle than the M-type, built around the concept of being able to carry an 8-tonne payload over rough terrain. Here a prototype vehicle is seen on test in 1977.

year right through until the mid-1980s.

The civilian TM range was also extended at the top end in 1977 by the introduction of the TM4400, designed to run at up to 44 tonnes, as then being permitted in Italy. It had an even more powerful Detroit Diesel, the 8V-92, of 12-litre capacity, developing 380bhp, making it by far the largest and most powerful Bedford yet.

As the 1970s drew to a close, Bedford was thus offering a wider range than ever, stretching from the ½-ton Chevanne to the 44-tonne gross version of the TM tractive unit. As well as the main production models, mostly selling in very large numbers, there were several of the 'niche' ventures which had grown in favour during Bob Price's era as Managing Director. In addition to those already mentioned, there was a joint venture with Lucas in the development of battery-electric vehicles, using the CF as basis, in which Geoff Harding, well-known in the bus industry as an innovator, and formerly Director of Operations of SELNEC PTE, was the leading light on the Lucas side.

Overall, 1978 was quite an encouraging year for the company, not only in terms of output, with total Bedford production at 117,443, up from 91,747 in 1977 and the second highest total ever (beaten only by the 1971 figure of 126,394), while Vauxhall was at 144,579, much the same as in the two previous years. There had been an operating profit of £11.8 million and although this came down to £2 million after interest charges and other adjustments, this followed a run of years when the company had failed to break even. Some major plans for expansion on the bus side were afoot, and the future doubtless looked quite promising.

Unfortunately 1979 was to prove disappointing. Industrial unrest was a major cause of this, it being reckoned that some 48,000 vehicles were lost in production terms, largely due to a national road haulage strike, a dispute at the Luton plant in March, engineering industry disputes in the summer and a 12-week dispute at the Ellesmere Port plant in the autumn. Vauxhall output was not greatly down at 142,582 but the Bedford figure dropped to 87,650. More seriously, the net loss was some £31.3 million. This did not augur well and, in addition, industry in general was being increasingly hit by the general depression, the worst experienced since the 1930s, which was to have drastic effects on commercial vehicle sales in general, not least those of Bedford.

The electric version of the CF was the result of a six-year joint project with Lucas and sought to broaden the concept of battery-powered vehicles beyond that of the very slow milk-float. A 50mph top speed and acceleration lively enough to allow the vehicles to keep up with the general flow of traffic was available but the 50-mile range before batteries needed recharging was still a factor severely restricting their use to very short-range work. This one was used experimentally by the Austrian Post Office. As happened with other similar projects both before and since, the prospect of much more widespread use proved to be a false dawn.

The TM continued to appeal as the basis for van bodywork. This Luton van operated by Kay-Metzeler Ltd and dating from 1978 was based on a TM1700 with Bedford 500 engine.

The key market for which the TM was largely intended when first introduced was the heavy-duty artic and some progress was made in capturing business of this type, even if not as much as had been hoped. This is another instance of a TM3800 with the 8V-71 engine working for a brewery group. The amalgamations and alliances within that line of business were already producing some intriguing juxtapositions of names – here the sleeper-cab equipped tractive unit carries the John Smith's name but the semi-trailer side-sheet has that of Hofmeister Lager.

THE TL RANGE AND THE FATEFUL 1980s

Bedford's final new range of models appeared in 1980. This was the TL, essentially a straightforward replacement for the TK, though in fact the latter continued in production in diminishing numbers for certain applications until the mid-1980s and the final wind-down of Bedford production as part of the General Motors empire. The brochure describing the new range was quoted as being published by 'Bedford Commercial Vehicles, Vauxhall Motors Limited, Luton, England', a form of words that was to be used in the period up to 1982.

It is clear that the concept was one of a new range which was intended to inherit the character of the TK, with layout and styling which seemed to underline the resemblance, even though it was very largely a new design. There was one fundamental difference, that being the provision of a tilt cab, the feature in which the TK had been unable to match competitive models, notably the Ford D-series. Yet even in this respect, a TK feature was retained in the continued provision of lift-up flaps to allow routine maintenance without tilting the cab with the latter's inevitable disturbance of items within. It was also possible to avoid faults which had been found in other tilt-cab designs in such respects as making it non-tamper proof and easy to operate without any need for what might be dirty hands to touch any part of the well-trimmed cab interior.

The range extended from 5.7 to 16.2 tonnes gross in terms of load-carrying models and, in much the same way as the TK, split broadly into groups using 16-in (in some cases 17-in) as opposed to 20-in wheels (or the equivalent 22.5in to suit tubeless tyres). There was a range of engines to suit the various weight ratings, most of which had a familiar ring about them, even though the designations had altered, most now having D or P added to signify whether diesel or petrol.

Among diesels, there were what was now called the 220D 3.6-litre four-cylinder unit, the 330D 5.4-litre six and at the top end of the range, the 8.2-litre Blue Series engine, hitherto called the 500. Petrol engines continued to be available to a limited degree, what was now called the 214P offered for lighter models being the 3.52-litre six-cylinder unit which, in essentials, was the old '28hp' engine first seen in 1938. The 300P was no longer offered on the British market but was available for export in mid-range models.

The range offered was as follows, the main designation being derived from the design gross weight in tonnes, sometimes rounded up or down slightly to give a round figure, TL570 having an actual gross weight of 5.69 tonnes, for example:-

Badge designation	Type number & engine	Wheelbase	Tyre size	Notes
TL570	DDG 214P	9ft 7in (2.921m)	7.00-16	
	DHG 220D	9ft 7in (2.921m)	7.00-16	
TL750	DDL 214P	11ft 3in (3.429m)	7.50-16	
	DHL 220D	11ft 3in (3.429m)	7.50-16	
TL860	DJA2 330D	11ft 3in (3.429m)	7.50-16	German spec.
	DJA3 330D	12ft 7in (3.835m)	7.50-16	German spec.
	DLA2 8.2	11ft 3in (3.429m)	7.50-16	German spec.
	DLA3 8.2	12ft 7in (3.835m)	7.50-16	German spec.
	DFM2 300P	11ft 3in (3.429m)	7.50-16	Not UK
	DFM3 300P	12ft 7in (3.835m)	7.50-16	Not UK
	DJM2 330D	11ft 3in (3.429m)	7.50-16	
	DJM3 330D	12ft 7in (3.835m)	7.50-16	

Note. Above TL860 models intended for 7.50 tonne gross weight; similar models with 8.25-16 tyres suitable for 8.64 tonne gross or 8.99 tone gross for German specification DLA models.

Badge designation	Type number & engine	Wheelbase	Tyre size	Notes
TL1000	DLW3 8.2	12ft 7in (3.835m)	8.25-17	German spec
	DFN3 300P	12ft 7in (3.835m)	8.25-17	Not UK
	DJN3 330D	12ft 7in (3.835m)	8.25-17	
TL1020	DLW3 8.2	12ft 7in (3.835m)	8.25-17	German spec
TL1260	DJR6 330D	10ft 0in (3.048m)	9.00-20	
	DJRA 330D	11ft 6in (3.505m)	9.00-20	
	DJR1 330D	12ft 7in (3.835m)	9.00-20	
	DJR3 330D	13ft 11in (4.241m)	9.00-20	
	DJR4 330D	16ft 1in (4.902m)	9.00-20	

Equivalents to above models available with 8.2-litre engine as DLR6, DLRA, DLR1 etc. and, for export only, with 300P engine as DFR6, DFRA, DFR1 etc.

Badge designation	Type number & engine	Wheelbase	Tyre size	Notes
TL1470	DMT2 8.2	11ft 2in (3.403m)	11x22.5	
	DMT3 8.2	13ft 7in (4.140m)	11x22.5	
	DMT4 8.2	15ft 9in (4.80m)	11x22.5	
TL1630	DMV7 8.2	13ft 2in (4.013m)	11x22.5	
	DMVT 8.2	12ft 4in (3.759m)	11x22.5	
	DMV1 8.2	14ft 6in (4.420m)	11x22.5	
	DMV2 8.2	17ft 4in (5.283m)	11x22.5	
	DMV3 8.2	18ft 8in (5.690m)	11x22.5	
TL1630	DJQ8 330D	8ft 0in (2.438m)	7.50-20	Tractive unit
TL1930	DLR8 8.2	8ft 0in (2.438m)	8.25-20	Tractive unit

By that period, safety had become more of a public issue, duly addressed in terms of cab strength, availability of inertia-reel seat belts and elimination of sharp projections inside the cab. Another public image matter was the way in which some truck cabs had acquired what was thought to be an aggressive appearance. It is significant that the descriptive brochure, which itself might be thought a touch aggressive in language with its claim 'the truck that has everything right' with repetition of the word 'right' in

In typical Bedford fashion, TL prototypes in virtually finalised form were run in varied climatic conditions for two years or more before the final announcement. This S-registered (1977/8) example of a 16-tonne gross model marketed as the TL1630 was undergoing test in northern Norway. There had been tentative plans for a range extending right down to lightweight models using the TM cab but the in the event the TL had a clear 'son-of-TK' look about it, with similar outlines but more modern detailing as well as practical features such as the headlamps mounted in and protected by the sturdy front bumper which formed the front crossmember of the frame.

The key feature of the TL which immediately distinguished it from the TK was the tilt cab. Care was taken not only to make it easy yet safe to tilt, but also to eliminate any risk of unauthorised tampering with the mechanism. Yet for day-to-day servicing, the lift-up valances in the rear part of the side panels, so familiar to TK users, were retained.

The interior of the TL cab also had strong echoes of the TK, right down to the tartan seat trim. Much was made of the spaciousness, only part of the shelf behind the seats being visible here, and the headroom was claimed to be the best in its class.

engine set back far enough to retain the 'walk-across' facility and helping to keep the internal noise level down. Further effort had been put into this aspect of design, in which the TK had itself made a major improvement in its day. Now further attention was given to eliminating 'those little gaps that have been proved to let through most noise' to quote words from the brochure that have the ring of being written by engineers rather than advertising copywriters.

As so often the case with Bedford, association with car technology was evident in such points as the adoption of pendant pedals as part of the gap-sealing process, and a more substantial seal round the gear lever was another element in this, trivial-sounding yet remarkably important in making the driver's job less fatiguing. Another traditional Bedford virtue was evident in the front suspension, using long (70-in) springs having two separated tapered leaves and thus eliminating the inter-leaf friction inherent in the traditional multi-leaf spring.

All in all, the TL was thus a worthy successor to the TK, retaining its merits and adding some worthwhile new ones, while prices were only marginally higher for comparable models. Yet it never achieved comparable success, at least in part because the whole industrial economy in Britain was entering a period of depression that was to prove the worst since the 1930s. As factories ran into periods of falling orders for their products, the buying of new vehicles to deliver them tended to be among the first casualties. The output of TK models in 1978 had been 22,649, a remarkable figure for a model range that was basically eighteen years old even though progressively expanded and updated. It was up from 18,092 in 1987 and not too far below the average over that period. There was a drop to 16,114 in 1979 and in 1980 there were 10,627 TK and 3,509 of the then new TL. Then in 1981, only 4,077 TK and 4,052 TL were built. The TL did pick up a little when the worst of that depression was over, reaching 7,320 in 1984, but even this was a modest figure by the standards

the page headings, makes a point of the 'non-aggressive cab styling'. In fact this seems fair comment, for a clear echo of the functional look of the TK was evident, cleaned up in detail design in line with contemporary taste.

The basic form of the cab was as on the TK, with the

No significant change from the prototype design was evident in the production TL, save that discreet model identification plates were fitted to the doors, just below the front corner of the windows. Seen in this photograph dated October 1980 is a TL1260, rated at 12.35 tons gross and having the 330D engine, operated by Bakelite UK Ltd. Note the well roped and sheeted load, an art not so often seen nowadays as it used to be.

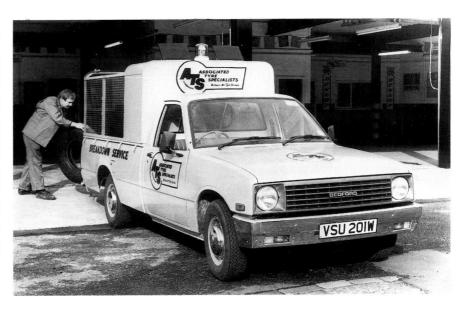

The KB26 1-ton pick-up showed no family resemblance to other Bedford or Vauxhall products and indeed was an Isuzu design, belonging to the period when many Japanese cars and small commercial vehicles had bland and 'forgettable' exterior styling. Its main virtue was what was described as one of the biggest cargo decks in its class. This one was operated by Associated Tyre Specialists (Scotland) Ltd. Isuzu had origins going back to the 1930s and had a range extending up to a six-wheel artic tractor unit with 16.5-litre engine and including buses, of which an underfloor engine was chosen as an option for a proposed heavy-duty bus range planned by Bedford though never put into production. Isuzu trucks were being assembled in Australia and also sold under the Bedford name.

of what had been the core of Bedford's truck business.

This time exports were not sufficiently strong to counter the trend, even though the TJ range, by then all exported, actually outnumbered TK plus TL output in 1981 at 8,360, itself well down on the 15,694 of the TJ range built in 1978. Many of Bedford's strongest overseas markets, notably in Africa, were themselves running into serious financial problems and sales to countries such as Nigeria, once so strong, had dropped back. Stronger competition was another factor, not only from European countries but particularly from Japan, whose motor industry had proved so adept at getting its products into hitherto impregnable markets. Even within the United States, Japanese cars had taken a significant share of a market which had been almost exclusively met by products of General Motors, Ford or Chrysler, so the whole basis of the GM empire was less secure than it had been since its early days.

It was a matter of some foresight in this context, though perhaps not a good omen in the long term for Bedford, that

GM had acquired a 35% shareholding in Isuzu in 1971, and indeed this could be regarded as a parallel to the much earlier investment involved in acquiring control of Vauxhall and Opel in Europe.

Van developments

It was perhaps symptomatic that in 1980 Bedford began producing the KB26 1-ton pick-up of Isuzu design, using a 1,584cc petrol engine – this followed the assembly of various Isuzu-designed models in Australia by Holden, GM's subsidiary there, from the late 1970s, marketed under the Bedford name, thereby cutting into sales of Dunstable products. The KB was introduced on the British market in April 1981 and two years later an improved version with five-speed gearbox and square instead of round headlamps was introduced. Meanwhile in 1982 a 4x4 version, the KB41, had been added, both types being available with an Isuzu 1,951cc diesel engine, the models then becoming KBD26 and KBD41 respectively.

This line-up of TM-hauled car transporters of The Autocar Transporters Group was doubtless posed to convey something of the spread of Vauxhall Motors products as they stood at the beginning of the 1980s, with Cavalier cars and HA and CF vans readily identifiable. The Cavalier was proving very successful, though as an Opel-based design its export potential was less beneficial to Vauxhall than a home-grown product. The HA was to live on until 1983 and the CF, with styling and other changes in the pipeline, was still an important model.

The CF van was given a face-lift in 1980, introduced at the Paris Motor Show that year and reflecting European sales of the model, sold on the Continent through the Opel network. Opel was also responsible for the standard petrol engine and the 2.3-litre diesel, described as a General Motors unit, was based on Opel designs. Output of this model remained lively, at 37,772 in 1980, though dropping to 21,618 in 1981 in response to the depression.

In July 1982, the Astra van was introduced, derived from the Vauxhall Astra car introduced in 1980 and in turn based on the latest version of the Opel Kadett. This had front-wheel-drive with transversely-mounted engine, both features new to Bedford. A 1,297cc engine was standard for the model rated at up to 1,470kg and a 1,598cc engine for the 1,550kg version, though there was also a diesel option, also of 1,598cc. The Chevanne was thereupon withdrawn but the venerable HA lived on for another year before being withdrawn from sale in 1983. The Astra van had high standards of handling and roadholding and sold quite well, output running at over 16,000 in 1983 and 1984.

Competition in the coach market

The picture regarding bus and coach chassis sales was at least as depressing as that applying to the truck range. Part of this was due to the same general cause, for operators were suffering – rising unemployment meant fewer people to carry to and from work, and even though Bedford had not been in that line of the business to any great depth, the coach operators were also finding that their business was suffering as people did not travel for pleasure so much. Independent operators were relatively more involved in coaching, and this was where Bedford's strength on the passenger side had been. The total number of coaches of all makes placed in service in Britain fell from about 2,600 in 1979 to only a little over 1,500 in 1981.

However, there was another important factor in what was an even greater collapse of what had been the very strong hold that Bedford had on that market. In 1980, for the first time, the Leyland Leopard took first place in home market sales of single-deck models, with the Bedford YMT in third place behind the Leyland National. The Leopard gained slightly in such a comparison in being used for both bus and coach bodywork, though by 1980 it was almost entirely as a coach that the Leopard was expanding its sales success. An important element was the policy of the National Bus Company, expanding its coach activities, for it standardised on the Leopard, but a new factor was an increasing tendency for independent operators to switch to heavier-duty chassis for coaches. To some degree, this was a reflection of growing interest in high-specification coaches, resulting in body weight going above the recommended gross weight for a Bedford chassis, and also in some cases the choice of 12-metre models, legal since 1968 and initially only taken up by a few users but becoming more widely favoured by the late 1970s.

More importantly, operators had found that heavier-duty models stood up to continuous high-speed running on motorways better than the Bedford and Ford models and even though they cost more initially, the overall costs, and damage to goodwill caused by breakdowns, had begun to work out in favour of the extra initial investment.

During the period from about the mid-1970s, the Bedford Y-series coach models began to get a reputation for suffering from engine troubles, often relatively minor-seeming in their initial cause as water or oil pump failures. The problem was that extensive engine damage could result from either, and the water pump failures were apt to end with the fan breaking away and slicing through the radiator. It only took a few such incidents, with passengers stranded and becoming impatient until a relief coach could be sent out, and the matter was raised at a high level via

A factor which influenced some operators to cease buying Bedford coaches around the beginning of the 1980s was the absence of a model designed to accept 12-metre bodywork, which grew from being a very limited market in Britain to one quite widely favoured, even among small operators, by about 1980 as well as being widely used abroad. However, an enterprising operator and dealer, Tricentrol, with one of its premises conveniently situated in Dunstable, carried out approved conversions of the YMT model, increasing the wheelbase from 18ft 6in to 20ft, and 20 left-hand drive examples with two-speed rear axles were exported to Greece for use on a service between Thessalonika and Athens. The 50-seat body was by Ioannidis of Thessalonika.

CPT, the operators' trade association.

When engineering representatives of operators and manufacturers met, there was a good level of understanding and the solutions were recognised on both sides. However, both Bedford and Ford seemed unable to bring changes to overcome such problems into effect quickly, so they tended to recur for a time, during which the firms' reputation slipped further. Although Leyland was itself far from perfect in such respects it, and increasingly Volvo, tended to reap the benefit of such disaffection with what still tended to be called 'lightweights'.

The combination of these factors resulted in a drop in Bedford bus and coach chassis output, at first mild but later catastrophic. In 1978 a total of 4,294 passenger chassis, including 2,341 of the NJM (SB5) almost entirely for export, and 1,045 of the YMT, were produced. In 1979 there was a fall to 3,523. It is noteworthy that in that year, out of 2,057 SB5 models built, 1,380 were supplied to Pakistan and 360 to Bangladesh, exported in CKD ('completely knocked-down') packs of twelve chassis at a time. There were also 255 BLP, which was what British users would have identified as the VAM, though by then fitted with the 8.2-litre engine, and 156 of these were also in CKD packs for Australia. The model continued to be built in small numbers until 1985.

In 1980 to 1982, the successive totals of all passenger models built were 1,743, 761 and 534. This was an astonishing drop, reflecting an unprecedented collapse in home-market demand and worsening world trade conditions. Its severity made it more difficult to obtain backing for investing in a more radical redesign programme, indeed undermining the case for the expansion into heavy-duty bus production that was being proposed.

Turbocharged Bedford diesels

General adoption of turbocharging for Bedford truck diesel engines was announced in May 1981. Quite apart from being a means of increasing output, it was easier to meet forthcoming noise standards and turbocharged diesels were becoming much more common in the whole commercial vehicle industry.

The power increases over the previous engines were often quite modest, making it clear that this had not been the main objective. The four-cylinder 3.6-litre, formerly 220D, now called 3.6/70TD went up from 65bhp to 72.3bhp at the same governed speed of 2,600rpm. The corresponding six-cylinder 5.4-litre unit, hitherto 330D and henceforth 5.4/105TD went from 98bhp to 107.3bhp, also at 2,600rpm. These two were described as the Red Series engines and the 8.2-litre continued to be called the Blue Series engine, again offered in two basic ratings. The new 8.2/130TD used in some medium-range TL models had a very slightly increased output of 130.1bhp compared to the previous equivalent version's 127.5bhp, at an unaltered 2,650rpm. The higher-rated version was now called 8.2/175TD and here the installed power ratings varied slightly depending on installation between 171.2 and 173.1bhp, both at 2,500rpm, the previous unblown version used in the early top-of range TL models giving 150.5bhp, also at 2,500rpm.

The turbocharged engines were also made available for passenger models though here the pattern was rather more complex. Early leaflets issued in 1981 referred to the 8.2/175TD unit as being fitted to the YMP and YMT models (the YMP was really what had hitherto been the YMQ, the final letter being changed to conform to international regulations on model designations).

Later in the year, however, there was a new YNT

The military endorsement of turbocharged engines in the TM 4x4 model provided a confidence-building basis for the decision to offer basically similar units in civilian models. Production of the initial order for 2,000 placed by the Ministry of Defence for Army use got under way in 1981, one of the completed vehicles being seen here. During 1982, 940 TM 4x4 models were built, accounting for almost 70% of total TM production that year. The model had the high-rated version of the 8.2-litre engine, also used for the YNT and, later, the YNV coach chassis, developing 204 to 206bhp at 2,500rpm, the precise figure depending on the installation. The standard main gearbox in this model was the Turner M6, which had suffered teething troubles when tried in passenger models but these had been overcome when used in prodution of TM 4x4 models, in which it was very successful.

Some versions of the new range of turbocharged engines were only marginally more powerful than their predecessors but the 8.2/205TD, seen here in the form used in the YNT, increased the power output considerably over the previous top-output engine of the same basic design. The foresight in planning for this possibility when the basic engine design was laid down thus paid off, although a larger-capacity Bedford-made engine would have been useful in meeting the increasing need for higher power in heavier vehicles.

model, with a much higher-rated 8.2/206TD version of the 8.2-litre engine, developing 206bhp at 2,500rpm. It was noteworthy that, despite the reduction in governed speed from the 2,800rpm used in previous Bedford coach diesels, this produced considerably higher power than the 160bhp of the naturally-aspirated 8.2-litre engine (8.2/160D) still standard in the YMT and the YMP. Both of the latter chassis were now also available with the 8.2/175TD, as

mentioned above and sometimes called the 'low-blow' turbocharged engine. In each case, the chassis with turbocharged engines were given higher-geared rear axles so that coaches travelled at almost exactly the same road speed with the new lower engine speed, making travel more restful and reducing that element of stress on engine items directly related to rotational speed. The additional power was available when needed but at the legal 70mph maximum on a level motorway a typical coach did not need all that was available and the new set-up was a better proposition for engine life and reliability.

British coach operators, themselves attempting to survive in a difficult economic climate, were becoming more demanding. One fresh demand was for a short coach of more up-to-date specification than the VAS, which was still being built in modest numbers. Tricentrol, an enterprising coach operator with a base in Dunstable, shortened YMP 10-metre chassis to 8-metre length and, conversely, also offered a lengthened version of the YNT to cater for operators who wanted a 12-metre coach. Inevitably such conversions were produced on a small scale, though it is significant that they were mentioned in Bedford's April 1982 coach brochure, glossier than ever and giving no clue to the fall in business. Sales remained very depressed by comparison with the heady days of the 1970s and although improving a little in 1983, the increase was almost entirely export-led, over half of the output of 1,010 that year being accounted for by the 600 SB-type chassis, which even at that late date included 15 petrol examples and thus were almost to the original 1950 specification.

The YNT, with 8.2/205TD engine, was Bedford's top-of-the-range coach chassis in the 1982-84 period, but the numbers built remained at around a modest 150 or so per year. This one supplied to G. K. Kinch of Loughborough had Plaxton Supreme V bodywork. The turbocharged 8.2-litre engine was $1\frac{1}{8}$in taller than the unblown unit and was mounted ½in lower in the frame, which made using it to replace engines in older vehicles difficult. As released for production, the YNT had the new Turner M6 gearbox as standard but it was troublesome initially and the ZF S6-65 was substituted. The rear axle, basically the KM unit, had a new hypoid gear set in place of the original spiral bevel unit and this had ratios which permitted the use of direct-top gearboxes in place of the previous overdrive type. At the same period the lighter bus chassis received a new version of the medium hypoid axle having oil-filled hubs.

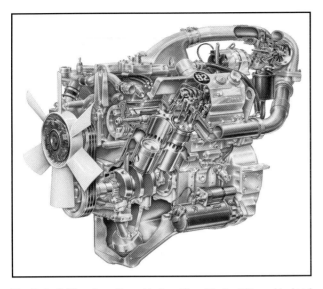

The Detroit Diesel continued to be offered in the TM, and indeed the October 1982 TM brochure quoted five such options, from the 6V-71 of 7-litre capacity, by then developing 221bhp at 2,100rpm to the 12-litre 8V-92TA giving 386bhp at 1,900rpm. The suffix T signified turbocharged and A indicated aftercooled but perhaps the most interesting versions were the two 6V-92TTA 'Torque Tailored' engines, where the torque was tuned to peak at 1,300rpm, the same speed as on the Cummins E-series engines by then also offered in the TM, though of course still sounding as if running much faster because of the two-stroke effect. In the case of the 236hp version the peak torque was 934 lb.ft, substantially higher than the 835 lb.ft given by the Cummins E255 engine producing 245bhp. Seen here is one of the turbocharged Silver Series 6V-92 units, then recently introduced.

Above: The range of 14-litre Cummins straight six-cylinder engines was more to the taste of most British hauliers. By 1982 the TM was available with versions in three rates of tune, all turbocharged. The top-of-the-range E370 developed 351bhp at 1,900rpm and, perhaps more importantly, 1,120 lb.ft of torque at 1,300rpm, only marginally less than the 8V-92TA's 1,190 lb.ft and was well maintained at even lower speeds – just the thing for lugging a fully-laden artic across hilly terrain.

Below: By 1982, a new heavy-duty TM artic was more likely to have a Cummins engine, a unit already well established and respected among British hauliers, even though the Detroit Diesel was very reliable and hard-wearing.

TM developments

As the 1980s began, to a large degree the TM was being sustained by the Ministry of Defence contracts. In the civilian heavy commercial vehicle market it had never made the hoped-for impact. As Pat Kennett put it in *Truck* magazine in April of that year "the long-haul men simply don't like the Detroit two-stroke diesel" – about 350 TM models in heavy artic form were being sold per year in a business where, at that stage, around 2,000 each were being sold by Volvo, ERF and Seddon-Atkinson, with Leyland not far behind and DAF, Scania and Mercedes-Benz all well ahead of Bedford. As the recession soon began to bring all these figures down, the competition simply became more intense.

Although the turbocharged 8.2-litre engine had won the support of the MoD and was available for the lighter models in the range up to 26-tonne tractive units, that left the prestige articulated market in the 32-tonne class and above in need of a suitable engine.

To compete more effectively, Cummins in-line six-cylinder engines were being offered, notably the E290 engine of 14-litre capacity with an installed power rating of 277bhp at 1,900rpm for the 38-tonne model. This was much more acceptable, and Cummins had built up a first-class reputation with engines in this class, produced in Britain at the company's works at Shotts, Lanarkshire since 1956. It was much more in line with the traditional

British concept of a big diesel truck engine despite its American origin and the use of the Cummins system of camshaft-operated injectors. However, from the Bedford perpective it had the disadvantage that, as a proprietary engine, it was available in several competitive British-

The Ministry of Defence orders for the TM 4x4 greatly helped in keeping production up to economic levels. This portrait of military attitudes was at the handing-over of the first batch of vehicles in 1981 – in 1982, almost 70% of TM output was 4x4, almost all for the Army.

thereafter. The extent to which the Ministry of Defence orders contributed to the total can be judged from the situation in 1982, when a total of 1,357 TM models were produced and 940 of these were of the 4x4 type, almost all military. In 1983, the total of this range built dropped to 677 and by 1985 it was down to 380, barely more than one per day.

On the other hand, the lighter M-type 4x4, still using the TK-style cab, continued to attract business, regularly outnumbering TM output of all types, no doubt at least partly because it was much less expensive. Although basically a military vehicle in concept, it was also favoured by contractors and public utility concerns requiring cross-country capability. In 1980, 3,726 M-types were produced and although this fell somewhat the pattern during 1983 to 1985 was one of rising demand, reaching 3,094 in the latter year, a healthy figure for a specialised type of vehicle that had been in production since 1970. With the general adoption of turbocharged engines, this model was fitted with the 5.4/105TD as standard in its later years, though the 300 cu in petrol engine, by then called the 4.9/115P, was an option.

Overall, Bedford's position had fallen well behind Ford. For 1981, as the recession began to bite, the United Kingdom figures for new registrations issued by the Society of Motor Manufactuerers and Traders showed the relative positions. Among car-derived vans, Ford's figure was 18,762 and Bedford's 10,437. At the 'non-car derived van' level – in other words the Transit and CF class, Ford had 32,490 and Bedford 12,196. Among 'trucks, rigid', Ford, helped by its new Cargo range, had put 10,242 on the

built chassis such as ERF, Seddon-Atkinson and Leyland, already well entrenched in this market, so the TM was still fighting an uphill battle in securing a large-enough hold on the market. In 1983, the smaller Cummins 10-litre straight six was also added for appropriate models in the TM range, notably the TM3800 38-tonne tractive unit.

In practice, even with these attempts at broadening the appeal, it was a losing battle, and although TM output in 1981 was 1,691, the best figure since 1978, it declined

The M-type, though a niche product apt to be out of the public eye as an off-road vehicle, and visually belonging to an older design generation, was still selling well, even in the difficult 1980s. By that period it was known as the M1120, in line with the gross-weight-related type numbers of the time, and was being produced in numbers of around 1,800 to 2,200 per year with occasional upsurges beyond the 3,000 mark. It conformed to an old Bedford tradition in offering value for money, with cross-country performance meeting military requirements and well-proved units at a modest price for such a vehicle of around £16,000 in chassis cab form. It made a very useful means of carrying supplies around a major constructional site, such as when building roads, as in the case of this Tarmac vehicle seen in 1982.

road to Bedford's 6,771, and only among the much more limited numbers of artics did Bedford show up better at 615 against Ford with 303 – both were small players in that league against Volvo at 1,552 and Leyland Vehicles at 1,418. Leyland Vehicles were also knocking at the door in the truck class with 5,765, this being largely due to models such as the Terrier and it was known by then that a new medium range exploiting the possibilities of Leyland's T45 cab was being developed.

The early 1980s were a difficult period for all British makers, and Bedford's position remained relatively depressed, with total output back around the 50,000 mark reminiscent of the 1950s when the business had a much narrower and more standardised range. In 1983, the most numerous truck model produced was the TJ range reminiscent of those days, with 6,336 produced, though the TL was not too far behind at 5,959. The TK was still being sold in modest numbers, 1,162 being built that year. In 1984, the TL did rather better at 7,320, which was just as well, as TJ production dropped to 2,639 – as ever, overseas sales tended to vary quite sharply due to economic or political events.

Top right: Efforts were made to sell the TM 4x4 model as a heavier-duty commercial equivalent to the M-type, but its cost, almost double that of the lighter model, limited its potential. Note that Bedford's name for this model was actually TM 4-4.

Centre: In May 1981, the TL range was expanded by the appearance of the first 6x2 version, as seen here. It had left-hand-drive, being one of a number that were to be specially bodied for soft drinks and brewery industries overseas.

Although the TJ, introduced in 1958 and itself an update of earlier designs, had been dropped from the home market in 1976, it was still selling well abroad to the end of Bedford as part of GM – this tipper was shown on the front of a brochure dated April 1982. In 1983, the TJ was actually Bedford's best-selling truck range, with 6,336 sold, slightly more than the still relatively new TL, though the latter was on an upward trend and greatly outnumbered the TJ in 1984. The TJ had scarcely altered and its relative simplicity was an asset in many overseas markets.

It is interesting to examine the price ranges of the various models on offer, taken from a home market price list dated 1st Janaury 1983. It included wording to the effect that it was "published by Bedford Commercial Vehicles, Luton, Beds" and then in smaller type "Division of General Motors Overseas Commercial Vehicle Corporation. Incorporated in the U.S.A. with limited liability." There was now no mention of Vauxhall Motors Ltd in publicity material, though the griffin emblem remained. These changes were in effect from that date.

There were some 125 models for which separate prices were quoted, quite apart from extensive factory-fitted option price lists for each range. It was a very different world from the beginning in April 1931 when there had been just two models, alternative wheelbase verions of the original 2-tonner, priced at £198 and £210, figures which wouldn't cover the addition of a side loading door on a CF van in 1983, illustrating the vast effects of inflation.

It is impractical to list all the models and prices but the following is intended to give an indication of representative figures. In general, the prices given are the lowest for the model and engine type quoted and, for example, longer-wheelbase variants were usually slightly more.

Model	Engine	Price
HA van	1.3/45P	£3,120 to £3,474
Astra		
van	1.3/75P	£3,892
	1.6/55D	£4,267
CF230	1.8/65P	£4,444
up to		
CF350	2.3/60D	£7,606
KB pick-up		£4,053 to £4,697
KB 4x4 pick-up		£5,217 to £5,861
TK570	3.6/90TD	£8,426
TK750	3.6/90TD	£9,470
TK860	5.4/105TD	£10,022
TL570	3.6/90TD	£8,876
TL750	3.6/90TD	£9,920

TL860	5.4/105TD	£10,472
TL1000	5.4/105TD	£11,173
TL1260	5.4/135TD	£12,947
TL1500	8.2/175TD	£16,401
TL1630	8.2/175TD	£17,554
M-type		
4x4	5.4/105TD	£16,090
TM 4x2		
TM1700	8.2/175TD	£18,736
	8.2/210TD	£22,398
	DD 6V71(222)	£25,136
	Cummins	
	10-litre	£26,951
TM1900	DD 6V92(266)	£28,039
TM 6x2		
TM2600	8.2/175TD	£22,429
	8.2/210TD	£23,822
	Cummins E290	£31,007
TM 6x4		
TM2600	8.2/175TD	£23,165
	8.2/210TD	£25,250
	DD 6V71(222)	£28,254
	Cummins E290	£32,491
TM tractor units		
TM2500	8.2/175TD	£18,928
TM3250	8.2/210TD	£21,424
TM3650	DD 6V71(222)	£24,011
	DD 6V92(236)	£25,634
TM3800	Cummins	
	10-litre	£25,364
TM4400	DD 6V92(266)	£27,303
	Cummins E255	£28,497
	Cummins E290	£28,652
	DD 6V92(313)	£29,063
	Cummins E370	£31,493
TM 4x4		
TM 4-4	8.2/205TD	£31,790
Bus and coach chassis		
VAS(PJK)	5.4/105TD	£9,239
SB(NJM)	5.4/105TD	£10,091
YMP	8.2/175TD	£13,880
YMT	8.2/175TD	£15,568
YNT	8.2/205TD	£17,663

The CF had received a style of grille with prominent 'Bedford' lettering which was closer in style to that of most of the larger models but in 1982-3 the petrol version still used the 2.3-litre inclined engine with belt-driven overhead camshaft originally introduced for the Vauxhall Victor FD car, though the diesel used a vertical unit of Opel origin. This CF350, with 3.5 tonne gross weight capability, demonstrates its capabilities by conveying a small concrete mixer for County Plastering, of Luton.

Right: The TK continued in production through the early 1980s even though the TL was effectively its successor, in models ranging from TK570 up to TK1630, plus the TK1930 tractor, these being slightly cheaper, model for model, than the equivalent TL. The TK750 shown on the right featured on the front cover of a brochure dated February 1982. Despite minor changes such as a mildly revised grille, mirrors, flashers, sidelamps and badging, it was very obviously the same animal as introduced almost 22 years earlier.

Below: The complexity of the TK range as still being produced at the beginning of 1982 is conveyed by the series of diagrams shown below, though some versions were offered only for export. There were a total of ten engine options with nominal power ratings from 65 to 175bhp, including the 3.5 and 4.9 litre petrol units and the 3.6, 5.4 and 8.2 litre diesels, all the diesels being produced in a range of power ratings. There were five main gearbox types and various axles to suit the different sizes and weight ratings, including two-speed units and others with differential locks, towards the top end of the range. By September 1982, the TK models offered in Britain had been cut back to the TK570, TK750 and TK860, and total TK output fell from 4,077 in 1981 to 1,162 in 1983, though the type continued to figure in the lists of models produced, with 831 in 1984 and 674 in 1985.

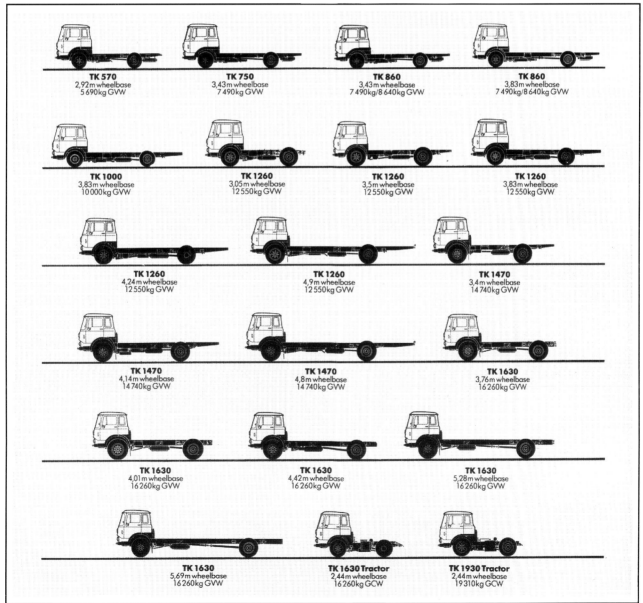

The early 1980s were difficult years for British commercial vehicle builders, with the home economy severely depressed and hence it was made more difficult to provide the volume of sales needed to allow export models to be competitive against makers whose home market was still buoyant. Accordingly, the TL took longer to become a familiar sight on the streets than had the TK. Even so, scenes such as these gradually became quite commonplace. The TL570, like its TK counterpart, was a handy vehicle for urban delivery work with its 112in (9ft 7in) wheelbase. The example shown on the left was operated by Tolerhire on behalf of Times Newspapers Ltd.

The TL750, as shown below, had quite wide appeal because its gross weight rating was low enough not to require a Heavy Goods Vehicle driving licence. No doubt the 'Turbo' lettering displayed by 1984 appealed to some budding boy racer drivers, even if the 90bhp of the standard four-cylinder diesel, though well up on earlier equivalents, hardly made it quite the GT their imagination might have expected; turbocharging having been adopted more as a means of meeting legislation than to increase performance. Note that from the 1985 models the side and flasher lamps were now separate and tucked closer into the cab corners, making them less vulnerable to being damaged.

Pickfords had been a household name in the removal business for generations – the firm's origins can be traced back to 1756 or even earlier. It had come under the control of the four main-line railways in 1933 and thus went through a spell of being part of the State-owned transport set-up from 1948 before re-emerging as a separate concern. It tended to have quite a mixed fleet though various series of Bedford models were represented over the years. The body on this 1985-type TL750, though of traditional Luton form, had side access doors.

Although diesel engines were not only standard but greatly in the majority, it was still possible right up to the final year of Bedford being part of GM to specify what by then was called the 3.5/80P six-cylinder petrol engine for the lighter TL, TK and TJ models where quiet running or fuel availability influenced the choice. In reality, this unit was what had begun life in 1938 as the '28hp' engine and then became known in the 1950s, 1960s and 1970s as the 214 cu in unit. Latterly it developed up to 83bhp at 3,400rpm, only modestly increased from its advertised output in 1938 of 72bhp at 3,000rpm, though at that earlier date figures were of the more flattering gross kind. There had been many minor changes in the period, almost spanning half a century, such as the use of an alternator instead of a dynamo and more effective lubricating oil filtration – some were also to meet modern requirements on emissions. Among the latter were revised ideas on crankcase ventilation. Ironically, while the old Bedford petrol engines tended to fume a little from the combined breather and oil filler on the rocker cover even when in good order and running well, the 3.5/80P with its more elaborate 'fume-consuming' set-up proved apt to build-up pressure within the crankcase and hence to throw oil out via the rear main oil seal.

3

An attempt to reinvigorate Bedford's export bus business in Africa, the Middle East and Asia was announced in the Autumn of 1983 with this 6.05-metre wheelbase chassis intended for 11-metre bodywork. It was publicised as type BOV, that being the basic code, but was derived from the TM range, using the 8.2-litre engine in its normal position at the front but with set-back front axle to permit the provision of an entrance opposite the driver. The chassis was to be supplied complete with the TM front and windscreen assembly as shown.

A demonstrator was built on the BOV chassis in 1983 by Robert Wright & Son (Coachworks) Ltd, of Ballymena, Northern Ireland, for use in Lagos, Nigeria, producing quite a neat-looking vehicle, the TM front giving it a clear identity as a Bedford product and suiting the body styling surprisingly well. It had seats for 41 passengers but was designed to carry up to 100, the majority standing. The body used Alusuisse modular aluminium construction.

Passenger sales doldrums

Bedford passenger chassis output picked up in 1983, just scraping into four figures at 1,010, thanks to one of the periodical upsurges in SB demand from export markets, though at 585 of the NJM diesel-engined model even this was not at the really big scale of earlier years. The YNT figure that year was a mere 167, this very modest total being the highest annual figure reached by this model, the front-line Bedford coach chassis at the time. The total of Y-type models that year was 204, comparing very poorly with the 1,192, mainly YMT, five years earlier.

The single-deck bus market in Britain was severely depressed at that time, but coach demand had recovered to some degree, the partial deregulation, mainly relating to the longer-distance services, that had occurred as the result of the Transport Act 1980 having stimulated demand for travel on express coach services. The main beneficiary proved to be the NBC coaching arm, National Express (which owned few vehicles of its own but whose livery was used on many supplied by other NBC subsidiaries), which gained much of the extra traffic because of its network linking well-established coach stations.

In terms of new vehicles, Leyland picked up most of the extra business with healthy orders, at first for the Leopard and then for a new underfloor-engined model with many affinities to the Leopard but having air suspension as

standard, for which Leyland's old model name, Tiger, was revived. In 1983, the underfloor-engined Tiger took first place among single-deck sales in Britain with over 700 delivered, of which about half were coaches for NBC subsidiaries. Yet from Bedford's viewpoint it was equally significant that Volvo, which had begun selling underfloor-engined coach chassis in Britain in 1972, had reached the position of seeing its B10M model, also new in 1980 and with air suspension, become the most popular choice among independents by 1982. The trend to heavier-duty chassis was clearly established and Volvo's success in this market was a portent for the future with implications for the whole British bus and coach manufacturing industry.

An attempt to breathe new life into the export side of the bus industry was made in 1983 with a model derived from the TM truck range. It was publicised as BOV, that being the generalised code leaving the choice of engine open – had it gone into production the models planned would have been BMV, as the engine would have been the 8.2-litre in either unblown 160 bhp form, as on the prototype, or turbocharged to 173 bhp, either of which units had the engine code M, or BNV when fitted with the 205 bhp version. The prototype had an Allison MT643 automatic, available only with the 160 bhp engine, but the ZF 56-65 six-speed synchromesh unit was offered with all three engine ratings.

Wright of Ballymena sprang into prominence quite rapidly in the early 1980s and was at first quite strongly associated with Bedford chassis, initially with some decidedly utilitarian bus bodies. However, this striking coach body, called the Contour, was produced with backing both from the Northern Ireland Development Corporation and Vauxhall Motors; the latter providing expertise in regard to the styling. The example shown, supplied to Cedar Coaches of Bedford on a YNT chassis, is seen at Brighton at the 1984 British Coach Rally where prizes were being handed out by John Fielder, organiser of the rally, on the right.

It was anticipated that many would be bodied in the destination country, and it was descided to provide a front panel and windscreen assembly, rather in the manner adopted by Mercedes-Benz and other continental makes on some of their bus chassis. The first vehicle to be bodied was intended as a demonstrator, receiving a body by Wright of Ballymena. It was bodied to a specification to suit operation in Lagos, Nigeria, but unfortunately the political and economic situation was unhelpful and what had been a good market for Bedford became virtually closed. It is understood that 50 BOV chassis were built, the remainder being bodied by Ikarus, the major Hungarian concern which was opening up to business in non-Communist countries as part of an easing of economic relations which took place several years before the eventual collapse of the Cold War. These too remained unsold.

The YNV Venturer coach chassis

A serious attempt to recapture a firmer hold on the coach market, hitherto dominated by Bedford for most of its existence, was made in October 1984, when the YNV 12-metre model with air suspension was announced. For the only time, a Bedford passenger model was given a name, Venturer, clearly intended to follow in the 'V' tradition associated with the happy days of Vista and Vega, though those were Duple body names despite the clear intent of alliteration with Vauxhall.

The choice of Venturer seemed rather odd to some of the older generation of bus people, for it had been Albion's standard name for its double-decker chassis in the later 1930s and up to 1951, when the model was dropped soon after Leyland took over – Albion was another firm which

An old-established independent bus operator in County Durham, the Langley Park Motor Co, chose a Y-type chassis with Duple Laser bodywork, normally a coach design but in this case with bus seats, for use on its service into Durham City. The fleetname Gypsy Queen had been in use for about half a century.

The Venturer YNV coach chassis had a specification which compared well with contemporary top-grade models in most respects, notably its suitability for 12-metre bodywork and air suspension. Undoubtedly, some potential buyers were discouraged by the continued use of the Bedford 8.2-litre engine and doubt as to whether its 205bhp in turbocharged form was enough to give adequate performance with typical mid-1980s coach bodywork. If weight was allowed to go up to the 16.25 tonnes permitted on optional tyres, it probably was not. It might have been wiser to put more emphasis on the concept of the model as a middleweight coach for it was possible to select modern and well-finished if not over-elaborate bodywork that kept the gross weight well below this maximum, and it would then perform very agreeably. The original intention had been that the Venturer would have an horizontal engine, with a choice of the turbocharged Bedford 8.2-litre, which would have been made available in horizontal form for the purpose, or an Isuzu unit – the latter concern having a suitable six-cylinder engine already developing 240bhp, although the latter would have made the chassis price comparable to that of a Volvo. Neither of the projects was approved, the 'payback' period being judged too long for the horizontal 8.2 while the TM episode discouraged a move into a more expensive sector of the market.

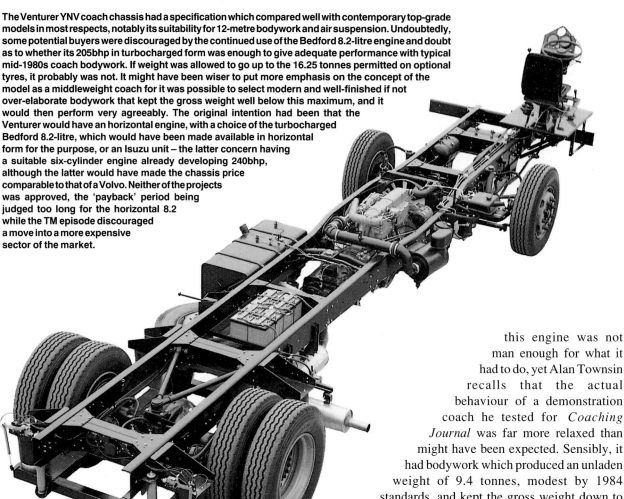

this engine was not man enough for what it had to do, yet Alan Townsin recalls that the actual behaviour of a demonstration coach he tested for *Coaching Journal* was far more relaxed than might have been expected. Sensibly, it had bodywork which produced an unladen weight of 9.4 tonnes, modest by 1984 standards, and kept the gross weight down to 14.6 tonnes as tested, which was equivalent to a full 51-passenger load with about 24kg of luggage each so it was by no means an unrealistic test. The body was an example of the Duple Laser design, which might also have helped in terms of wind resistance by virtue of its swept-back windscreen, but again this seemed sensible as a realistic choice for the kind of work such a coach might be expected to do.

Even so, there had been speculation that the Cummins LT10 10-litre engine might be offered, particularly as it had been made available in TM-range models. It was available in various power ratings but the 250bhp version was an obvious choice and might well have attracted quite a number of operators, allowing use of the full gross weight figure without the doubts about performance that undoubtedly contributed to the poor sales performance. It is perhaps unfair to judge decisions with the benefit of hindsight, but even though some of the profit would have gone to an outside engine maker, increased overall demand might well have resulted had the Cummins been offered.

The specification of the YNV chassis in other respects matched up well to contemporary practice albeit a little late in responding to demand trends. The 12-metre (39ft 4in) overall length had been legal in Britain since September 1967, and demand for coaches built to it was initially very small, at first tending to be confined to specialised cases such as the Scottish Bus Group services linking London and Edinburgh or Glasgow, Bedford logically judging it to

tended to use names beginning with V for its passenger models, Viking still being used for a popular truck-based export model in the Leyland Bus era, and for an inline rear-engined, somewhat spartan, chassis built for the Scottish Bus Group. The Albion Venturer never became a very well-known type, which may have influenced Bedford to adopt the name, unused since the early 1950s, for its new model – yet ironically, Bedford's version did not reach anywhere near even the fairly modest numbers of Albion's Venturer; over 400 of the most popular CX19 type had been built, though only a few preserved examples survived into the Bedford Venturer era.

Yet the YNV deserved to succeed considerably better than it did, for it offered a good specification at a chassis price, £24,111 at the time of annoucement, which was low by the standards of the opposition. In earlier times, that had been a typical General Motors formula for success. The most obvious question mark lay over the choice of engine, which was the same Bedford 8.2/205TD unit as used in the YNT. By 1984 standards, an output of 204.3bhp at 2,500rpm was no longer high for a 12-metre model that could weigh up to 15.5 tonnes gross, that being the rated maximum figure on standard tyres.

Operators may well have shied away on the basis that

The Duple Laser 2 body in 51-seat form was chosen for Bedford's own demonstrator YNV coach, a shrewd choice in the sense that its unladen weight of 9405kg allowed the gross weight with a simulated full passenger and luggage load to be kept to 14.6 tonnes. The well-raked windscreen probably also helped in cutting down wind resistance. The Laser had first appeared as one of a pair of new Duple designs to replace the Dominant series of coach bodies in 1982, and was revised in detail in 1984. The YNV with Laser 2 body seen here was for Youngs of Cambridge. A 'Venturer Turbo' plate was supplied for attachment to the front grille – this being Bedford's only named coach chassis, though several earlier types often took on Duple's body names as unofficial titles.

The YNT continued in production alongside the YNV, the sales pitch for it taking the line that it was "the best-riding steel-sprung coach available on the British market". It was also claimed that the power to weight ratio was among the best among British 'middleweight' coaches, again a rather limited claim by that date though the 205bhp engine had less to do than in a YNV; the chassis weight was 4.47 tonnes, a typical complete coach around 8.5 tonnes and the gross weight 12.5 tonnes. This 1985 example had Plaxton Paramount bodywork – both the leading coach bodybuilders were introducing new styles to replace those that had survived with little change though the 1970s, the Paramount having been introduced at the 1982 Show. The Y-type models were not always easy to get through the tilt test, especially if fitted with the taller types of body. The two Venturer prototypes had Plaxton Paramount bodies, one with a 3200 body similar to that shown but the other had the higher 3500 and did not pass until a Telma retarder was added, acting as ballast.

be insufficient to justify producing such a model at that time. Yet it had increasingly gained favour towards the latter part of the 1970s, tending to supplant the hitherto dominant 11-metre length and some of Bedford's loss of business was probably related to non-availability of a standard chassis to suit this length.

Similarly, the air suspension had become a feature which was felt essential for the more upmarket type of coach travel offered by many operators. Over the years, Bedford had often offered better standards in this respect than more expensive models – traditionally, Leyland coach chassis, and in particular the Leopard, tended to have a reputation for being rather hard-riding, so it was unfortunate that for some years Bedford was 'behind the game' in this respect. The air system had four rolling-diaphragm spring units for the rear axle and two for the front, the latter being at mounted at the rear of two-leaf springs which provided axle location. There was a facility for raising the ride height by 75mm to accommodate uneven surfaces, notably when boarding or leaving ferries. The ride standard achieved was very good, with none of the excessive wallowing softness that can make some air systems prone to inducing travel-sickness.

In other respects, the design was to a high-quality contemporary standard, with an air-assisted clutch and a ZF S6-65 six-speed direct-top synchromesh gearbox, direct air-pressure brakes having a twin-cylinder water-cooled compressor and steering with integral power assistance.

Despite its merits, the YNV did not even do as well as the YNT, though the combined output of Y-types did rise a little to 304 in 1984, of which 124 were YNV and 122

YNT. Yet that was the only year when the numbers went into three figures, the output of YNV for 1985 being a very poor 36 and in the January to June 1986 period there were just three. It is understood that 200 YNV chassis were actually produced in a one-off run, but that it took several years to sell them. By that time the bus market was collapsing as the Transport Act 1985 brought the prospect of deregulation and the privatisation of NBC, while the coach industry went through another spell of poor confidence and limited orders. It was scant comfort that by then Ford had succombed entirely as a coach chassis maker – ironically it was the Ford Transit that benefitted strongly from the move into minibuses made by NBC in particular as its reaction to the prosepct of deregulation.

It was ironic that, despite all the modern technology of the Y-series models, culminating in the Venturer YNV, Bedford's top-selling passenger chassis every year in the 1978-85 period was the SB in its NJM form, built almost entirely for export. In 1985, some 501 such chassis left the factory, compared to only 127 of all variants of the far more 'advanced' Y-type mid-engined models. When production ended in 1986, some 57,129 SB chassis had been built. Among the few home market users of the type in the later years was the British Army, and it was apt in more ways than one that Marshall christened its bus design for the model the Campaigner. In later years the SB (NJM) chassis, as still offered on the British market in the form shown above, had the 5.4/105TD turbocharged version of what had been more familiar in earlier days as the 330 diesel and an Eaton five-speed gearbox as standard. By then the gear-change linkage was similar in principle to that used on TK and TL models and there was a spring parking brake to meet contemporary legislation. There had been quite extensive changes to both the SB and VAS brake systems to meet EEC requirements during the 1970s and early 1980s and the driving position was revised with steering column and pedals moved forward and upward to improve close-range vision. Even so, in essentials, they were based on 1950s concepts.

Reorganisation of Bedford as a directly-run division of General Motors rather than simply a commercial-vehicle marque name of Vauxhall Motors Ltd was proclaimed in 1985-season brochures under the heading 'Geared to the needs of the future', an ironic statement when it is remembered that the decision to shut down truck and bus production was taken in the latter part of the following year. Hitherto, there had been no imposing doorway as shown in this picture accompanying the statement, yet the immense successes of earlier years were fast disappearing.

The van scene in the early 1980s

If the truck and especially the coach scenes were rather depressing in the early 1980s, the van picture was rather brighter. The Astra van was selling well, the 15,989 produced in the first year, 1983, being improved upon in succeeding years. A Mark II version was introduced in October 1984, retaining the running gear of the earlier model but with improved body design which showed that it was possible to reconcile a good aerodynamic design with 66 cu ft load-carrying capacity. Its versatility was further widened in August 1985 when a high-roof version became available. All of these, like Vauxhall cars of the period, were closely related to Opel products, being designed by that concern.

The KB, together with its four-wheel-drive variant, continued as a relatively small-scale 'niche' market vehicle of which a little over 1,500 per year were being produced in the 1983-85 period.

The CF was improved in a series of stages over the years. By 1984 it had become CF2 with a choice of 2-litre petrol or 2.3-litre diesel engine, both Opel-designed vertical units with chain-driven overhead camshaft. The front grille assembly, with headlamps and bumper could be removed by undoing eight bolts for improved access to the front of the engine and other items. The CF2/230, 250 and 280 models had front disc brakes, the heavier CF2/350 and 350L had self-adjusting drum brakes all round.

The KB continued as a 'niche' product, the KB41 seen here offering the benefit of four-wheel drive at a modest price (£5,217 plus VAT in January 1983).

Despite the split from Vauxhall, much of what remained of Bedford's success was still bound up with that concern, and indeed Opel car designs – the Astra van became Bedford's top-selling model in 1984, after being only just behind the CF in 1983. The resemblance to the Estate version of the Vauxhall Astra car is strongly evident in this view of the L model which had car-like trim details. Such a model had obvious merit when 'image' was regarded as important, quite apart from being agreeable to drive.

Although the CF2 introduced in 1984 looked almost identical to its immediate predecessor, it had an Opel-designed 2-litre petrol engine as standard, mounted vertically instead of inclined as in the earlier versions with their Vauxhall-derived inclined engines. This is the CF2/250 short-wheelbase (106in) version.

In addition to the longer 126in wheelbase versions, the CF2 was also available in CF2/350L form with 140-in wheelbase but only as a chassis with cab or cowl, as seen here.

However, the most striking development of that period was the introduction of the Midi van, announced in the Autumn of 1984 and put into production in the Spring of 1985. This was another Isuzu design, though there was clear evidence of GM involvement in regard to styling, with a characteristic well-rounded shape having a distinct family resemblance, viewed from a Bedford perspective, to the JJL bus. This time, however, it was to become much more familiar and indeed still is. There was clear confidence in its success, with a £70 million investment programme at the Luton plant to build it.

In terms of layout, the concept could almost be described as a scaled-down TK, with the engine set back so as to be positioned beneath the front seats, allowing easy access from either side.

Japan, with crowded streets in its cities, had fostered the development of compact and, in particular, narrow van designs, several having been on the British market for some time; some were very small. The Midi was aimed at a mid-range market, with payload in the 1 to 1.2-tonne class, with alternative 2.35 and 2.69 metre wheelbases. The Isuzu engines were a 1.8-litre 76bhp petrol unit or a 2-litre 57bhp diesel, both with a five-speed gearbox noteworthy for having steering-column control so as to facilitate driver entry or exit from either side.

The CF2 interior was neatly finished, even in the low-cost CF2/230 Fleet model seen here.

Jon Barrass, writing in *Motor Transport's* 'Which Van?' review in 1985, pointed out that the short-wheelbase Midi diesel had almost directly comparable gross weight to the CF2/250 diesel, the Midi figure of 2,550kg being 20kg less, but its payload capacity was 1,065kg, 50kg more than the CF. The overall body width was considerably less at 1.69 metre compared to 1.93 metre yet total load volume was only mildly down at 5.2 cu m, compared to the CF 5.9 cu m. The cost of the diesel Midi short-wheelbase model was £6,275 compared to £6,578 for the equivalent CF2/250 diesel.

He reported that Bedford expected the Midi to take a significant proportion of CF sales, and indeed that was exactly what happened. The CF total output figure of 15,598 in 1984 dipped quite sharply to 7,915 in 1985, while Midi output went up from the first example which came down the line on 20th December 1984 to 12,037 in 1985. Both were well behind the Astra van however, of which 21,531 were produced in 1985, to which 3,799 of the Astramax version were added.

The total Bedford van-class output in 1985 was 46,847, in which were also included 1,560 KB and a final handful of five HA, a model of which general production had eded in 1983. That year the total truck and bus output was 14,799, very slightly up on the 14,274 of 1984, but a very poor showing compared to the 46,790 of 1978. The writing was on the wall, though the end was to be swifter than anyone imagined.

The first Midi to come down the line, on 20th December 1984. Despite the £70 million investment in the plant created to build it and the effort put into a celebratory air to the proceedings, the thoughtful look evident among some of the bystanders reflected a new situation in which 'Bedford' was becoming little more than a name applied to products assembled at Luton but no longer designed there. Within two years the death knell was to fall on all but van and light commercial production.

The Midi's styling had a clear General Motors look about it, and especially in this 15-seat personnel carrier form there was a distinct hint of the JJL bus that had aroused so much admiration and interest, but this time set to become a very familiar sight.

19 THE END OF AN ERA

The overall position of Bedford must have been causing concern to GM headquarters since the catastrophic fall in output in 1981 and the subsequent failure to make any significant recovery. For a complex combination of reasons, including many beyond the control of its management, or even that at General Motors, Bedford's strong position of earlier years had vanished. Yet it still had much going for it, not least the immense resources of design and marketing skill, related to sales all over the world, both at Luton and available to it within GM. Although sales were very low, there were occasional flashes of interesting activity. Among them were the efforts of the Special Vehicles Operations group which built 20 in-house short YMPs to replace the Tricentrol conversions, and 50 export bus versions of the TM truck, one bodied by Wright and the remainder by Ikarus. They did not sell and later passed to AWD. A late success was the sale of 200 VAS (PJK) to Morocco.

Then what was clearly seen as a major opportunity for a strengthening of the General Motors position in regard to commercial vehicles in Britain arose because of events quite outside anything related to Dunstable or Luton and centred more on Westminster.

The re-election of Mrs Margaret Thatcher's Government in 1983 resulted in a strengthening of the policy of privatisation and deregulation. The British Leyland Motor Corporation had been formed in 1968 as a merger, at that time under private enterprise but with the approval of the then Labour Government, of the Leyland Motor Corporation (including AEC, Albion and Scammell commercial vehicles as well as Leyland itself plus, on the car side, Standard-Triumph and Rover, including Land Rover) with British Motor Holdings. The latter was itself the result of a merger in 1966 in which the British Motor Corporation was the senior partner – the car makers Austin and Morris were the biggest names in BMC, though it also included the BMC truck factory at Bathgate which was a direct competitor with Bedford, having developed from Austin's commercial vehicle department and Morris-Commercial. The other partner in BMH was Jaguar Cars, the latter by then owning Daimler, including its successful bus business, and Guy trucks.

BLMC become a nationalised concern in 1974 when huge losses made by its car division, mainly Austin and Morris, threatened to sink the whole conglomerate had not the Government stepped in. Leyland's Truck and Bus Division had been making substantial profits but these had been diverted to support the car business – indeed an unsuccessful attempt had been made to hive the division off and keep it in private ownership at that time.

There had been a number of reorganisations and closures of various factories in attempts to rationalise the complex organisation, beginning in the late 1970s, the commercial vehicle side being split as Leyland Trucks and Leyland Bus, but heavy losses continued to be made, still mainly related to car production. Mrs Thatcher was determined that the whole organisation should be sold off, either complete or in parts.

Early in 1986, it became known that General Motors had made an offer to buy Leyland Trucks on condition that Land Rover was included – it was said that the price offered was £230 million.

Had this gone through, it would have given GM a modern heavy truck assembly plant at Leyland as well as a much stronger foothold in the heavy end of the European truck business than had been possible with the Bedford TM as a haulage vehicle. Yet conversely the success of the TM as a 4x4 might well have been a basis for expansion in conjunction with Leyland's own activities in that field. Indeed with Land Rover, there would have been scope for a whole range of cross-country vehicles of all sizes. Leyland had engines covering power ratings not covered by Bedford and although their development had been hampered by lack of cash, GM funds had the potential to put that right. Leyland had made significant inroads into Bedford's traditional strength in the mid-range truck market with models in part derived from BMC origins, but with proper backing the combined Leyland-Bedford organisation should have been able to win back business from Ford.

But it was not to be. There was a remarkably emotional outburst by various Members of Parliament and others, centred on the proposed sale of Land Rover, "a British institution", to a foreign buyer. Yet there seemed to be no comparable concern over the future of Leyland Trucks, nor any recognition that Bedford, in General Motors ownership since its beginning in 1931, was a major supplier of trucks to the British Army and had been since the dark days of 1939-45, when the standard Army lorry was a Bedford. That was quite apart from its immense export successes and future potential in that direction, even if in eclipse at that time. Proposals for the British Government retaining a 51% share in Land Rover were put forward, but GM made it clear that its offer was for an outright take-over of both and was not negotiable.

A graphic account of the complex manoeuvrings involving counter-bids for different combinations of BL divisions appears in Doug Jack's book *Beyond Reality – Leyland Bus – the twilight years* but the end result was that the Government got cold feet and decided in April 1986 not to accept any of the offers then being put forward for Leyland Trucks or Land Rover. In Doug Jack's words, "the General Motors team returned to Detroit in disgust, having refused to accept any compromise deal". It has even been suggested that there was an element of reaction to that rejection in GM's subsequent decisions on Bedford.

Even so, this failure left Bedford's problems unresolved and indeed highlighted the growing crisis. Unease rumbled on until 9th September 1986 when a grim statement was issued "Bedford Commercial Vehicles announced today that in the light of continued losses it is to phase out the production of its medium and heavy duty trucks and its bus chassis range by the end of this year". In justification, it was pointed out that losses in the three years from September 1983 amounted to £187 million. It was added that the production of military trucks and CKD packs for export would continue, as would the availability of replacement parts and full service support. Yet clearly all of these could only be living on borrowed time once the core activity had gone.

That was a devastating blow to thousands of people, not least the employees at the Dunstable plant. It was revealed that a meeting had occurred the previous week between trade union representatives at Bedford Trucks with Robert Stempel, General Motors Vice-President for operations outside North America. The unions put forward a plan involving the introduction of a new cab already developed by Bedford engineers on existing chassis, but this was rejected. That appears to relate to what was sometimes called the 'World Truck' project, with the new cab but having a new chassis which would have used proprietary components including ZF gearboxes and Rockwell axles.

It was pointed out that the company had lost a number of dealers. Mr Stempel also revealed that a replacement for the CF2 would probably be an anglicised version of another design from Isuzu and indeed subsequent van-building under both Bedford and Vauxhall names has been based on similar designs.

It also came to light that at the time of the talks between GM and Leyland there had also been conversations between Mr Stempel and his team and the DAF concern in Holland, later to emerge as the purchaser for Leyland Trucks, and with the Paccar group which included the American Kenworth and Peterbilt truck concerns and which had acquired the old-established Foden concern.

After the announcement, output of Bedford chassis at Dunstable was wound down, though the military contracts for TM 4x4 and 6x6 models and the M-type 4x4 continued, together with the overseas-related models such as the TJ and the SB and VAS passenger models. It was anticipated that complete closure would have occurred in December 1988.

The AWD era

A year after the GM announcement of the phasing out of Bedford trucks, it was revealed that discussions were being held by Paul Tosch of GM with David J. B. Brown, an engineering entrepreneur, on the purchase of the truck business.

Mr Brown (not to be confused with an earlier David Brown whose firm had produced gearboxes under that name, based in Huddersfield, and then moved into the car business with Aston Martin and Lagonda) had set up DJB Dumpers in 1973, selling his house to put up £60,000 of capital. The concern specialised in all-wheel-drive dump trucks in a niche not covered by concerns such as Caterpillar or International Harvester, which had diversified into part of this market. He also set up other enterprises, notably Artix and Multidrive, mainly related to similar activities.

Eventually, on 26th November 1987, it was announced that Mr Brown had bought the Dunstable truck and bus plant. Output would be continued, those vehicles sold in the United Kingdom being badged as AWD and those exported badged as AWD-Bedford. GM continued to market its vans in Britain under the Bedford name.

Plans were announced by AWD for building 8,000 vehicles in the first year, of which 1,000 were to be for the

The AWD-built range had an obvious resemblance to its Bedford forbears, inevitably so as many parts including the cab pressings and other visible items continued to be of unchanged design. The TL cab is readily identifiable here, though the Bedford grille panel had given way to a plainer style with AWD lettering. The two teddy bears were not standard, however!

UK civilian market and by the Autumn of 1988 it was announced that there were 47 AWD dealers. At first it was possible to operate on the momentum of the old Bedford set-up to some degree, some engines still being in stock, for example, though a policy of using Perkins units was adopted for new production. The remnants of Bedford Engineering, latterly under the direction of Dr David Rees as the first British Chief Engineer for some time, were also acquired by Mr Brown, but this became a separate contract design business, serving both AWD and Artix.

Work was put in hand on the reintroduction of the TL and updating of the TJ range. A couple of export bus chassis were schemed and plans made for Perkins-engined versions of the SB and VAS and one of the JJLs was repurchased but Mr Brown preferred to concentrate on the possibility of competing for the Ministry of Defence order for the M-type replacement, unfortunately without success. The reduction in scale was drastic, with 38 people who could be counted as belonging to the engineering department as compared to the 1,600 under Vauxhall, and inevitably this limited both what could be done and the methods that could be used.

What was announced as the first major order for AWD trucks, 20 7.5 tonne TL models with demountable box bodies came in October 1988 from a truck hire firm, John Dee, via the dealers Sherwoods of Darlington. There were announcements of a European dealer network, a proposed 38-44 tonne range and planned sales campaigns in Spain, Greece and then eastern Europe.

In the event, although there was limited sales success it was far short of what was needed for continued operation. Cut-backs in staff, which included early retirement for 80 people in 1991 were not enough to prevent receivership, which came on 4th June 1992.

Marshall SPV

Four months later, on 12th October 1992, the business was purchased by Marshall of Cambridge. This brought echoes of earlier times, though the thread of continuity was probably more that of the practical business of providing bodywork for military Bedford vehicles than of the JJL bus, even though there was still interest in a vehicle of that type.

Bedford was now described as 'a division of Marshall SPV Ltd', the address being quoted as Airport Works, Cambridge, though a new truck division office was opened in Stevenage early in 1993. The AWD dealer network was not retained but the parts operation was purchased from GM, which had distributed parts for AWD.

The model ranges being offered early in 1993 were those developed under AWD and now standardised on Perkins engines:- the TJ2 (visually still much as the TJ when introduced in 1958), the MT (developed from the M-type) and the TL; the Perkins Phaser 6-litre engine being the power unit for most standard models. Sales became very small, though Fullers, the London brewers, bought a batch of TL 17-21 models.

Four years later the TL 17-21 was the only model available for the UK market, though TJ, TL and MT models were being built for export. There were twelve sales outlets, 85 for parts, but many Bedford operators were finding parts difficult to obtain.

Meanwhile it was announced in May 1996 that the Lex group would be selling certain Isuzu trucks and, more significantly, and ironically in view of earlier history, that there were plans for production of a range of models of Isuzu design to be produced at the old Leyland plant acquired by Leyland-DAF. As we go to press, Marshall is reported to be planning to close Bedford truck production.

Under Marshall SPV, the range offered continued to reflect its origins. The TJ export range had become TJ2 and the 11-tonne gross models continued at first to be available with the Bedford 5.4/100D engine and Bedford four-speed gearbox, producing a vehicle which in essentials was largely as built by Bedford in the 1960s, and retaining the cab whose origins could be traced to a 1947 Chevrolet design.

Meanwhile, in Britain, Bedford became purely a name associated with small vans. The Rascal, introduced in 1986 and seen here, was another result of GM investment in a Japanese maker, being based on the Suzuki ST90, though again managing to acquire a touch of GM looks, even further scaled down to the microvan class. This early example was supplied to the East Midlands division of British Gas.

It is planned to examine the final Bedford years and the AWD and Marshall continuation of the story plus a review of preserved and working Bedfords with the facilities for their support in more detail in Volume 3.

INDEX

VOLUME THREE

A third volume, to be published in 1998, will take a retrospective view of Bedford. It will deal in greater detail with events during the final years under General Motors ownership, followed by the transfer of truck production to AWD and then in turn to Marshall. A review of Bedfords in service, including many still in use and preserved in Britain and abroad will include many colour illustrations. The remarkable growth in the preservation of Bedfords of widely varied types will receive special attention, as will the specialist concerns able to supply spare parts and other services.

Reserve your copy now to void disappointment.

Venture *publications*

128, Pikes Lane, Glossop, Derbyshire, SK13 8EH

Printed by The Amadeus Press Ltd, Huddersfield